ACADEMIC FREEDOM IN HIGHER EDUCATION

This timely book explores the challenges facing universities and individual scholars through an examination of the history and theory underlying the concept of academic freedom.

Freedom of speech is widely viewed as a central attribute of contemporary liberal democracies in which — within limits — differing opinions have the right to be articulated in public without fear of reprisal. Academic freedom, long regarded as central to the idea of the university, is, on the other hand, a right which must be earned through the acquisition of expert knowledge and the application of intellectual rigour in teaching and research. Both hard-won freedoms are argued by many to be under serious threat.

The expert contributors to this book, from different global regions, examine both the importance of academic freedom and the severe threats universities face in this context in the twenty-first century. With its interdisciplinary perspective and cross-national emphasis, central issues in this text are illustrated through detailed examination of case studies and consideration of wider developments in the academy. Adopting a *longue duree* approach, rather than discussing the details of fast moving controversies, the analyses offer insights for an educated public about an issue of pressing, contemporary significance.

This book will be of interest to researchers, policy makers, staff and students across higher education and to members of the general public, who are concerned about these important and contested matters.

Maria Slowey is Emeritus Professor, Higher Education Research Centre, Dublin City University, Ireland and Visiting Professor at the Universities of Florence, Italy, and Glasgow, UK.

Richard Taylor is Emeritus Professorial Fellow, Wolfson College, Cambridge University, UK.

ACADEMIC FREEDOM IN HIGHER EDUCATION

Core Value or Elite Privilege?

Edited by Maria Slowey and Richard Taylor

Routledge
Taylor & Francis Group

LONDON AND NEW YORK

Designed cover image: Reproduced by kind permission of the artist
Francesca Wilkinson Shaw

First published 2025
by Routledge
4 Park Square, Milton Park, Abingdon, Oxon OX14 4RN

and by Routledge
605 Third Avenue, New York, NY 10158

Routledge is an imprint of the Taylor & Francis Group, an informa business

© 2025 selection and editorial matter, Maria Slowey and Richard Taylor;
individual chapters, the contributors

British Library Cataloguing-in-Publication Data
A catalogue record for this book is available from the British Library

ISBN: 978-1-032-42550-4 (hbk)
ISBN: 978-1-032-42551-1 (pbk)
ISBN: 978-1-003-36326-2 (ebk)

DOI: 10.4324/9781003363262

Typeset in ITC Galliard Pro
by KnowledgeWorks Global Ltd.

For David Watson (1949–2015)

CONTENTS

ABOUT THE EDITORS

Maria Slowey is Emeritus Professor, Higher Education Research Centre, Dublin City University, Ireland and Visiting Professor at the, Universities of Florence and Glasgow. She was previously Vice-President (DCU), and Research Dean, Professor and Director of Adult and Continuing Education (Glasgow University). She is Senior Editor of *Studies in Higher Education*, elected Fellow of the Academy of Social Sciences, and member of the International Adult Education Hall of Fame.

Richard Taylor is Emeritus Professorial Fellow, Wolfson College, Cambridge University. He was Professor and Director of Continuing Education and Lifelong Learning at Cambridge, and before that held a similar post at Leeds University, where he was also Dean of Faculty. He is author or co-author of 14 books on adult and higher education, politics, and peace studies; and was Chair of the Board of Trustees of the Workers' Educational Association (WEA), and Chair of the Executive Committee of the National Institute of Adult Continuing Education (NIACE).

CONTRIBUTORS

Wietse de Vries is a full professor at the Benemérita Universidad Autónoma de Puebla, Mexico. His area of interest is how public policies affect higher education institutions and their actors (students, alumni, academics, and administrators). He is (still) a National System of Researchers (SNI) member.

Ellen Hazelkorn is Joint Managing Partner, BH Associates education consultants. She is Professor Emeritus, Technological University Dublin (Ireland), and Joint Editor, Policy Reviews in Higher Education. She is Research Fellow, Centre for International Higher Education, Boston College, USA, and member of the Research Management Committee and Advisory Board of the Centre for Global Higher Education (CGHE), Oxford.

Alan Haworth's books include *Anti-Libertarianism: Markets, Philosophy, and Myth* (1994), *Free Speech* (1998), *Understanding the Political Philosophers: From Ancient to Modern Times* (Second Edition 2012), and *Totalitarianism and Philosophy* (2020). All are published by Routledge. His most recent book is entitled *Political Philosophy After 1945*.

Liz Jackson is a Professor in the Faculty of Education at the University of Hong Kong. She is also Immediate Past President and Fellow of the Philosophy of Education Society of Australasia (PESA) and the Acting Editor-in-Chief of Educational Philosophy and Theory.

Andrea Pető is a historian and a Professor at the Department of Gender Studies at Central European University, Vienna, Austria, a Research Affiliate of the CEU Democracy Institute, Budapest, and a Doctor of Science of the Hungarian Academy of Sciences. Her co-author on the chapter in this book is **Rebeka Bakos,** a Hungarian sociologist who, in 2023 applied to the doctoral program of sociology at the Eötvös Loránd University in Budapest. Her research interests are the migration motivations and strategies of minorities living in Vojvodina. She currently works as an editor for a Hungarian newspaper in Serbia.

Peter Scott is Emeritus Professor of Higher Education Studies at University College, London. Previously he was Vice-Chancellor of Kingston University. He has served as Commissioner for Fair Access in Scotland, and board member of the former Higher Education Funding Council for England. His most recent book is *Retreat or Resolution: Tackling the Crisis of Mass Higher Education* (2021).

Evan Smith is a research fellow in history at the College of Humanities, Arts and Social Sciences at Flinders University, Australia. He has published widely on the history of political extremism, social movements, national security, and borders. One of his recent books is *No Platform: A History of Anti-Fascism, Universities and the limits of Free Speech* (2020).

ACKNOWLEDGEMENTS

The original idea for this book came from our friend and colleague, Michael Newman. We are grateful to Mike for the suggestion, and for his invaluable help and advice during the gestation of the book.

Thanks are also due to all our contributors who, without exception, have been collegial and efficient in this collaborative project.

We are grateful to Lucia Vazquez Mendoza, post-doctoral researcher, Dublin City University, for her willing assistance in preparing the final manuscript for submission; and to the Editorial team at Routledge Education, Sarah Hyde, Molly Selby, and Rhea Gupta, and the input of Nashra Khan and the production team at the final stages of the process.

The cover image of the book has been reproduced by kind permission of the artist Francesca Wilkinson Shaw.

Finally, this book is dedicated to the memory of our friend and colleague, David Watson. David, a historian by background, published extensively on higher education, held many senior roles in British higher education, and was knighted for his services to the field. However, more importantly from our perspective, David was a consistently progressive and eloquent advocate for access to a liberal higher education *for all*, coupled with a deeply rooted commitment to the ideal of academic freedom.

Maria Slowey and Richard Taylor
Dublin, Ireland and Pooley Bridge, UK
March 2024

FOREWORD

There are few, if any, concepts so central to the university in liberal democracies as academic freedom. Academic freedom is the oxygen of discovery and pedagogy. The free interplay of ideas and the collegial, expert contestation of research findings is essential for the furtherance of knowledge, understanding, and indeed to the never-ending pursuit of truth. Similarly, in the teaching context, all ideas and theories should be open for debate.

Universities in the twenty-first century are undeniably more important – economically, socially, educationally – than ever before. Moreover, they are far larger than at any previous time, with more than half of the age cohort attending in most developed societies. The research carried out by universities is critically important in what is, by general agreement, a global knowledge society. The United Nations Development Goals, blueprint to preserve our biosphere and planet, have further amplified demands for innovation and newly skilled graduates.

At the same time as universities enjoy this unprecedented prominence and importance, there are very real threats to academic freedom: these are both 'external,' principally from governments seeking to steer universities in particular directions, but also from commercial interests and public pressures, and 'internal,' through a series of pressures to conform in various ways to the mainstream in research and teaching cultures.

Whilst virtually all academics, policy makers, and university leaders agree that academic freedom is foundational to the academy, not only it is hard to define precisely but also it is often only when it is threatened that the need for constant vigilance becomes evident.

Nevertheless, there would be general agreement with the EUA statement that 'Scholars need freedom of thought and inquiry to advance knowledge, as well as the freedom to communicate the results of their work and educate the next generation of critical thinkers. .... underpinning this is institutional autonomy, which shields higher education and research institutions from political and economic interference and ensures the self-governance of the scientific community' (EUA, 2019).

This is therefore a timely and important book for all those concerned with the roles that universities play in the modern world. The expert authors, from a range of disciplines, across diverse societies and nationalities, differ in focus and perspectives: but all agree that the protection and development of academic freedom is essential if universities are to fulfil their central roles in relation to the pursuit and dissemination of independent knowledge in the interests of the wellbeing of current, and future, societies.

The book deserves a legacy beyond life on the shelves. It deserves tangible impact, inspiring greater collective actions by university communities to sustain academic freedom: garnering of new empirical evidence of its value sufficient to persuade sceptical policy makers to refine academic autonomy measurement tools to capture growing subtle infringements, new strategies to broaden societal appreciation of its intrinsic value, and a wider sharing of policy principles to combat self-censorship on university campuses – to name a few. As these initiatives emerge, the authors can justifiably lay some claim to the famous epitaph: *si monumentum exegesis, circumspici!*

Michael B. Murphy,
President European Universities Association (2019–2023)

PART I

Academic Freedom

The Issues

1

INTRODUCTION

Academic freedom: core value or elite privilege?

Maria Slowey and Richard Taylor

Introduction

Academic freedom has long been regarded as a core value of universities in Western societies. At first sight, it may appear to be not only an uncomplicated but also an uncontentious concept: an (almost) *a priori* attribute of universities across the widely differing societies that constitute the Western world.

However, as so often with 'foundational values' over different historical periods and in diverse contexts, on closer examination the concept and practice of academic freedom is riven with complexity and contradiction. Moreover, it is held by many to be possibly under greater threat today than at any period since World War II.

In this introductory chapter, we begin with a historically contextualised definition of the concept of academic freedom, its interaction with, but differences from, the more generalised societal value of free speech, and the salience of both for the contemporary university.

In recent times, across liberal democracies, the university – and its underlying value structure – has been held by some, largely on the left of the political spectrum, to be both conservative and elitist. Conversely, many on the right have seen the contemporary university as embodying a middle-class, liberal, 'politically correct' culture, divorced from the concerns and perspectives of 'ordinary people,' and imposing, at least implicitly, a uniformity of ideological view.

In both cases, for different reasons, a common critique is that academic freedom has been used (or misused) as a type of protective 'smokescreen' for the preservation of closed systems of thought and approach – in effect, different forms of elite privilege.

DOI: 10.4324/9781003363262-2

These ideas are explored and contested below. Our argument is that the importance of asserting and protecting academic freedom is central to the preservation of many of the core values of the university.

The nature of contemporary higher education, including universities, has of course changed radically in the decades since 1945, not least in terms of the diversity of types of institution, the rapid and dramatic expansion of student numbers, and the increasingly central role universities are called upon to play in the economy and society. The university has thus had to adjust to very different societal contexts. There have been, and continue to be, associated and severe threats to the preservation of the characteristics that make universities distinctive. These threats have come both externally (since the late nineteenth century, primarily from the State) and internally (from a complex of cultural and political self-censorship within the academy).

Can academic freedom, in any meaningful sense, survive in this changed context? *Should* it remain a core value of the contemporary university? These questions shape the discussion in this introductory chapter.

The first part of the chapter provides an overview of the origins and definitions of the idea – and ideal – of academic freedom. The second clarifies important distinctions between academic freedom and the associated, but wider, principle of free speech. In democratic societies, free speech is, or ought to be, a universal right, subject only to legal constraints. Academic freedom, on the other hand, for both institutions and individuals – as members of the academy, teachers, researchers, and (in some important respects) students – is a right which has to be earned through the acquisition of expert knowledge and the application of intellectual rigour in teaching and research. The objective here has always been the pursuit of knowledge and 'truth' through scholarship, and the dissemination of knowledge and understanding.

The third part outlines threats to this concept of academic freedom, both explicit and implicit, and emanating from both external and internal sources. The fourth part offers our rationale for this book, its interdisciplinary, international, comparative perspective, and structure, and notes briefly the content and approach of each of the following chapters.

We conclude with a robust defence of the centrality of academic freedom within the university, characterised by the free pursuit of knowledge and the associated, never-ending, quest for 'truth.' Such institutions and cultures are key elements of civil society and thus of a wider, vibrant liberal democracy.

Origins and definitions

Although academic freedom is universally held to be a defining characteristic of the university, it is notoriously hard to give an exact definition, even when confined to the context of the contemporary university in liberal democratic states.[1] A good starting point is the assertion, by Karl Jaspers, that 'it is a human right that the search for truth should be preserved everywhere unfettered' (translation in Beaud, 2020, 612). It is from this *a priori* assertion that the university, as an institution, and those individuals engaged as members of academic staff ('faculty,' in American terminology) have the right, and indeed the duty, to pursue the search for truth as they see fit, free from interference or pressure from both external agencies (for example, the State) and internal cultures or interests (for example, Trustees, Governors, or 'Management'). Thus, the university should provide the environment whereby, through free enquiry seeking truth via the acquisition of knowledge and understanding,

> scholars who are dedicated to the life of the mind [are able] to follow the argument where it leads, unfettered of received wisdom and popular views of political connections and regardless of the practical, social or moral implications of their conclusions.
>
> *(Shweder, 2016, 190)*

The self-determining aspect of academic freedom is emphasised by Marginson (2008): defining academic freedom as an 'activity space of research and scholarship in the university domain' means that this activity should, at least in some respects, be 'conceived, directed and executed by scholars and researchers themselves' (269).

Some analysts point to increasing isomorphism in contemporary university structures, governance, and modes of operation as they – and, also, national policy makers – respond to powerful global forces in increasingly similar ways (Schofer and Meyer, 2005). However, even allowing for such common trends, the current formation of universities is also reflective of particular historical and cultural traditions, which, in different ways, have contributed to notions of academic freedom. While the Western medieval university was, of course, closely associated with the church and also linked to local territorial states, this dual relationship provided a degree of independence.

> That crucial sliver of space between the two larger players, church and state, enabled them to develop partial institutional autonomy and a more complete academic freedom. In legal terms the mediaeval universities were incorporated entities, formalising their independent status.
>
> *(Marginson and Yang, 2020, 7)*

There are generally held to be, in broad terms, four archetypical models of higher education traditions (Zgaga, 2009): those with a focus on education for elite careers (Napoleonic); those emphasising the creation and maintenance of knowledge (Humboldt); those focusing on students' personal development (Newman); and those with an emphasis on preparing students as 'civic actors' (Dewey).

Altbach (2001) in an influential overview of global developments in higher education drew attention to the important, yet necessarily broad, range of interpretations of academic freedom.

> Those entrusted with teaching and research in higher education, it is claimed, have a special obligation to dedicate themselves to truth and objectivity in all their scholarly work. These critics argue that academe and politics should not be intertwined. Universities are not political institutions, and those involved in the academic enterprise need to recognize that academe's survival depends on its ability to keep an appropriate distance from partisan politics. Others have a more absolutist view of academic freedom and feel that faculty members should have the right to participate in any activities they deem appropriate, and that representative bodies of the faculty may similarly be engaged. There is as yet no consensus, and as a result, there is considerable debate about the appropriate limits to academic freedom.
>
> *(Altbach, 2001, 208)*

Across all of the archetypes and international variances, the practice of academic freedom is associated with three key features: first, students should be taught how to think and think *critically*; second, the scholar must be free to pursue research as he or she determines, with the overriding objective, as noted, of the pursuit of truth through the acquisition of knowledge and understanding; also, that the teaching provided should be informed by such research, thus creating – ideally – a symbiosis between teaching and research; and, third, this 'community of scholars' must be free from external or internal interference.

As Reichman has observed, citing the USA 1915 *Declaration of Principles on Academic Freedom and Academic Tenure*,

> once appointed, the scholar has professional functions to perform in which the appointing authorities have neither competency nor moral right to intervene. The responsibility of the university teacher is primarily to the public itself and to the judgment of his [sic] own profession.
>
> *(Reichman, 2021, 10–1)*

However, as numerous analysts have argued, this is an ideal to be striven for, an aspiration: it has never been truly realised – nor probably can it ever be. Academic staff, and of course students, are human and subjective, however conscientiously they may strive for objectivity. Moreover, there are numerous interpretations of what should properly constitute 'impartiality' in any context, including teaching and research.

There are further caveats and problems with the 'intellectual probity' of the concept of academic freedom. As Scott (2019) has argued, a central contradiction, or at the very least, a limiting factor, of academic freedom is that free inquiry is essential to its definition, but it is inquiry patrolled and legitimated by disciplinary authority – a disciplinary authority that, in turn, warrants autonomy, the freedom of scholars from external pressure. The university provides knowledge essential to the operation of democracy, but knowledge production is not a democratic process because it rests on the expertise of researchers and teachers (Scott, 2019, 5).

Moreover, definitions and criteria for achieving such expertise tend to be in the control of those who are senior and, it is to be presumed, respected by peers in their relevant disciplinary area. They are thus in a position not only to act as gatekeepers within their own disciplines but also to engage in power struggles with other disciplines – for example, as illustrated in Clark's (1983) classic discussion of the power of 'academic oligarchies' and Becher and Trowler's (1993) 'academic tribes and territories.' To add to the problems, despite a rhetoric in recent decades of the importance of interdisciplinarity, associated conceptual and methodological approaches often remain marginal in the academy (Slowey, 2023). Arguably also, disciplines have tended to become ever more specialised and self-referential. For those academics who might wish to pursue research outside these increasingly restricted parameters, opportunities are curtailed, not least in terms of external funding. These problems apply especially to younger, more junior academic staff (Haviland *et al*, 2017).

The 'appropriateness' of research inquiries and of teaching curricula is thus determined to a large extent by the generally accepted norms, criteria, and overall culture of the discipline concerned; and these are 'policed,' sometimes explicitly, more often implicitly, by the university's hierarchical academic structures (Faculty Committees, Quality Assurance Committees, Senates and the like). Once again, academic freedom is something of a paradox. As Sitze (2017) observes, free inquiry in academia is predicated on voluntarily assumed forms of unfreedom that are unique to the academy. There is arguably an in-built conservatism in the criteria employed in the academy to determine what is deemed 'appropriate' in terms of quality and the advancement of knowledge in any given discipline. Clearly, this can be seen pejoratively, from the point of view of those who would see the academy as challenging orthodoxies and presenting radical reinterpretations of social, cultural, and, indeed, scientific realities. More positively, of course, academics can be seen as truth seekers who are equipped to judge the abilities of their peers (Dewey, 1976).

Academic freedom and free speech

There is thus a variety of perspectives on what properly constitutes the theory and practice of academic freedom in the university context. It is clear, however, that academic freedom is widely regarded as a particular subset of the more general societal right to free speech. Academic freedom can be exercised only within the university, and only by those who are deemed to be appropriately qualified to gain entry to the academic profession. As has been argued, academic freedom even then is constrained and restricted in a number of ways.

Free speech, in contrast, as noted earlier is, or should be, a fundamental right of *all* citizens in liberal democracies. Within very broad limits, widely differing opinions – whether they be political, religious, social, or moral, or some combination – can be articulated in the public domain without fear of reprisals from governments or other State institutions.

Since the Enlightenment movements of the late eighteenth and early nineteenth centuries, freedom – of the individual and of the wider society – has been a fundamental principle. For Immanuel Kant, for example (as cited in Williams, 2016, 5), '...people's awakening from their self-imposed immaturity [required] nothing but freedom. For people to take control of their own lives... [they needed] the freedom to make public use of one's reason in all matters.' Some 80 years after the publication of Kant's major work *A Critique of Pure Reason,* Mill (1859), in his classic text *On Liberty*, similarly argued that

> Persons of genius, it is true, are, and are always likely to be, a small minority; but in order to have them, it is necessary to preserve the soil in which they grow. Genius can only breathe freely in an atmosphere of freedom.
>
> *(1859, 60)*

> Precisely because the tyranny of opinion is such as to make eccentricity a reproach, it is desirable, in order to break through that tyranny, that people should be eccentric. Eccentricity has always abounded when and where strength of character has abounded; and the amount of eccentricity in a society has generally been proportional to the amount of genius, mental vigour, and moral courage it contained. That so few now dare to be eccentric marks the chief danger of the time.
>
> *(1859, 62)*

Whether or not it might be in any way desirable for the university to be formed of 'eccentric geniuses' is, of course, a moot point. However, this is clearly distinct from the formal processes of research and teaching, where the parameters of academic freedom are necessarily more professionally constrained, as noted, by the accepted disciplinary criteria of relevant expertise.

Thus, both academics and students, in their capacities as citizens, should have the absolute freedom to express opinions, take part in pressure group or (legal) demonstrations, and contribute to political, polemical, or propagandist writings in support of any cause, however contentious (or indeed, as the majority of people might think, untenable and/or undesirable). As cited in Scott (2019, 136), Stanley Fish observed 'Freedom of speech is not an academic value. Accuracy of speech is an academic value, completeness of speech is an academic value; relevance of speech is an academic value. Each of these is directly related to the goal of academic inquiry: getting a matter of fact right.' Freedom of speech is, in this context, quite different. It is about the right to express an opinion, whether right or wrong, in a public forum, debating and arguing with others.

However, exercising these freedoms – for outside speakers at student-organised events, for example – has not always been straightforward. How far, for example, should those espousing fascist, racist, misogynist, or sexist perspectives be allowed to put forward their views in the university environment – even if their public pronouncements remain formally within the boundaries of the law? Once again, a conceptual challenge involves separating wider rights of free speech, from those arising from the more specific concept of academic freedom. Academic freedom has to be concerned with protecting those whose thinking may well challenge established orthodoxies: yet it also has to be assumed that this right has been earned through peer recognition and associated academic recognition based on methods, standards, and accepted procedures of relevant disciplines.

External and internal threats to academic freedom

Clearly, universities have never been so prominent and highly valued as they are today, not only in Western societies but also globally. As Scott, puts it, the

> development of mass higher education has produced what is arguably the university's golden age. The achievements of the medieval university, so unlike its modern form but nevertheless its nominal ancestor, were insignificant in comparison.
>
> *(Scott, 2021, 2)*

Included among recent achievements, most importantly, is the increase in the numbers of students, and the proportions of young people gaining access, as well as the opening of universities to significantly wider sections of the population previously underrepresented or excluded from higher education. On the positive side, universities have never played such a significant role in both society and the economy; their research expertise and their resources of technical, scientific, and professional knowledge have never been so widely deployed and so highly regarded and influential; their social as well as their educational roles figure prominently in the institutions and life experiences of almost all aspects of society, from large corporations, to cultural organisations (including modern media), to the caring professions and the service sector; in the 'scientific age,' universities have an unparalleled influence upon decision-making in the State; and, quite simply, they are very considerably larger than ever before.

On the negative side, however, there are undoubtedly challenges to the underpinning values and culture of the university. In 2023, 22 countries and territories were identified where universities and scholars enjoyed 'significantly' less freedom than a decade previously, while, overall, academic freedom was regarded as having 'stagnated' in 152 countries: often from what was defined as already being at a 'low level' (Kinzelbach *et al*, 2023). Many of these threats centre on the concept and practice of academic freedom, and they come from both outside and inside the university: with tensions between the mission of higher education institutions to produce and disseminate knowledge and simultaneously respond to societal needs. Many such contemporary pressures, as Picard and Goastellec (2014) put it, 'take the form of external demand to increase support for innovation needed to stimulate national economic growth as well as train a highly-skilled workforce to meet the ongoing needs of the labour market' (205).

More broadly, such tensions can be seen as the incursion into the heart of the university's culture of ideologies and practices associated with late capitalism and neo-liberal policies. In their penetrating analysis of 'academic capitalism,' Slaughter and Rhoades (2004) showed the ways in which the boundaries between public concerns and private gains were dissolving as, with a view to income generation, research was increasingly 'redirected' towards market interests: they make a strong case that, without a renewed understanding of academic freedom, and commitment to tenure (in the USA system), universities were in danger of becoming more like knowledge 'factories' than spaces for debates on the diversity of truths.

This type of marketisation of higher education has proceeded apace throughout the Western world, resulting in

> a growth in managerialism… imposing ideas and practices from the private world of business… This has led to the demise of the university as a republic of scholars… or as a cultural institution to be replaced by a corporate organization opened up to stakeholders and the evaluative State.
>
> *(Clancy, 2021, 171)*

Most Western governments, and increasingly the wider cultures of their societies, have prioritised STEM (science, technology, engineering, and mathematics) subjects and the associated research. This has been seen as enhancing the economic efficiency of modern, technologically complex, societies; and such approaches have been justified in instrumental, utilitarian terms. Such has been the dominance of this approach that the whole internal culture of the university has been affected: for example, the criteria for excellence applied in science and technological disciplines have replaced, at least in part, the criteria used in the inherently different areas of the arts and social sciences. This is apparent in the value attributed to published research articles in high-status academic journals, as opposed to scholarly monograph studies; and also in the criteria used for the promotion of junior staff to more senior level positions in the academy.

The irony of reducing public investment in universities being accompanied by increasing requirements for accountability is widely acknowledged. Inevitably, this has shaped, at least partially, the nature of the research undertaken by academic scholars. As Rostan (2010) has observed, the 'quest for external research funding and the links with the economy consequently confront academics with alien demands and expectations' (586). Similarly, such influences have not infrequently had a negative impact upon degree course planning, with priority given to subject areas deemed to be 'relevant' to such outside interests.

These factors, combined with the overwhelmingly neo-liberal ideological orientation of many Western governments, have resulted in an increasingly utilitarian, instrumental culture in higher education.

Within this constraining and negative context for academic freedom, there has been a marked reduction in the proportion of academic staff who hold tenured, full-time posts and who consequently lack the freedom to determine their research (and teaching) priorities. Similarly, there is a growing number of 'teaching only' academic staff and others on short-term research contracts who do not, by contractual definition, enjoy the privileges of their permanent/ tenured colleagues.

Inevitably, given all these factors, there has been a growth in a corporate style of management in the academy, usually accompanied by more hierarchical and managerially determined decision-making structures, with a corresponding diminution in the autonomy, and thus the academic freedom, of individual scholars. And, in consequence of this complex of negative external forces, fee-paying students in particular can be seen, and increasingly see themselves, as 'customers' in the 'marketplace' of higher education. (In Europe, perhaps this is most notably the case in the UK, especially England, as a result of the imposition of high levels of student fees.)

The original liberal conception – admittedly always, as noted, an aspirational ideal rather than a reality, of the university as 'a community of scholars' – often seems distant in the early twenty-first century. Rather than challenging orthodoxies in teaching and research, it can seem that in many respects the university is at risk of becoming dangerously conformist.

If these negative *external* factors provide a difficult environment for the protection and development of academic freedom within the culture of a liberal university, then the *internal* threats are equally daunting, if less obvious. At the core of these internal threats has been an emerging university culture of what some define as self-censorship (for example, Bloom, 1987; Russell, 1993).

In many respects,

> the final decades of the nineteenth century and the first decades of the
> twentieth century represent the heyday of the liberal academic project.
> Scholars were becoming increasingly confident in espousing a notion of
> secular truth and had a strong concept of their own role in relation to its
> pursuit through knowledge.
>
> *(Williams, 2016, 35–6)*

As late as 1957, the philosopher John Anderson could state with confidence
that academic freedom

> does *not* mean that academics have the same standing "before the law" as
> any other citizen; it means that they have a special province, a field in which
> they can say: "*We* are the experts here; *we* can tell you (the Law, the State)
> what has force, what *runs*, in this department of social activity".
>
> *(cited in Hayes, 2009, 107)*

If universities are considered to be the 'intellectual conscience' of a nation,
then the preservation of their intellectual freedom and autonomy is of para-
mount importance (Shattock, 2012).

However, we must never forget that for much of their history, universities
in the Western world were elitist enclaves of almost entirely male, white academics, drawn overwhelmingly from the upper echelons of society. Moreover,
the culture of these institutions was intellectually and socially overconfident,
if not arrogant. But, in the context of academic freedom, they had a kernel
of unshakeable liberal beliefs: they saw universities as being essentially sites of
(protected) free inquiry and the pursuit of truth through the acquisition of
knowledge; and the means of achieving these goals was through the free inter-
change, in a community of scholars, of differing opinions, ideas and themes.
'Socratic dialogue' was accepted as the mode of both teaching and scholarly
research endeavour.

Paradoxically, as universities began their long ascent in the public domain
to becoming recognised as central institutions in society for both economic
and social reasons, so increasing public investment in both teaching and research was defined and justified in largely utilitarian terms. The chief criterion
became the 'useful' advance of scientific and technological knowledge. The
very essence of the university was 'undermined by the imposition of instrumental objectives' (Williams, 2016, 43).

There were several other factors, in the decades since 1945, that have severely undermined the liberal conception of the university and, with it, the
belief in the centrality of academic freedom. In the Cold War period, for example, the rise of McCarthyism led, *inter alia*, to the widespread questioning of

whether proper academic objectivity could ever be attained by Communists, so-called Fellow Travellers, and other left socialists.

In this context, even more destructive intellectually than the directly political attacks were two other factors. First, the undermining of the whole Enlightenment idea by the devastating experience of the Holocaust and its aftermath in what was generally held to have been one of the societies whose culture stemmed centrally from the Enlightenment and whose contributions to Western civilisation were unquestionably so significant. The Holocaust was seen by many influential thinkers – Adorno and his Frankfurt colleagues, for example – as connected with scientific thought and rationality, leading to the growth of post-modernist critiques in some disciplines.

Second, and inexorably following from these positions, there developed a post-modern questioning of all established truths and even more of any of the grand narratives (whether political or religious) stemming from the Enlightenment. Intellectual relativism became the order of the day and this self-doubting (rather than properly self-critical and openly questioning) environment led often to a defensive retreat into illiberal positions (Taylor *et al*, 2002); as Peters (2017) puts it: 'in the era of post-truth it is not enough to revisit notions or theories of truth, accounts of "evidence", and forms of epistemic justification as a guide to truth, but we need to understand the broader epistemological and Orwellian implications of post-truth politics, science and education' (565).

In this context also, it has been suggested that perhaps a reason for the continuing influence in some circles of Habermas may lie in

> the impulse to avoid relativism – whereby there is no truth but many truths. No correct moral judgement but only a competing clamour of different value claims – has been an important part of what has kept Habermas spinning his web of words for more than half a century. Habermas's fight against the relativism of postmodern thought is central to understanding his work.
>
> *(Jeffries, 2017, 359)*

Several linked but different elements combine: first, as noted, there has been, at least, a degree of acquiescence on the part of some (possibly many?) academics in the narrowing of both research and teaching priorities to areas perceived as more instrumental, vocational, and/or scientific; secondly, the relativism referred to has often combined, unhelpfully, with students' views of themselves as 'customers' effectively to exclude from the curriculum opinions, or indeed whole areas of intellectual inquiry, as being 'beyond the pale'; and finally, the growth of an individualistic, atomised culture has contributed to undermining the concept of a collective, disinterested pursuit of truth, through knowledge acquisition.

Arguably, a further result of this climate of individualism has been the emphasis upon so-called 'identity politics' and associated campaigns for the need for 'safe spaces'. Callan (2016) makes a case for squaring this particular circle by distinguishing between what he refers to as 'dignity safety'– to which everyone has a right – and 'intellectual safety,' which is against the ethos of free enquiry and 'repugnant' to any education worth having: as he puts it, 'intellectual safety' in education 'can only be conferred at the cost of indulging close-mindedness and allied vices. Tension between securing dignity safety and creating a fittingly unsafe intellectual environment can be eased when teaching and institutional ethos promote the virtue of civility' (64).

A final instrumental challenge for the operation of academic freedom in contemporary universities lies in the rapid step-changes being made in technological developments in AI. Related issues were already in evidence over two decades ago.

> Are professors entitled to academic freedom in the cyberclassroom? Does the cyberprofessor have the freedom to design and deliver a course without external restriction from sponsors (often profit-making companies), especially when development costs may be high? Who owns knowledge products developed for Internet use? These are questions that impinge on traditional ideas about academic freedom, and need to be answered as higher education moves to new modes of delivering knowledge.
>
> *(Altbach, 2001, 208–9)*

As we noted at the outset, universities are called upon to play more important and influential roles in society than ever before, and yet, at the same time, their fundamental values and identity are, arguably, more threatened than at any time since the end of World War II. It is for this reason that we decided to join with expert colleagues, from a variety of disciplines and countries, to discuss and analyse the current state of academic freedom in the academy.

Purpose and structure of the book

There is an extensive literature on the theme of academic freedom, much of it emanating from the USA and concentrating almost exclusively on the American experience. Our book aims to make a distinctive contribution to this debate by adopting both international and interdisciplinary perspectives: the authors are experts based in Europe (the UK, Ireland, and Hungary), Mexico, Australia, and Hong Kong, and their analyses draw on a range of disciplines: political science, sociology, history, philosophy, higher education studies, and gender studies.

The following two chapters in this **Part** of the book explore in more detail the historical and philosophical underpinnings of academic freedom and free speech. They interrogate the ways in which these issues have been approached over time.

In the first of these, Peter Scott (Chapter 2) adopts a historical approach and traces the (elusive) concept of academic freedom from the medieval to the modern world. He delineates the challenging context for academic freedom in contemporary higher education, where other agendas, including democratic accountability to the State, 'restorative justice,' and respect for once subordinated non-elite groups are all deemed to have a high priority in the academy. Moreover, the intellectual climate – with successive waves of post-structuralism, deconstructionism, and other similar intellectual currents – potentially undermines more traditional forms of scholarly inquiry and scientific reason. Scott makes the case that, whereas institutional autonomy has been reduced in mass systems, academic freedom has only exceptionally been directly attacked – although sometimes subtly eroded as much from within as from without. He traces the shifting foundations of academic freedom, free speech, and the associated dilemmas posed for universities from four interlocking perspectives: external structural pressures; externally derived ideological interventions; internal structural changes; and internally generated ideological effects.

In Chapter 3, Alan Haworth examines the philosophical origins of the concepts of free speech and academic freedom, centring on J.S. Mill, but encompassing also the perspectives of other influential thinkers. He analyses the differences between 'the liberty of thought and discussion' and the concept of academic freedom. The emerging social class structure of the late nineteenth century facilitated, so Mill argued, a new taste for discussion, and this held the key to social progress and acted as an antidote to 'the tyranny of the majority.' How relevant are such arguments to twenty-first century conditions?

In **Part II**, the general issues analysed above are illustrated through a detailed examination of two contrasting cases over the post–World War II period in British higher education: from the 1940s through to the 1990s. The lasting implications for contemporary debates are discussed in each.

In the first of these, Richard Taylor (Chapter 4) analyses a controversial episode in the UK where it was alleged by some that there was systemic discrimination against left-wing academics in university extramural departments, particularly those who were associated with the Communist Party. Their legitimacy as university professionals was queried because of their ideological perspectives in the early Cold War era (the late 1940s through to the mid-1950s). Such departments were engaged in educational provision in inherently contentious contexts, with a variety of social and state bodies: for example, trade unions, social workers, the police, and the armed services. Moreover, in the immediate post-war period, Britain still had an extensive Empire in Africa and elsewhere: such departments were also often involved with government in higher educational provision where it was inevitable that issues of colonialism and the demands for independence would arise.

Although framed in a specific historical and organisational context, the issues raised about the appropriate limits, if any, to academic freedom have continuing relevance for the university system.

So-called 'cancel culture' and 'no platforming' have become issues of considerable contention in universities and wider society in most liberal democracies in the twenty-first century. In Chapter 5, Evan Smith provides a historically contextualised analysis of this phenomenon, and the controversies that have surrounded it for some time in the UK. He provides detailed evidence that this issue is not in fact a recent phenomenon but had been both prominent and contentious over many decades. The application of 'no platforming' has revealed tensions within the student movement – and wider society – over how it should be used and who should be targeted.

The case raises several important issues. Specifically, should the rights of an individual transcend those of the wider academic community, including black and ethnic minority students and staff, to learn and teach in a secure environment? There are, it is maintained, relevant and politically significant implications for academic freedom in contemporary higher education institutions in the UK and elsewhere.

In **Part III**, the discussion is internationalised and brought up to the contemporary period. The chapters draw on contrasting experience and debates on issues relating to academic freedom in Mexico, Hong Kong, and Hungary. In Mexico, in the 2020s, there is a populist, left-leaning government; in Hungary, in contrast, the government is populist and right-leaning; and in Hong Kong, while there is a historical background of liberalism in a colonial context, its recent absorption into the People's Republic of China has created a complex situation for many in the academy.

In Chapter 6, Wietse de Vries investigates the situation of academic freedom in Mexico under a populist regime that, he argues, seeks to redefine from a political perspective what the parameters of academic freedom and research should be. These developments affect not only freedom of speech, but also freedom of thought, exploration, and research. Thus, while the Government permits people to say whatever they want (and even defends their right to do so), it discourages, directly or indirectly, research on certain topics. De Vries points to issues of 'self-censorship' in the academy as a good deal of serious research from the past has been condemned as 'neo-liberal science,' not only by the State but also by the management of certain universities and some academic peers.

Liz Jackson, in Chapter 7, contrasts the idealised perspectives of academic freedom, with academics' concrete experiences, drawing on her knowledge of both Hong Kong and the USA. She sees academic freedom more as 'a capability': the extent to which a person has academic freedom can be dynamic and not confined to legal rights. In particular, the capacity to exercise academic freedom hinges on such factors as the forms of knowledge that are valued within a given social context, and by whom; and what influences scholars to be silent or self-censor, even when academic freedom is formally operative.

In Chapter 8, Rebeka Bakos and Andrea Pető adopt a critical and comparative perspective on a contemporary crisis confronting long-held European values, as they consider the treatment of refugee scholars in Hungary, under two interrelated aspects of the Orbán government's policies: a traditionally anti-refugee stance, and also what they argue is an illiberal approach to academic freedom. They make the case that, while Hungarian refugee policy had become increasingly restrictive since the 2015 refugee crisis, there was an apparent shift in governmental attitude in 2022 with the beginning of the Russian invasion of Ukraine. Through analyses of governmental policies and in-depth interviews with several migration experts, the chapter explores the extent to which Hungary is prepared to receive refugee academics compared with their reception across the European Union (EU) in general and Romania and the United Kingdom in particular.

The chapters in **Part IV** highlight specific contemporary developments in higher education which carry significant implications for academic freedom – conceptually and in practice.

Increasing proportions of higher education academics (lecturing staff) and researchers are employed in contingent – that is, short-term, temporary, and/or part-time – positions. Taking up this theme in Chapter 9, Maria Slowey addresses the question of the extent to which the core principles of academic freedom apply in practice – if at all – to such members of the university. In exploring this issue, she draws on a consultation exercise conducted to elicit the views of experts in higher education research from 11 countries: in Europe – Denmark, Germany, Italy, Ireland, Slovenia, Sweden, Switzerland, and the United Kingdom; Japan; South Africa; and the United States. She analyses their conceptions of academic freedom – safeguards and threats – and their views on the implications for the rights and protections for those sometimes referred to as the 'academic precariat.'

The use, and misuse, of global rankings over recent decades is taken up by Ellen Hazelkorn (Chapter 10). These rankings have had a profound effect upon the shaping of global higher education and the science landscape. They are, in part, reflective of the increasing trends of globalisation in higher education, as in many other sectors, and have led to broader conversations about knowledge creation and dissemination. Several issues arise, amongst them: how is the concept of 'excellence' to be determined? And how important are factors such as 'student employability' or 'public impact'? Similarly, new forms of publishing (pre-print, for example) reflect new practices for sharing research and making research results publicly available: but might these lead to a narrowing, rather than a widening, of public access? Moreover, there is evidence of increasing links between rankings, publishing, and 'Big Data,' creating huge repositories which are usually held behind 'pay walls.' The monetisation of higher education data highlights its value beyond the higher education community and governments, and thus, at least implicitly, militates against the spirit of academic freedom.

Finally, as editors, in Chapter 11, we reflect on the analyses in the preceding chapters, and reassert the importance of academic freedom and the need both to reaffirm and to protect its centrality in the next stage of development of the university in contemporary society.

Concluding comments

As noted above, the shape of higher education has changed radically since the mid-twentieth century. Participation rates in higher education in most Western societies now exceed over half of the school leaving age cohort. We have argued that, while many of these developments have been socially advantageous – in terms, for example, of widening access – it is our contention that, in a number of crucial respects, certain freedoms of central importance to the academy have simultaneously been threatened.

Universities have become far more enmeshed with different arms of the State – reaching beyond the confines of ministries of education to the ministries of finance and others concerned with economic development, at regional, national, and international levels. Despite levels of funding waxing and waning over time, states have become increasingly involved in steering higher education through accountability and quality assurance regimes. All this has led inexorably to the State having both a more significant 'stakeholder' role and what is potentially a worrying degree of ideological dominance in the academy.

This dominance has had several negative consequences, in the context of the debate over academic freedom – and more generally, free speech – in the academy. First, the State (via government departments and agencies) tends to prioritise investment in research and teaching in those areas deemed to be 'in the national interest': this decision-making process is permeated by ideological positions and assumptions, whether explicit or implicit. In this way, dissident voices and 'awkward' research are often marginalised or excluded altogether. Second, and more amorphous but even more important, the State exercises a powerful influence on the cultural parameters of discussion in universities. This is usually an implicit process: but on occasion it becomes explicit, as in the specific case studies which are considered in this book. Third, many states and regional bodies, such as the EU, have in recent years prioritised instrumental, sometimes narrowly vocational, agendas for higher education, with implications for the wider development of knowledge and critical thinking. Fourth, associated with the knowledge economy there has been an increasing focus on intellectual property rights, commercial 'spin-out' companies, and the like. Directly or indirectly, in many countries this has led to the prioritisation of

STEM subjects at the expense of disciplines perceived to be 'less relevant.' Fifth, there has been a rapid growth in the application of 'objective,' algorithmic-based indicators of quality – particularly of research – on both individual academics and universities. This has had the negative effect of constraining and bureaucratising behaviour at both institutional and individual levels – particularly in relation to research.

Whatever their various differences, virtually all higher education systems in the Western tradition share core values, including, as noted, centrally their explicit commitment to free speech in general and academic freedom in particular. In this respect, there are close parallels between the challenges facing universities and those more generally facing the liberal democracies of which they are a part. As Douglass (2021) discusses, the growth of populism and neo-nationalism poses threats as

> isolationist, anti-globalist leanings of neo-nationalist governments have a significant impact on universities, which are inherently globally engaged institutions. The impact is not only felt in illiberal democracies. In Europe, for example, restrictions on civil liberties, including the persecution of academics, affects the global flow of talent mobility.
>
> *(ix)*

Of course, far more serious problems, in the context of free speech, academic freedom, and much else, exist for universities and other social and political institutions in contemporary societies characterised by totalitarian and/or authoritarian regimes of varying degrees of barbarity. Globally, the academic community is proactive in working to support colleagues and students under threat through the important contribution made by networks such as Scholars at Risk Network (SAR 2024) and the Universities of Sanctuary movement (2024).

Whether such ideological repression can be challenged successfully and overcome – as a consequence of such international actions, or through the democratisation of access to knowledge and information, or access to education, or through some other social mechanism – is a subject for another, wider, study. Here, as stated, the focus is more narrowly on problems and issues associated with academic freedom and free speech in universities in modern liberal societies. Inevitably, however, higher education's international reach, underpinned by core values, leads to a particular responsibility to engage with such major challenges.

Note

1 While a great deal of what is broadly termed 'higher education' takes place in institutions *other* than universities – colleges, polytechnics, specialist and technological institutions, and the like – the focus here is mainly on universities.

References

Altbach, P. (2001). Academic freedom: International realities and challenges. *Higher Education, 41*, 205–19.

Beaud, O. (2020). Reflections on the concept of academic freedom. *European Review of History: Revue Européenne d'Histoire, 27*(5), 611–27. https://doi.org/10.1080/13507486.2020.1823650

Becher, T., and Trowler, P. R. (1993). *Academic tribes and territories: Intellectual enquiry and the culture of disciplines* (2nd ed.). Buckingham: SRHE/Open University Press.

Bloom, A. (1987). *The closing of the American mind*. New York: Simon and Schuster.

Callan, E. (2016). Education in safe and unsafe spaces. *Philosophical Inquiry in Education, 24*(1), 64–78.

Clancy, P. (2021). The governance of European higher education in transition. In H. Eggins, A. Smolentseva, and H. de Wit (eds), *Higher education in the next decade: Global challenges, future prospects* (167–85). Leiden: Brill.

Clark, B. (1983). *The higher education system: Academic organization in cross-national perspective*. Berkeley: University of California Press.

Dewey, J. (1976). Academic freedom. In J. A. Boydston (ed), *John Dewey: The middle works, 1899-1924. Vol. 2: 1902-1903* (53–66). Carbondale: Southern Illinois University Press. (Original work published 1902).

Douglass, J. (2021). *Neo-nationalism and universities: Populists, autocrats, and the future of higher education*. Baltimore: Johns Hopkins University.

Haviland, D., Alleman, N. F., and Allen, C. C. (2017). 'Separate but not quite equal': Collegiality experiences of full-time non-tenure-track faculty members. *The Journal of Higher Education, 88*(4), 505–28.

Hayes, D. (2009). Editorial: Academic freedom. *British Journal of Educational Studies, 57*(2), 107–10.

Jeffries, S. (2017). *Grand hotel abyss: The lives of the Frankfurt school*. London: Verso.

Kinzelbach, K., Lindberg, S. I., Pelke, L., and Spannagel, J. (2023). *Academic Freedom Index 2023 Update*. FAU Erlangen-Nürnberg and V-Dem Institute. https://doi.org/10.25593/opus4-fau-21630

Marginson, S. (2008). Academic creativity under new public management: foundations for an investigation. *Educational Theory, 58*, 3.

Marginson, S., and Yang, L. (2020). *The role of higher education in generating 'public' and 'common' goods: A comparison of Sinic and Anglo-American political cultures*. Centre for Global Higher Education Working Paper No.52. Oxford: Centre for Global Higher Education.

Mill, J. S. (1859). *On liberty*. London.

Peters, M. A. (2017) Education in a post-truth world. *Educational Philosophy and Theory, 49*(6), 563–6. https://doi.org/10.1080/00131857.2016.1264114

Picard, F., and Goastellec, G. (eds) (2014). *Higher education in societies: A multi scale perspective*. Rotterdam: Sense.

Reichman, H. (2021). *Understanding academic freedom*. Baltimore: Johns Hopkins University Press.

Rostan, M. (2010). Challenges to academic freedom: Some empirical evidence. *European Review, 18*(S1), S71–88. https://doi.org/10.1017/S1062798709990329

Russell, C. (1993). *Academic freedom*. London: Routledge.

Schofer, E., and Meyer, J. W. (2005). The worldwide expansion of higher education in the twentieth century. *American Sociological Review*, 70(6), 898–920.

Scholars at Risk Network (SAR). (2024). https://www.scholarsatrisk.org/

Shweder, R. A. (2016). To follow the argument wherever it leads: An antiquarian view of the aim of academic freedom at the university of Chicago. In A. Bilgrami and J. R. Cole (eds), *Who's afraid of academic freedom?* (190–238). New York: Columbia University Press.

Scott, J. W. (2019). *Knowledge, power, and academic freedom.* New York: Columbia University Press.

Scott, P. (2021). *Retreat or resolution? Tackling the crisis of mass higher education.* Bristol: Policy Press.

Shattock, M. (2012). *Making policy in British higher education 1945-2011.* Buckingham: Open University Press.

Sitze, A. (2017). Academic unfreedom, unacademic freedom: Part one of two. *The Massachusetts Review*, 58(4), 589–607.

Slaughter, S., and Rhoades, G. (2004). *Academic capitalism and the new economy: markets, State and higher education.* Baltimore: Johns Hopkins University Press.

Slowey, M. (2023) Intersectionality: Implications for research in the field of adult education and lifelong learning. In K. Evans, W. O. Lee, J. Markowitsch, and M. Zukas (eds), *Third international handbook of lifelong learning.* Cham: Springer. https://link.springer.com/referenceworkentry/10.1007/978-3-031-19592-1_5

Taylor, R., Barr, J., and Steele, T. (2002). *For a radical higher education: After postmodernism.* Buckingham: SRHE and Open University Press.

Universities of Sanctuary (2024). https://universities.cityofsanctuary.org/

Williams, J. (2016). *Academic freedom in an age of conformity: Confronting the fear of knowledge.* London: Palgrave Macmillan.

Zgaga, P. (2009). Higher education and citizenship: The full range of purposes. *European Educational Research Journal*, 8(2), 175–88.

2

ACADEMIC FREEDOM AND THE DILEMMAS OF THE MODERN UNIVERSITY

Peter Scott

Introduction

Academic freedom and free speech have acquired a painful resonance in the present age of competing internationalisms and populisms. On both the right, in particular, and the left, sadly, it no longer commands universal assent. For the right, now influenced as much by free-market neo-liberal thought as nostalgia for the conservative order of a hierarchical society, academic freedom has become a problematical ideal. In the eyes of the conservative right, ideas and their expression that could safely be permitted within the closed conversations typical of elite university systems appear more threatening in the more open landscape of mass higher education systems. For the market, or neo-liberal, right academic freedom has come to be regarded almost as an indulgence, a leftist bulwark against the rightful demands for universities and academics to demonstrate the impact and utility of their teaching and research (preoccupations, to be fair, that are shared by many on the left).

For the left, perhaps less concerned now with its historic mission to create space for dissidence if not resistance to build a new and better world and more preoccupied with asserting socio-cultural identities than with addressing class-based economic inequalities, free speech has also become an equally problematical ideal. After all, it can be used to challenge these identities and associated feelings, and even to decry and deride their legitimate force. Free speech is now as likely to be seen as a means whereby elites can 'put down' marginalised and disempowered minorities as one of the most important core liberties. Thinking and speaking the unthinkable has taken on a darker hue.

As a result, both academic freedom and freedom of speech have become shrouded in the fog of so-called 'culture wars.' Both left and right have

DOI: 10.4324/9781003363262-3

contributed, although the latter in greater measure. For the left, fighting 'culture' wars is a symptom of the shift from class-based to identity-based politics, perhaps a silent confession that the reordering of society on the basis of greater equality has become an impossible project. For the right, fighting 'culture wars' has the advantage of drawing attention away from the failure of neo-liberal capitalism to produce the levels of economic growth needed to ensure that for the majority of the population living standards, and life chances, were continuously improving. The collapse of Communism was succeeded two decades later by the 'failure' of welfare-state capitalism, the latter the result of unconstrained, even triumphalist, free-market ideology. For the right also, the urge to emulate, through unconsidered but respectful parody, the ideological frenzy of the Republican Party in the US in thrall to Donald Trump has also proved irresistible. It is in this context that the UK Government legislated on free speech and academic freedom in higher education, to be enforced by a State-appointed Director of Free Speech and Academic Freedom. The fact that the UK Conservative Party, ostensibly committed to shrinking the State, should acquiesce in such an enlargement of State power is an indication of the toxic power of 'culture wars.'

On the surface, of course, nothing substantial has changed. Only the most authoritarian states openly deny the need for academic freedom (Altbach, 2001). But many governments, even in liberal democracies (to their shame, perhaps), have introduced ever more intrusive systems of accountability, some of which tip over into outright surveillance, in their higher education systems. Typically, four broad justifications are offered:

- The first is that the State, as the guardian of the interests of taxpayers (a conveniently ill-defined category), must ensure value for money when it funds universities directly or through students. The operation of universities must be as efficient as possible to secure the greatest possible benefits from the public funds they receive.
- The second is that the neo-liberal State, as the guardian of the interests of the customers of higher education (predominantly students, although in practice they are rarely consulted about their own best interests), must regulate universities – as if they were providers of 'knowledge' products and services.
- The third justification is that, in the same vein, governments have a responsibility to ensure the academic quality of the higher education and research it funds, whether directly or indirectly, and if possible to 'drive up standards.' They are therefore obliged to promote assessment systems that measure, for example, the student experience or the quality of research.
- The fourth is that, even in democratic states forced to compete in a global knowledge economy, governments are entitled to set the broad priorities that universities, and therefore individual scholars and scientists, should

follow. 'National needs' must be identified, policy initiatives promulgated, and funding programmes developed. Universities, preferably 'world-class,' have become the battle fleets of global competition in terms both of economic success and of the 'soft power' of geopolitical influence in the twenty-first century.

It is the same with free speech. Only authoritarian states deny its legitimacy. Its protection is solemnly mandated in national constitutions and international statements on human rights. Formally, it is unassailable. In practice, of course, limits have always been set, from the proverbial denial of the right to shout fire in a crowded theatre to criminal sanctions against threatening behaviour or 'hate' speech. However, in recent years further encroachments have been made. Governments, fearful of radicalisation which has been given a sharper focus by the presumed clash of civilisations on the international plane and closer to home by the revival of anti-democratic movements (on occasion thread-barely disguised as ultra-conservative political parties), have imposed new restrictions. New laws to ban particular forms of free speech have been passed, and new initiatives developed to 'de-radicalise' those at risk of radicalisation.

High-tech firms and social media, which once defended the internet as a censorship-free zone of unmediated exchange, now struggle to introduce effective restrictions on hate speech and fake news. Even universities, despite their stake in free and critical enquiry, seek to manage their academic workforces in new and more intrusive ways in order to maximise their 'performance.' They may also vet speakers invited by their students' unions, often on the grounds of an assumed threat to public order. Students' unions and societies, in turn, may 'no platform' speakers with unpalatable ideas that are seen as a threat to some students' feelings and standing. Individual students denounce teachers who in their view pose similar threats. In short, everyone – governments, the media, universities, and students – supports free speech. Everyone accuses others, not themselves, of denying free speech. But, when it comes to restrictions on free speech, everyone is at it.

It is in this turbulent context that academic freedom and free speech must now be framed. The Magna Charta Universitatum Observatory, originally established to commemorate the 900th anniversary of the University of Bologna, Europe's oldest, in 1988, has recently redrafted its founding statement on institutional autonomy and academic freedom – a clear demonstration that simply restating the tired formulas of the past is no longer adequate (MCU Observatory, 2020). Half a century ago or more, two decisive movements were launched that continue to reverberate in their impact on our understanding of academic freedom. The first, the drive to mass higher education, has fundamentally reshaped the academic and wider intellectual and even social landscapes. At its simplest, academic freedom, in some form, is now enjoyed by a greatly expanded academic population. The second, the assertion that consensual pragmatic politics (generally dominated by the technocratic centre) would prevail, the so-called 'end of ideology,' an assertion repeated again in a modified form after the fall of Communism in vainglorious claims about the 'end of history,' has proved to be a hollow promise (Bell, 1960, latest edition 2000; Fukuyama, 1992). Not only did the neo-liberal assault on postwar welfarism, beginning in the 1980s, reignite political conflict, but also the more recent prominence of social media has enabled ever more exotic forms of evidence-lite ideology to thrive.

But both movements, the one that has triumphed and the other that failed, have fundamentally shifted the terms of engagement for defining and defending academic freedom. Because mass systems have penetrated so deeply into contemporary societies, older ideas of universities as protected and preserved spaces apart, 'cities [of the intellect] on the hill,' have fallen away. Instead, higher education is embedded in society to a degree that makes new forms of accountability – or, more even-handedly, of engagement – inevitable. At the same time, traditional notions of academic freedom, rooted in mutual respect for the independence of distinctive domains – law, culture, education, and the rest – were especially reliant on a pragmatic political consensus among elites. The crumbling of that consensus and the re-emergence of ideological confrontation have undermined the mutual respect and tacit conventions that sustained academic and other freedoms in their traditional forms.

Academic freedom in history

For most of their history, universities have enjoyed some form of institutional autonomy. But the concept of academic freedom was a comparatively recent arrival and cannot be fully understood in its modern sense before the nineteenth century. The relationship between institutional autonomy and academic freedom has always been complex. It cannot be justified to assume that the former is a precondition of the latter, as demonstrated by the contemporary experiences of the late twentieth and early twenty-first century managerial university.

However, what did distinguish medieval European universities from the court or monastery-based schools in earlier centuries, and also from the contemporary (and often more advanced) centres of learning in the Islamic world and east and south Asia, was that they were established as independent and organisationally distinctive corporations. In this regard, universities were not unique or exceptional; the European medieval world was littered with corporations, for cities and distinctive (if subordinate) jurisdictions, merchants, and craftsmen. It was not intended that universities should be free to pursue heretical, or deviant, ideas. The independence they sometimes asserted from kings and other secular authorities, which was highly limited in practice, was a reflection of their wider allegiance to church and papal authority. Medieval universities were as often the enforcers of orthodoxy as its challengers.

Speculative thinking was as likely to emerge in Moslem Cordoba or Samarkand as Christian Paris or Oxford. Aristotle was preserved as a window into classical civilisation in the former; in the latter, the austerities of St Augustine and rejection of the pagan world prevailed (Marmura, 2002).

It was in the sixteenth and seventeenth centuries that the right to speculate, without excessive restriction by the church, the precursor of academic freedom and free speech in a modern sense, was first clearly articulated by scholars such as Erasmus, Spinoza, Bacon, Descartes (and, in relation to the press, Milton). The splintering of medieval Christendom into Protestant and Catholic nations (or, more accurately dynastic states) greatly facilitated this shift. So too, of course, did a new breed of experimental and observational scientists such as Copernicus, Kepler, and Galileo – and later, Newton. However, universities as institutions, although many were established during this period, played a relatively passive role in this process. Instead, these early stirrings of academic freedom and free speech arose in a wider intellectual milieu that had its beginnings in the Renaissance. Although some of these scholars and scientists had loose connections with universities, their more substantial affiliations were found in informal intellectual salons and, in the seventeenth century, scholarly colleges and academies, of which the prototype was the Royal Society in England. This intellectual orientation continued for much of the eighteenth century, with universities very much in a supporting role.

Academic freedom in an explicitly modern form was first articulated in the early nineteenth century by Wilhelm von Humboldt, a founder of the University of Berlin in 1810 and one of the key reformers of the Prussian state after its defeat by Napoleon at the Battle of Jena four years earlier (Fuller, 2009). Von Humboldt defined academic freedom in terms of the freedom to teach (*Lehrfreiheit*) and freedom to learn (*Lernfreiheit*). Both these freedoms were focused on students and teachers, not researchers. They did not necessarily entail the freedom to research and, crucially, to publish, which today are more typically associated with the exercise of academic freedom. The development of these latter freedoms was assisted more by the abolition of censorship, the exercise of free speech in a wider sense, than by a particular focus on academic freedom within the context of universities.

In von Humboldt's formulation, academic freedom had both idealistic and utilitarian dimensions. Not only did these freedoms reflect what were regarded as philosophical truths and the advance of liberal ideas but also they were seen as likely to promote the most advanced and successful forms of education. Therefore, these freedoms to teach and learn, now entrenched in powerful institutions, the reformed and newly established universities of the nineteenth century, were regarded as essential for the building and strengthening of nation states. It should be noted that during this period universities were dominated by the natural and technical sciences, fuelling and fuelled by industrialisation, as well as the liberal arts, philosophy, and law, designed to produce more efficient national elites. Any associations with 'thinking the unthinkable,' or countering intellectual hegemonies, were only faintly present.

It was only in the twentieth century that these associations came to the fore in debates about academic freedom, which was defined as much in terms of resistance to potential or actual State demands (or restrictions by university managers or trustees) as a positive right. It was in 1915 that the new American Association of University Professors (AAUP) published a statement on academic freedom, its so-called '1915 Declaration of Principles.' This statement further defined the Humboldtian freedom to teach as freedom of inquiry and research, freedom of teaching within the university, and freedom to speak in the wider public world (Wilson, 2016). These principles were repeated in a more nuanced form in a revised statement in 1940, emphasising that the freedom to teach was limited to the subject matter in the class but that institutions should never seek to restrict the right of academic staff to the free speech enjoyed by all citizens.

In the early 1950s, Columbia University hosted the American Academic Freedom Project. One of its most impressive outputs was a historical survey of academic freedom (Hofstadter and Metzger, 1955). In the US, protected tenure of academic posts became, and remains, a bulwark of academic freedom. Consequently, the more recent growth of a non-tenured and often casualised academic workforce is a key element in the debate about the state of academic freedom in the mass higher education systems of the twenty-first century. (See Chapter 9 by Maria Slowey).

In Europe where, with the exception of the UK, university teachers were civil servants until at least the end of the twentieth century, the defence of academic freedom against State encroachment was less straightforward. In Germany, Humboldtian principles withered in the face of the Nazi tyranny. In the Soviet Union from the 1930s onwards – and its eastern European hinterland, between 1945 and 1989 – there was no suggestion that universities had any freedom except to conform to the social principles established by the Communist state. In the liberal democracies, academic freedom was seen in the context of the wider democratic freedoms respected by these states. State bureaucracies, responsible for still relatively elite university systems, had little interest in imposing any form of intellectual conformity, as opposed to administrative regularity. Indeed, they were generally less threatening, and potentially intrusive, than university administrations, boards of trustees or State Governments in the US where much expanded mass systems of higher education first developed. By the end of the twentieth century, there was general acceptance of the principle of academic freedom, even if it required redefinition to match changing circumstances, as the Magna Charta's first Bologna Declaration in 1988 (MCU Observatory, 1988) and UNESCO's 1997 attempt to establish an international standard on the status of higher education teachers, suggest (International Labour Office, 2016). As the twenty-first century dawned, the principle seemed beyond challenge.

Academic freedom today

After this brief historical review, the rest of this chapter addresses these shifting foundations of academic freedom and free speech in the twenty-first century, as well as the dilemmas of the universities, from four interlocking perspectives:

- External structural pressures – such as the need for greater efficiency, accountability, value for money, improved graduate employability, assurances of quality, and demonstrations of impact.
- Externally derived ideological interventions – for example, the subordination of educational or idealist goals to instrumental ones, such as job-related and knowledge production goals, and also bans of 'under-performing' courses, the imposition of 'free speech' codes, and the demands of new social movements.
- Internal structural changes – for example, the development of more elaborate management structures to reflect the increasing scale and complexity of universities, along with the erosion of a shared academic culture and the fragmentation of the academic profession.
- Internally generated ideological effects – notably the rise of so-called 'managerialism' and the reconceptualisation of universities as corporate organisations.

These perspectives, which overlap and bleed into each other, can best be represented in the following diagram:

A1 External structural pressures	**A2 External ideological interventions**
B1 Internal structural changes	**B2 Internal ideological effects**

In the light of these multiple pressures, new rationales will need to be developed to re-invigorate the ideal of academic freedom, and free speech, while also relating these rationales to the social purposes of mass higher education. It is only by acknowledging the force of these pressures, and even their legitimate claims on the university, that such rationales can be successfully developed. That must be the starting point.

A1   External structural pressures

Accountability, efficiency, and performance

It is important to draw a distinction between institutional autonomy, which has clearly been reduced in mass systems, and academic freedom, which has only exceptionally been directly attacked but has sometimes been subtly eroded as much from within as from without. States were initially most concerned to ensure proper accountability for the public funding that universities received.

They had little intention of influencing academic priorities and, as such, their concern had limited implications for academic freedom. However, this focus on *accountability* was soon extended, perhaps inevitably, to a desire to promote greater *efficiency* in the operation of universities, which required assessments to be made of the viability and value of university departments and programmes. The need to develop 'business cases' came to be emphasised, which meant that what were once purely academic judgments now had to be complemented by measures of operational efficacy, which, in turn, began to erode the principle of academic freedom in its purest forms. In a third stage, the focus on efficiency widened yet further to an emphasis on *performance*, whether measured by student opinion or more formal assessment tools, which eroded the principle and practice of academic freedom in more fundamental ways.

This three-stage evolution from accountability to efficiency, and finally to performance, can be illustrated by the experience of universities in the UK.

Accountability. Although they had received state funding since before World War I, and that funding had become the major and then predominant source of their income after 1945, no attempt had been made to either trespass on their institutional autonomy or restrict academic freedom. In 1963, responsibility within government was switched from the Treasury to the expanded Ministry of Education, now the Department for Education and Science (DES). Although this switch had few immediate consequences, in the longer term it opened up the possibility of more activist, and interventionist, policies being pursued. During the same period, new universities were established, which were state-sponsored and almost entirely state-funded. Of more immediate significance was a decision three years later to open up university accounts to the scrutiny of the Comptroller and Auditor General (CAG) and thus the House of Commons Public Accounts Committee (PAC). This is an example of the first: *accountability* – although, in practice, the CAG and the PAC only took notice of the most egregious examples of the misdirection of public funding (Shattock, 2012).

The second stage (*efficiency*) developed in the course of the 1980s when the increasing number of students and universities (and the former polytechnics, which developed into a parallel sector of higher education) led to increasing budgetary pressures – and, as a result, greater pressure to promote the most efficient use of scarcer resources. The universities themselves took the lead initially, commissioning a series of efficiency studies culminating in a final report, the Jarratt report, later seen as the portent of a wave of managerialism (Committee of Vice-Chancellors and Principals, 1985). For this reason, the efficiency drive can also be regarded as an endogenous trend, although this sector-led process was largely driven by a desire to pre-empt State intervention. Its agents, notably the intermediary body responsible for distributing institutional funding, the University Grants Committee (UGC) also sponsored the efficiency drive.

The third stage, the shift from efficiency to *performance*, began in the late 1980s and 1990s, partly because of the drive to develop more transparent and formulaic funding systems (of which the first of many subsequent research assessment exercises was a prominent feature). Universities naturally sought to maximise their State income in accordance with these new systems. Therefore, the now ubiquitous performance indicators were born – in part imposed on UK universities by the State, directly or more often through its subordinate agencies; and in part as management tools within institutions. Performance indicators and metrics of all kinds, have now become pervasive.

Employability and impact

A second structural pressure, which also has its origins in the quest for accountability, is the desire to align the priorities of universities, and as a result their academic shape, with the perceived needs of society and the economy, whether expressed through political direction or market influences. This alignment typically has been interpreted in broad-brush rather than fine-grain terms. No sustained attempts have been made to shape the balance of students, the pattern of courses or the production of graduates to projected workforce demands – with some important exceptions such as medicine and other healthcare professions and school teaching, areas in which the State itself is often the major employer.

However, this desire for broad alignment between university priorities and socio-economic needs has been expressed through several important policy discourses and agendas. Inevitably, these structural pressures bleed into more openly ideological choices.

- The first is a growing emphasis on the instrumentality of higher education. Almost without prompting, universities justify themselves, and the funding they receive, in terms of their utility. They have espoused a language of value for money, social responsibility, and economic multiplier effects. Where students are charged tuition fees, as they are in England, they are encouraged to regard these fees as an investment that will pay off in terms of well-remunerated graduate jobs. This discourse has been internalised to such an extent that it has lost all novelty. It has become a 'given.' It has also become the standard whereby Governments justify increased public funding for universities.
- The second agenda (or discourse) is closely related. This is the increasing emphasis on the employability of graduates. It is no longer sufficient to argue that the principal benefit of a higher education is that students learn cognitive and critical skills as a result of a close encounter with a body of knowledge. Instead, it is often expected that they will be taught explicit job skills that will enhance their position in a competitive graduate labour

market. Increasingly, success is defined not simply in academic terms but in terms of future careers. This change mirrors a more fundamental shift, from regarding a university education as a process centred on the cultivated individual to a product centred on 'economic man [and woman].'

- The third agenda, or discourse, is the emphasis on the impact of research (Khazragui and Hudson, 2015; Murphy, 2022). This has opened up a new divide, between more impactful (for example, engineering, business, and health) and less impactful (humanities and some branches of natural sciences) research. It has also tended to reverse (or try to reverse) the natural order of scientific enquiry, in other words no longer to start with questions and proceed to answers. Perceptions of society's needs now shape research agendas more insistently than the curiosity (and creativity?) of scientists and scholars.

All three agendas, or discussions, have important implications for academic freedom if it is defined in Humboldtian terms, the freedom to teach and the freedom to learn. None of them, at any rate in a moderate form, is necessarily incompatible with academic freedom. But they all raise important questions. Of course, it can be argued that in mass higher education enrolling millions of students, in a society increasingly shaped by the life choices of university graduates and in a global skills- and knowledge-based economy, States have not only a right, but even a responsibility, to secure a broad correspondence between the priorities for universities, in terms of teaching and research programmes, and the general good of society. Equally, students in a mass system have the right to expect universities not to be indifferent to their career ambitions. The key questions are on what terms and by whom within the public realm that right and responsibility are exercised.

The rise of metrics

Academic freedom has always been exercised through the power of scientific communities that frame the choices of individual academics. But these communities had, and have, an ambiguous effect – both protecting and defending the freedom of teachers and researchers, but also setting limits to what is acceptable (and therefore deserves protection). The main instrument for setting these limits has always been peer review, serving as a gatekeeper to who gets appointed to academic positions and promoted and what gets published in journals and books. Once, in elite university systems, disciplinary communities operated through loose networks of informal patronage within which hierarchies, which certainly existed, were largely tacit.

However, the development since the late 1980s in the UK, and in many other countries over a similar period, of formal assessment systems, initially for research and later for teaching, has changed not simply the rules of the game but the game itself. Once tacit routines have been superseded by management systems. Although peer review remains the main method for determining quality, in appointments, promotions, and publications, it has been harnessed (and subordinated?) by these management systems. In short, formal assessment systems have been imposed on universities – 'the march of the metrics' as explored in Chapter 10 by Ellen Hazelkorn.

Formal assessment has taken several forms. Some have been largely internal to the academic system – such as new approaches to course design. For example, loosely cumulative three- or four-year undergraduate programmes have been replaced by more tightly structured, often modular, patterns of study, and (over?) specified 'learning outcomes' have been identified. New professional roles have developed in quality assurance and learning and teaching to manage and police these changes, which have received substantial encouragement from outside, from the State and its agencies. What might otherwise have been a flexible evolution has become a quasi-compulsory framework.

However, a greater change has taken place in the domain of university research. In research-intensive universities, which are generally also those with the greatest prestige, it is research, not teaching, that counts. In the UK, it is impossible to exaggerate the impact of successive research management regimes, initially the Research Assessment Exercise (RAE) and later the Research Excellence Framework (REF) (Elton, 2000), on the strategies and priorities of universities and the lives and careers of researchers. These regimes are managed by State agencies while still relying on peer-review judgments to determine the quality of research in university departments within a matrix of disciplines (or 'units of assessment' in official language). Similar, although typically less detailed (and therefore less intrusive), regimes have been developed in other countries. One example is the *Excellenz* initiative in Germany.

The actual quality grades, or 'scores,' of departments and the putative grades for individual researchers determine the fates of both. High-performing departments attract additional investment, often in the form of additional academic posts, and also externally funded research grants. Poorly performing departments are restructured, or even abolished. The careers of individuals are made or marred. The highly rated are given time, and resources, to further develop their research. Their less fortunate peers are often loaded with extra teaching commitments. In both cases, their careers are now actively managed, which in day-to-day practice has eroded the autonomy they once enjoyed. Alongside these new assessment regimes, Governments, as has already been said, typically through research and innovation agencies, have developed research strategies that identify in advance the areas on which investment is to be focused. National initiatives and programmes now litter the research landscape.

Of course, it can be argued that any restrictive, even oppressive, effects of the closer management of teaching and, especially, research simply formalise and systematise the hegemony of elite groups within disciplines. But, alongside formalisation and systematisation, processes of intensification and externalisation have also taken place. Traditional disciplinary hegemonies and hierarchies, for all their chilling effects, were 'owned' by the universities themselves and the academic community at large. These new control regimes have been imposed from outside, albeit with the help of academics. It is for this reason that they can be described as a new game.

A2 External ideological interventions

Invading the 'private life' of universities

Martin Trow made an important distinction between the 'public life' of higher education – in other words, system-level governance, funding, and fees – and its 'private life' – the world of academic disciplines (and the main focus of Humboldt's freedoms to teach and to learn). But in mass systems it has become more difficult to define, let alone guard, the frontier between them.

What had begun in the 1960s as an essentially administrative process – a limited intervention in the institutional autonomy of universities to guarantee accountability and encourage greater efficiency – has become a much more extensive and intrusive intervention into their academic world. And not only the academic world at institutional level, but also departmental, course, and research group level, and even the level of individual academics whose teaching and research performance has come to be assessed in a detail once unimaginable. Of course, it can be argued that these formal methods of assessment have simply replaced older and potentially more discriminatory forms of informal judgment. Before transparent funding systems were developed, the UGC relied on what was revealingly described as 'informed prejudice.' But the visibility and specificity of contemporary performance indicators have produced a clear framework within which academic behaviour, at all levels including the individual, can now be managed. The effect is a curtailment of academic freedom, even in the absence of any ideological intention.

However, at some point structural and ideological restrictions on academic freedom can became entwined in a way that makes it almost impossible to tell them apart. A good example is the recent announcement by the Office for Students in England that new metrics will be developed to identify low-value courses, and that institutions offering such courses will suffer serious consequences (as yet, unspecified). In brief, the thresholds will be that 80 per cent of first-year students must progress to the next year, 75 per cent must complete their qualification and 60 per cent of graduates must be employed in 'professional' jobs (or go on to further study). These thresholds will be applied not simply to whole institutions, but also by subject and mode of study (Office for Students, 2022). Clearly, this amounts to a substantial invasion of institutional autonomy, which will impose a substantial bureaucratic burden and encourage data 'gaming' by institutions.

Such consequences are not directly relevant to the theme of this chapter, although in the absence of institutional autonomy academic freedom is at greater risk. Of greater relevance are the ideological assumptions underpinning this intervention.

- One assumption is that students must conform to a preordained pattern of study in short, linear progression and timely completion. Although this may reflect the wishes of the majority of students, it will be educationally damaging for others. It is also difficult to reconcile with the development of more flexible pathways into, through and out of a broader lifelong learning system.
- A second assumption is that success can be reduced to a well-paid career in an arbitrarily defined 'graduate' job – and that is the only reason students engage in higher education and achieve satisfaction, and the only way in which society benefits. At a technical level, the impact of either changes in occupational roles over the life cycle, or discrimination within the labour market, is taken into account. In normative terms, no weight is attached to other benefits that are not immediately instrumental to students or to society. In other words, an openly ideological and fiercely contested instrumentality is being imposed as the sole goal of higher education, under the guise of efficiency and accountability.

Direct ideological interventions

Direct ideological interventions, although still rare, are becoming more frequent. Of course, only in totalitarian States is the principle of academic freedom actively denied; and even in the largest example, China, there is still a productive scientific culture and vigorous intellectual culture within the bounds set by the Communist Party. In quasi-authoritarian States, both institutional autonomy and academic freedom have come under fire – but typically without explicitly contradicting the principles themselves. In Hungary, the long-running dispute between the Viktor Orban Government and the George Soros–funded Central European University was presented formally in terms of the validity of awards made by organisations in foreign jurisdictions (see Chapter 8 by Rebeka Bakos and Andrea Pető) – even if little attempt was made to disguise the Government's true motives, its struggle against cosmopolitanism (Foer, 2019). In Turkey, the Erdogan Government's sharp repression of intellectual dissent and stricter subordination of the universities were presented in terms of subversion of the State.

However, even in liberal democracies attempts to restrict academic freedom on openly ideological grounds have become more frequent since 2000. From the political right, there have been increasing efforts to combat so-called 'political correctness' in a self-declared 'war on woke' waged with especial relish by the Republican Party in the US and the Conservative Party in the UK. A particular target in the US has been critical race theory, a scholarly perspective that emphasises the pervasive impacts of racism. From the political left, there has been an increasing tolerance of so-called 'cancel culture,' under which it has become acceptable to censor (even silence) views that tend to offend the feelings of minority or marginalised groups (Mishan, 2020). The right has its own version of cancel culture – for example, when it seeks to ban so-called 'critical race theory,' which has already been mentioned. A particular example of these new conflicts is the confused, and convoluted, debate about biological sex and gender identity, which has given rise to accusations of transphobia. A small, but growing, number of academics have been caught uncomfortably in the middle of this debate.

The attacks from the right are merely one aspect of the wider advance of radical-right populism, in its revolt against multiculturalism (and so-called 'liberal elites'). The attacks from the left reflect the growing assertion of minority and marginalised groups, whether black and other ethnic minority groups ('Black Lives Matter') or LBTGQ groups, and their refusal to accept historical subordination. In other words, both of these ideologically inspired assaults on academic freedom, and in extreme cases free speech, arise from much more profound social movements and their political expressions. In turn, these movements reflect the increasing polarisation of society that stretches back to the erosion of the welfare state from the 1980s onwards but were turbocharged by additional economic strains created by the 2008 banking crisis and the subsequent actions of Governments. This polarisation has almost certainly been further intensified by the impact of the COVID-19 pandemic. It has also been powered, and to some degree legitimised, by the influence of unconstrained social media, which allowed extreme views a greater voice. The unrestrained attacks on doctors and clinicians by 'anti-vaxxers,' and opponents of public health measures, and the spread of fake news during the pandemic are the latest and most alarming example of the influence of social media.

In several instances, when individual academics have been censored, silenced or otherwise discriminated against, they have appeared not to be innocent bystanders caught in the crossfire but active adherents of the competing social movements, which is a further reflection of this polarisation from which the academic community cannot be insulated. The rise of these social movements against a background of increasing polarisation and the baleful effects on academic freedom raise an important, but also alarming, question. Does respect for academic freedom rest ultimately on wider socio-political conditions that no longer apply, in other words a consensual political culture and responsible media? This leads in turn to another challenging question – how can academic freedom best be protected in this more hostile environment?

B1 Internal structural changes and B2 internal ideological effects

In the next section, on the internal evolution of universities as institutions and of mass higher education systems, structural and ideological effects are even more difficult to disentangle. What some will regard as a blatantly ideological intervention, with potentially negative effects on academic freedom, will be regarded by others as a purely pragmatic response to changing circumstances (and, in practice, a means by which academic freedom is preserved). For this reason, internal structural changes and ideological effects will be discussed together. However, the duality of perspectives should be respected.

Four structural changes, and their potential ideological effects, will be considered:

- The growth of mass higher education systems, and the implications for the organisational culture of universities.
- The impact of these organisational changes on how universities are governed and managed, in particular the balance between academic and professional (and, indeed, hybrid) roles and the growth of a distinctive management class (and, arguably, of managerialist culture).
- The erosion of a sense of a shared academic culture, rooted in shared cognitive and professional norms, and the rise of contestation reflecting both the diversity of student populations and the porous boundaries between the academy and society.
- The changing relationships between mass systems, enrolling a majority of young adults, not only with the State and market but also with wider society.

Mass higher education

Between 1960 and 2020, the number of students in higher education increased more than 10 times over. In the UK, for example, it grew from fewer than 200,000 to more than 2.5 million. Similar rates of growth can be observed in most European countries and across North America. Expansion has been even more rapid in parts of Africa, Asia, and Latin America. The American sociologist Martin Trow, although not quite the first to use the term 'mass higher education,' was the most celebrated theorist of this phenomenal growth. In Trow's scheme of things, elite higher education (in practice, university) systems enrolling up to 15 per cent of young adults have been succeeded by mass systems enrolling up to 50 per cent (Trow, 1973). In practice, many countries now have participation rates in excess of 50 per cent, an evolutionary stage Trow labelled 'universal' higher education, although more recently an alternative label – high-participation systems – has become more popular (Marginson, 2016).

This explosion of student numbers over the last two generations, of course, has had profound social and economic effects, which are not the concern of this chapter. But it has also had two more immediate consequences that bear more directly on academic freedom. The first is the almost equivalent increase in the number of higher education teachers and – because of the continuing links between teaching and research – also of researchers. But it is not simply the scale of the academic profession that has been transformed, so too has its composition and, arguably, its values. As with the student body, many more academics are women. The proportion with tenure, or in permanent, positions has declined. The growth of externally funded research, almost as dynamic a process as massification itself, has led to the employment of a large number of dedicated researchers, only a minority of whom can aspire – or, indeed, want – to pursue once conventional academic careers. It can be argued that the degree of academic freedom appropriate for much smaller, and coherent, groups of academics – 'dons,' in traditional language – may no longer be appropriate for a much larger, and more heterogeneous, academic profession in mass systems, not only in practical but also in principled terms (as discussed further in Chapter 9 by Maria Slowey).

The higher education workforce has undergone not only quantitative expansion but also experienced qualitative change. There has been a rapid increase in the number of hybrid posts, part-academic, and part-time managerial, not only at the senior management level (Vice-Chancellors/Presidents and Deans) but also to service new hybrid roles in learning and teaching or quality assurance. The kind of academic freedom enjoyed by a much smaller and more traditional academic profession may no longer be appropriate, or even relevant, for many of these new groups and/or these new situations. To take a simple example, Deans in their academic role as professors are entitled to enjoy academic freedom, but in their managerial roles, they clearly have more constraining professional and institutional responsibilities.

Organisational change and 'managerialism'

The second consequence of massification is that universities have become much larger, more complex and more heterogeneous institutions. Their increased social and economic weight, and political and cultural significance, have led to new forms of external engagement, even entanglement. As a result, their organisational cultures have been transformed. Their leaders now have strategic responsibilities that demand more explicitly managerial responses. The traditional model of minimalist and symbolic leadership no longer applies. More elaborate management structures have been developed to handle not only the greatly increased number of students (and police new pedagogic practices) but also the many new roles taken on by the contemporary university – research management, innovation and technology transfer, community engagement.

As large organisations, and large employers, universities also have to comply with the wide range of externally set codes – for good governance, equal opportunities, fair employment, professional ethics, corporate responsibility, health, and safety – as well as satisfying the reporting and other requirements bound up with their receipt of public funding. They have been caught up in the so-called 'audit society' (Power, 1999). The cumulative effect of all these changes has been the need for universities to develop a much-enhanced management capacity, which sits uneasily beside the ideal of an academic collegium. Inevitably, the institutional foundations of academic freedom have shifted.

However, it may be wrong to view these changes associated with the growth of mass higher education systems in an entirely negative light. The famed 'donnish dominion' was as much a comforting myth as an empirical statement about how elite universities were managed in some imagined golden time (Halsey, 1995). A significant proportion of academic staff were never members of this supposed self-governing collegium, which tended to be dominated by senior professors who sometimes were not reluctant to exercise their powers of patronage. The academic freedom of more junior staff, often dependent on such patronage to advance in their careers, was often provisional and precarious. Unfair employment practices could also be found. That is why, during the years of student activism in the 1960s and 1970s, many junior staff were also activists, aiming to create the conditions of genuine academic democracy. It may even be that in the often-maligned managerial university of the twenty-first century the systematisation of academic authority, and therefore of limits to its exercise, may actually have conferred rights and benefits on more junior staff they did not enjoy within the informal, and therefore unchallengeable, regime of academic professional hierarchy.

However, a clear distinction needs to be drawn between the inevitable changes in the management of universities to meet the challenges of massification, and much more intense social engagement, and the ideological excesses associated with what is termed 'managerialism' (Deem et al, 2007). 'Managerialism,' rooted in neo-liberal conceptions, goes beyond a purely pragmatic adjustment to the need for strengthened management in large and complex institutions. For example, it can lead to significant restrictions on academic freedom, not simply in terms of encouraging 'efficient' teaching and 'productive' research but also protecting 'institutional reputation.' Universities, in protecting their reputations, naturally shy away from controversies, as Edinburgh University did when it removed the name of David Hume, Scotland's most famous philosopher, from a building because of a fleeting suggestion in one of his writings that black people were inferior to whites. Any large company would have done the same (BBC News, 2020). This was classic corporate behaviour.

In any case, this hardening of the corporate shell of the contemporary university, part the result of massification itself and part the result of the influence of neo-liberal ideas, has had serious consequences for academic freedom as traditionally conceived. First, as has already been indicated, the perceived need to manage academic performance, the systematisation of university teaching in terms of professional skills, prescribed contents, and explicit outcomes, and the ubiquity if not inevitability of university, departmental, subject, and course rankings are difficult to reconcile with the Humboldtian freedom to learn and to teach. Both have clearly to be circumscribed. Second, academics as employees are now seen as having new responsibilities to the universities that employ them. For example, they are expected to act in ways that do not damage institutional reputations, just like employees of other public and corporate bodies. This again is difficult to reconcile with the traditional model of academic freedom. While they may continue to be free to enjoy academic freedom within the restricted confines of their academic disciplines, their role as public intellectuals is clearly curtailed.

Diversity and controversy

Potentially this role has been further curtailed by the splintering of academic consensus, in terms both of content and of methods, and by the failure to contain the impact of ideological controversies. The first of these can be attributed to the development of mass systems. Students are now drawn from a much wider social spectrum, with different experiences and expectations. It can also be attributed to the intellectual dynamism of the modern university, which has accelerated the rise of new disciplines, and specialities within them, and the decay of old ones.

The result has been an increase in cognitive dissonance. Taken together, their effects have been unsettling. For example, the rapid increase in the number of women in mass systems has reflected new social norms about gender, which in turn has nourished new consciousnesses that can be simply labelled as feminism, which in its turn has led to the establishment of courses in women's studies and increasing emphasis on feminist perspectives in most arts and social sciences disciplines. A similar evolution can be observed with regard to the impact of the recruitment of much larger numbers of minority ethnic students, more muted perhaps until new momentum was acquired from recently renewed campaigns against racism.

In other words, the new demographics of mass systems have evoked powerful academic responses, both creative and destructive, in the curriculum and in research priorities. At one level, this has led to a welcome extension of academic freedom. But, at another level, this splintering of traditional academic culture has produced turbulence and provoked reactions that perhaps have led to academic freedom being sharply contested. Once again, the degree of academic freedom that was regarded as appropriate when it was exercised through established professional structures and relatively stable disciplinary communities may appear to be more difficult to accept, or to defend, when it is expressed through much more fluid and fragmented professional structures and more febrile disciplinary communities. An additional and disturbing factor is increasing methodological fluidity as ideas about contextualisation, relativism, and even subjectivity has come to challenge, or at any rate complement, more traditional forms of scientific enquiry. The cumulative effect of all these changes has been to problematise traditional ideas of academic freedom, rendering them anachronistic.

These doubts and conflicts have spilled over outside the academy. Mass universities are now so embroiled and entwined with wider society that it has become difficult to maintain conventional inside/outside demarcations. Confusingly, they have become technocratic instruments, in the sense that their production of research and graduates now shape the economy with an intensity unimaginable in the last century; but they have also become, to some degree, primary bases for new social movements, both direct sites and also through their graduates, in ways prefigured by the student radicals of the 1970s (as discussed in Chapter 5 by Evan Smith).

Universities and democracy

Elite universities were highly autonomous institutions within a civil society that itself enjoyed a stable life distinct from the State and the market. The mass universities of today are deeply embedded in society and the economy in ways that have resulted in the traditional rules of institutional autonomy having to be rewritten. At the same time, civil society has been squeezed between a State that has resisted all attempts to downsize and an increasingly aggressive market. The intrusion of the State into not only the public life of universities (for example, funding) but also their private life (for example, academic quality) has been considered earlier in this chapter. In this final section of this discussion of the endogenous forces that have acted on academic freedom, the focus is on how universities themselves now conceive their external relationships. A complex area, but two points in particular deserve to be discussed.

First, universities, certainly their leaders, habitually justify investment in higher education by the State and others in instrumental terms – as producers of the highly skilled (and entrepreneurial) graduate workforce required for a knowledge-based economy; of the science that is the basis of industrial innovation (and supposedly greater business efficiency); and of the technology and knowledge exchange, which makes universities anchor institutions within this new economy as well as major social actors within their communities. The economic footprint of universities in their cities and regions – purchasing power, staff and students consumption, business incubation, multiplier effects, and the rest – is also much emphasised. Students too are wooed not so much in terms of a university education being a rite of passage or an intellectual adventure, but of future employability and well-paid graduate jobs. The recruitment of international students is justified less in terms of intellectual pluralism or cross-cultural learning than of diplomatic 'soft power,' future economic advantage, and present profit making (for institutions, their regions and the country as a whole).

This sometimes overwhelming emphasis on the instrumental value of higher education, of course, is partly the result of the external pressures on universities – the demands for greater efficiency, improved accountability, demonstrable impact and relevance and (in more recent times) their ideological subordination. But it is partly also a reflection of how many people in universities, especially in leadership positions, now see the predominant roles of higher education. As a result, academic freedom is typically defended not so much as a public good or an individual right but in terms of the need to give scientists and researchers the space to engage in the most 'relevant' teaching and the most 'productive' research.

Second, the debate about accountability has been largely confined to the narrow balance between institutional autonomy, which although plainly in retreat is still a form of default setting for universities, and satisfying the requirements of State regulators and public and private funders. In other words, it is regarded as a zero-sum game. One objection to this is that it is a narrow interpretation of accountability. Subordination to the State tends to crowd out other potentially more open (and even-handed) forms of accountability – to staff, students, local communities, regions (and, of course, in an age of increasing global consciousness, about the wider world beyond national states). Yet this pluralism is not reflected in how accountability is generally exercised, or even conceived (Scott, 2021). A second objection continues this theme of pluralism. The autonomy–accountability nexus need not be seen as a zero-sum game whereby the freedom of universities can only be upheld at the expense of the containment of other interests. Once again, in mass higher education systems these relationships are more fluid and reflexive. If this is accepted, academic freedom takes on a new character. It too ceases to be a zero-sum game and becomes an arena in which truth(s) and respect can be carefully negotiated.

Conclusion

The approach taken in this chapter is that academic freedom must always be seen in context. To ground it simply in an abstract ideal, a natural right, does not advance our understanding much. In *On Liberty* (Mill 1991[1859]), the ur-text of liberalism (as discussed in detail in Chapter 3 by Alan Haworth) J. S. Mill argued that objectionable speech should be not only tolerated but also encouraged because it could lead to the discovery of new and better truth. Few would dissent from that principle, but they would quickly fall out about its practical application. Max Weber developed similar justifications for academic freedom in the late nineteenth and early twentieth century. As the American philosopher Richard Rorty has written: 'Philosophers on my side of the argument think that if we stop trying to give epistemological justifications for academic freedom and instead give socio-political justifications, we should be more honest and clear-headed' (Rorty, 1996 as cited in Lackey, 2018, 5). The historian Conrad Russell followed a similar logic in his book on academic freedom, which was provoked by the abolition of the celebrated buffer between State and universities, the UGC, in 1987 (Russell, 1993/2015). The three sections of his book were labelled 'ideals,' 'limits,' and 'mapping the borders.'

Academic freedom has always been lodged in its broader hinterland, both within higher education (now, of course, a mass system and no longer a small collection of elite universities) and in wider society (the shrill contests between 'populist' right and identity-focused left, set in the wider socio-economic order of the early twenty-first century). It is for this reason, to discuss academic freedom in its socio-political context, that this chapter has attempted to place the concept of academic freedom in its historical context, and also to consider the external forces that act on academic freedom from outside the academy, and the internal forces that have shaped the behaviour of universities and of individual academics.

In the past, a contrast was often drawn between narrow and broad definitions of academic freedom, illustrated, respectively, by two American scholars. Stanley Fish, literary theorist and newspaper columnist, came to the eventual conclusion in a set of lectures that academic freedom was in effect a tool; it had to be sufficient to allow academics to do their jobs (as academics) (Fish, 2014). The philosopher Martha Nussbaum has written about academic freedom more in terms of it being a right of academics to engage in wider social debate (Nussbaum, 2018).

In other words, is academic freedom essentially to be exercised within the restricted territory of academic disciplines – few would deny the right of the physicist or the historian to practise their expertise without external constraint – or should it be framed in terms of the rights of academics to engage as public intellectuals beyond perhaps the strict boundaries of their own expertise and acknowledged discipline? The latter interpretation leads to further complications. While academic freedom as a tool of the academic trade may deserve special protection, it is more difficult to argue that academics, when exercising their right to intervene in public controversies, deserve the same enhanced protection simply because they are academics. In short, is academic freedom claimed as a guild privilege or a democratic right? (See Maria Slowey and Richard Taylor, Chapter 11.)

Arguably, in mass systems the question is moot. In the humanities and social sciences, of course, it has always been difficult to determine the boundary between academic specialist and public intellectual. Even the most scholarly history potentially has contemporary resonances that intrude into public debate and, potentially, controversy. Sociologists and economists, however uneasy they may feel in the role, have little choice but to act to some extent as public intellectuals. Their research is almost inevitably an intervention in public debate. Even science and now engineering embrace ethical, legal, and environmental issues, which take them into the same treacherous territory. This recasting of many academics as public intellectuals, even pundits, raises important philosophical and ethical issues, which tend to erode simpler understandings of academic freedom (Melzer, Weinberger and Zinman, 2003).

But two developments have made this boundary even more fuzzy and porous. The first is that a combination of the proliferation of academic 'experts' (and their division into often warring tribes) and the intensified clashes between, for example, 'populists' and 'liberals,' fuelled of course by social media, in an age of crumbling consensus, has made it more difficult to stand aside. Their work even in the apparently most objective scientific fields is always at risk of being conscripted by one side or the other, with or without their permission, as the experience of the COVID-19 pandemic demonstrated. The second is that in mass higher education systems with more diverse student bodies new areas of study have developed that, however scrupulous they may be in their use of evidence, have clear agendas. Anti-feminists do not publish in feminist journals. As a result, the distinction between the academic as disciplinary expert and as public intellectual has been sharply eroding, which in turn has tended to negate the distinction between narrow and broad definitions of academic freedom, as a tool or as a right.

In conclusion, academic freedom cannot be treated as if it stands aside from the full range of human rights, in particular the free speech enjoyed by all citizens in a democracy. Admittedly, it may have special features – two, in particular, one functional and the other more idealist. First, academics, both as teachers and especially perhaps as researchers, need the maximum degree of freedom to pursue their disciplines, however uncomfortable that may be for others. Second, the autonomy of universities needs to be safeguarded alongside other key institutions in civil society but with special attention because of their responsibility to promote critical enquiry to probe the frontiers of existing knowledge.

If these special features are accepted as valid justifications of academic freedom, it is difficult to escape two conclusions. First, the excessive drive to greater efficiency, accountability, value-for-money, and, in particular, to re-conceptualise higher education as a 'market' that has characterised higher education policies in many countries – notably in England – undermines institutional autonomy and is a threat to academic freedom. Second, the substitution of managerial practices for collegial values as the key drivers in the governance of universities, and the imposition of line-management hierarchies and excessive performance review, are also difficult to reconcile with academic freedom. In short, marketisation and managerialism do not mix with academic freedom. Finally, of course, respect for academic freedom is closely related with respect for all human rights in democratic societies. The rise of various forms of 'populist' authoritarianism, the rise of conflictual politics, division into cultural 'tribes' – all inevitably undermine academic freedom.

References

Altbach, P. (2001). Academic freedom: International realities and challenges. *Higher Education*, *41*(1/2), 205–19.

BBC News. (2020, September 13). Edinburgh University renames David Hume Tower over 'racist' views. Retrieved from https://www.bbc.co.uk/news/uk-scotland-edinburgh-east-fife-54138247

Bell, D. (1960). *The end of ideology*. Cambridge: Harvard University Press.

Committee of Vice-Chancellors and Principals. (1985). Report of the Steering Group for Efficiency Studies in Universities [Jarratt Report]. London: CVCP. Retrieved from www.educationengland.org.uk/documents/jarratt1985/index.html

Deem, R., Halyard, S., and Reed, R. (2007). *Knowledge, higher education and the new managerialism: The Changing Management of UK Universities*. Oxford: Oxford University Press.

Elton, L. (2000). The UK Research Assessment Exercise: Unintended consequences. *Higher Education Quarterly*, *54*(3), 274–83. https://doi.org/10.1111/1468-2273.00160

Fish, S. (2014). *Versions of academic freedom*. Chicago: University of Chicago Press.

Foer, F. (2019, June). Viktor Orban's war on intellect. *The Atlantic*. Retrieved from https://www.theatlantic.com/magazine/archive/2019/06/george-soros-viktor-orban-ceu/588070/

Fukuyama, F. (1992). *The end of history and the last man*. New York: The Free Press.

Fuller, S. (2009). The genealogy of judgement: Towards a deep history of academic freedom. *British Journal of Educational Studies*, *57*(2), 164–77.

Halsey, A. H. (1995). *Decline of donnish dominion: The British academic professions in the twentieth century*. Oxford: Clarendon Press.

Hofstadter, R., and Metzger, W. P. (1955). *The development of academic freedom in the United States*. New York: Columbia University Press.

International Labour Office. (2016). *ILO/UNESCO Recommendation concerning the status of teachers (1966) and the UNESCO Recommendation concerning the status of higher-education teaching personnel (1997) – Revised edition 2016*. Geneva: ILO.

Khazragui, H., and Hudson, J. (2015). Measuring the benefits of university research: Impact and the REF in the UK. *Research Evaluation*, *24*(1), 51–6. https://ideas.repec.org/a/oup/rseval/v24y2015i1p51-62..html

Lackey, J. (ed). (2018). *Academic freedom*. Oxford: Oxford University Press.

Magna Charta Universitatum Observatory [MCU Observatory]. (1988). *Magna Charta Universitatum 1988*. Bologna: MCU. Retrieved from http://www.magna-charta.org/magna-charta-universitatum/read-the-magna-charta/the-magna-charta

Magna Charta Universitatum Observatory [MCU Observatory]. (2020). *Magna Charta Universitatum 2020*. Bologna: MCU. Retrieved from http://www.magna-charta.org/magna-charta-universitatum/mcu-2020

Marginson, S. (2016). The worldwide trend to high participation higher education: Dynamics of social stratification in inclusive systems. *Higher Education*, *72*(4), 413–34.

Marmura, M. (2002). Medieval Islamic philosophy and the classical tradition. In J. Inglis (ed), *Medieval philosophy and the classical tradition: In Islam, Judaism and Christianity* (pp. 17–28). London: Routledge.

Melzer, A., Weinberger, J., and Zinman, M. (eds). (2003). *The public intellectual: Between philosophy and ethics*. Lanham: Rowman and Littlefield.

Mill, J. S. (1991 [1859]). On liberty. In J. Gray (ed), *John Stuart Mill: On liberty and other essays* (pp. 5–128). Oxford: Oxford University Press.

Mishan, L. (2020, December 6). The long and tortured history of cancel culture. *New York Times Style Magazine*. Retrieved from https://www.nytimes.com/2020/12/03/t-magazine/cancel-culture-history.html

Murphy, M. (2022). Publicness and intellectual work: Rethinking academic freedom in an age of impact. In R. Watermeyer, R. Raaper, and M. Olssen (eds), *Handbook on academic freedom* (pp. 37–51). Cheltenham: Edward Elgar.

Nussbaum, M. C. (2018). Civil disobedience and free speech in the academy. In J. Lackey (ed), *Academic freedom* (pp. 170–85). Oxford: Oxford University Press.

Office for Students. (2022, January 20). *Consultation on a new approach to regulating student outcomes.* London: Office for Students. Retrieved from https://www.officeforstudents.org.uk/media/c46cb18a-7826-4ed9-9739-1e785e24519a/consultation-on-a-new-approach-to-regulating-student-outcomes-ofs-2022-01.pdf

Power, M. (1999). *The audit society: Rituals of verification.* Oxford: Oxford University Press.

Rorty, R. (1996). Does academic freedom have philosophical presuppositions? In L. Menand. *The future of academic freedom.* Chicago. University of Chicago Press.

Russell, C. (2015). *Academic freedom* (2nd ed.). London: Routledge. (Original work published in 1993).

Scott, P. (2021). *Retreat or resolution? Tackling the crisis of mass higher education.* Bristol: Policy Press.

Shattock, M. (2012). *Making policy in British higher education 1945-2011.* Maidenhead: Open University Press.

Trow, M. (1973). *Problems in the transition from elite to mass higher education.* Berkeley: Carnegie Commission on Higher Education.

Wilson, J. K. (2016). AAUP's 1915 Declaration of Principles: Conservative and radical, visionary and myopic. *The Journal of Academic Freedom, 7.* Retrieved from https://www.aaup.org/sites/default/files/Wilson_1.pdf

3

'FREE SPEECH,' ACADEMIC FREEDOM, AND THE PUBLIC SPHERE

Some reflections on principles

Alan Haworth

Introduction

I shall take it that a society which respects the liberty of speech and expression (or 'free speech' for short) will be one in which the freedom to perform certain acts is protected by law. The category of such 'protected acts' usually focuses on those which involve the use of language – in speech or writing. However, this might also be extended to include the liberty to participate in public demonstrations, for example, or the 'artistic freedom' to produce work, free from imposition by external arbiters of taste. So much is uncontroversial, or so it is assumed here. It is equally obvious, however, that more problematic is the question of precisely what types of action ought to be protected. Mere offensiveness of a statement, a joke, or some other remark is insufficient to warrant its prohibition. Equally, however, it is generally accepted in contemporary liberal societies that, for example, literary material which is racist in content ought to be removed from the public sphere. But what if the offensiveness is not just to someone's sense of taste or decorum but also to that person's deeply held religious beliefs? Or, conversely, what if one person's objection to a questionable joke on the grounds that it is not merely in poor taste but also racist is seen by another person as a case of exaggerated political correctness? We need rationally based principles to resolve such problems.

What, then, might such principles be? It is with that question in mind that, in what follows, I turn to the argument contained in the second chapter of J. S. Mill's *On Liberty*, the chapter entitled 'Of the Liberty of Thought and Discussion' (1859/1991, 5–128). It is an argument with a long pedigree – one which stretches back to the debates over religious toleration during the seventeenth century. With the assumption that length of pedigree

DOI: 10.4324/9781003363262-4

can be an indicator of breadth of influence, the significance of Mill's chapter is evident enough.[1]

Mill's argument has its limitations, however, and, given its widespread influence, it is important to explore precisely what those limitations might be. With this in mind, the discussion in the following section begins with an account of that argument and its implications for the idea that 'free speech' should be valued and protected. This leads on to a discussion of the implications of Mill's argument for 'academic freedom,' the central focus of concern in this book. In the final sections of this chapter, it is suggested that the value of academic freedom might best be understood not so much in the light of Mill's specific argument, but in the vision of the good society of which that argument forms a part.

The liberty of thought and discussion: Mill's consequentialist argument

Exactly what did Mill say? Towards the end of his chapter, he supplies a usefully succinct summary of its argument, stating that the necessity for freedom of opinion and freedom of the expression of opinion rests upon four distinct grounds.

1 That, 'if any opinion is compelled to silence, that opinion may, for aught we can certainly know, be true.' (Mill adds that, 'to deny this is to assume our own infallibility.')
2 That, 'though the silenced opinion be an error, it may, and very commonly does, contain a portion of truth; and since the general or prevailing opinion on any subject is rarely or never the whole truth, it is only by the collision of adverse opinions that the remainder of the truth has any chance of being supplied.'
3 That, 'even if the received opinion be not only true, but the whole truth; unless it is suffered to be, and actually is, vigorously and earnestly contested, it will, by most of those who receive it, be held in the manner of a prejudice, with little comprehension or feeling of its rational grounds.'
4 That, unless it is frequently contested, 'the meaning of the doctrine itself will be in danger of being lost or enfeebled and deprived of its vital effect on the character and conduct'; in other words, that it will degenerate into 'dogma.'

For the purposes of the present chapter, the notable features of these claims are as follows: first, Mill connects the importance of thought and discussion with the value of knowledge. It is, as he puts it, through the 'collision' of ideas that our chances of discovering new truths are increased. This means that his arguments can only carry conviction to the extent that knowledge (that such-and-such propositions are true) has value, and indeed Mill's view is exactly that. '[T]he well-being of mankind,' he wrote, 'may almost be measured by the number and gravity of the truths which have reached the point of being uncontested.' Against this, it might be argued that the liberty of thought and discussion may have desirable consequences other than the discovery of truth. It is obvious enough, for example, that it is a liberty which enables competing interest groups to articulate and express their preferences, and that it is thereby a liberty upon which the successful operation of any democracy must rest.

A second notable feature of Mill's arguments is that they are *consequentialist* in nature. In other words, he is claiming that, where the liberty of thought and discussion is exercised, new truths will emerge *as a result*. It is a feature which means that Mill's case – resting as it does upon an empirical claim – is open to the challenge that it requires evidence to support it. Consider, for example, the comforting platitude according to which, if fascists and their nasty like are granted full freedom of expression, people will recognise them for what they are and reject their views. It is a claim one encounters surprisingly often, and yet there is no good evidence to support it. On the contrary, the fact that fascists and the like do sometimes make political headway could easily be taken as evidence that the claim is false – or so it might well be argued. What *is* true, no doubt, is that the exercise of freedom of expression by fascists *sometimes* leads to the public exposure of their inadequacies, but that must surely depend upon contingent factors, such as the talent for eloquence possessed by this or that individual fascist and the similar degree of talent on the part of those who oppose them.

Does the consequentialist nature of Mill's argument add up to a reason for rejecting it? I do not think so, although much hangs upon how it is interpreted. Thus, if we take Mill to be arguing that the liberty of thought and discussion, through its exercise, must *inevitably* lead to the discovery of new truths – that the latter outcome is actually *guaranteed* – then he is clearly wrong. On the other hand, if we take him to be arguing that the exercise of the former liberty has a tendency to produce the latter outcome – generally, though not in every particular instance – then it seems to me that he is right. This point cannot be demonstrated *a priori*. It is notable, however, that Mill's argument rests upon an adversarial principle similar to that which lies at the core of many liberal institutions, including, notably in the context of the focus of this book, universities. This principle is well embedded in practice and there are some reasonable grounds for accepting it as 'well-tested.'

From 'thought and discussion' to 'academic freedom'

The expression 'academic freedom' is best construed as an 'umbrella term,' one which denotes a category which in fact includes a number of distinct liberties – liberties which are largely, or peculiarly, the province of 'the academy.' With that in mind, it should be noted that Mill's argument is *itself* a justification for academic freedom, *but only to a certain extent* – that is, to the extent that 'academic freedom' is understood to be the freedom of intellectuals (including academics) to engage in discussion as they pursue truth and understanding. As such, it has certain strengths, but it also has limitations.

Certainly, while it may serve as a defence of 'academic freedom' in that restricted sense of the expression, it is not so obvious that it can serve, as Mill intended, as a defence of 'free speech' more generally. That is because there are many acts of speech and expression which one might normally expect to be tolerated in a society which genuinely respected free speech, but which do not qualify as the exercise of thought and discussion in the pursuit of truth and understanding. In the modern world, there are, for example, plenty of individuals who believe that there are, at present, flying saucers circling Earth, or that they were once abducted by aliens, even that they can communicate with those aliens in the Venusian language. Individuals who subscribe to such beliefs frequently do so on the basis of conviction or faith and are unlikely to be swayed by challenges which invoke argument or evidence.

In short, in a society where the liberty of speech and expression is genuinely respected, there is a wide range of activities which one might reasonably expect individuals to be free to perform, and yet many of those activities fall, as it were, beyond the boundaries of Mill's argument. Certainly, there are many which by no means qualify as the exercise of academic freedom and, if they qualify for protection at all, it is on the grounds of Mill's 'no harm' principle, according to which, 'the only purpose for which power can be exercised over any member of a civilised community, against his will, is to prevent harm to others.' It is a principle which clearly distinguishes the expression of beliefs which lack rational justification, and which are also harmless – the belief in flying saucers being an example – from, say, the set of baseless claims which, together, constitute what has come to be known as 'Holocaust denial,' the latter being fraught with damaging and malign intent.[2]

The upshot of the argument up to this point, then, is that the exercise of discussion in the pursuit of truth is a rather specialised activity and one which supplies a model from which it is difficult to generalise without confusion. Two implications of this conclusion are especially worth emphasising here, each being relevant to the subject of academic freedom. The first is that, while it may be the duty of academics to take controversial claims seriously – claims which are controversial for good academic reasons that is – they have no special obligation to expose students to ideas which are questionable for other than academic reasons – which are offensive, unwelcome, distasteful, or otherwise unwelcome. It is important to stress the point, if only because it is so frequently argued that academics in particular have just that obligation.

By way of example, consider the following comment. It is drawn from a speech by the British Member of Parliament, Jo Johnson, in 2017, when announcing the introduction of a new government agency, the Office for Students.

> Shield young people from controversial opinions, views that challenge their most profoundly held beliefs or simply make them uncomfortable, and you are on the slippery slope that ends up with a society less able to make scientific breakthroughs, to be innovative and to resist injustice.

Johnson adds

> Whether it is Galileo's heretical rejection of geocentrism, Darwin's godless theory of creation or the bravery of dissidents resisting oppression all over the world, history shows the right to disagree is the cornerstone of intellectual and political freedom.
>
> *(Johnson, 2017)*

Johnson's remarks invite a number of comments, one being that – unlike believers in flying saucers or abduction by aliens – both Galileo and Darwin had good evidence with which to support their 'heretical' and 'godless' theories – the one having observed the moons of Jupiter and the other having taken detailed notes while voyaging on the *Beagle*. Another point is that he was confusing two separate ideas. One is the idea that the discussion of conflicting ideas is a useful aid to the pursuit of knowledge – the exercise of 'the liberty of thought and discussion' in pursuit of truth, in other words – and the other is political freedom from oppression. It is not so obvious that the argument of Mill's second chapter has anything relevant to say on the latter subject, the two activities – the pursuit of truth and resistance to oppression – being conceptually distinct activities (even though it can, of course, happen in practice that the former has a role to play in the latter). Moreover, none of this is to mention what is, apparently, Johnson's bizarre assumption that, unlike other citizens, students are incapable of reading newspapers or trawling the internet – activities in the course of which they inevitably encounter all manner of offensive and otherwise unwelcome material.

A second implication is that academic freedom – construed as the freedom of intellectuals to engage in the pursuit of truth and understanding – is consistent with autocracy and other forms of 'top down' government by this or that political elite. That is because it is a freedom which may be confined to a few – the members of small research institutes, for example, or, as in medieval Europe, monastic orders. Picture a society in which small groups of intellectuals, enclosed within the confines of various institutes, are happily engaged in the pursuit of truth. Suppose that, to the extent that they are successful, their efforts have exactly the results Mill ascribes to the liberty of thought and discussion – an increase in 'the number and gravity of the truths which have reached the point of being uncontested, a consequent contribution to the well-being of mankind,' and so on. Suppose that meanwhile, beyond the academy's walls, the greater part of the population get on with their lives. There would be autocratic rule, of course, but perhaps this would be widely ignored so long as the autocrat was 'benevolent.'

If the foregoing society is conceivable, then Mill's argument would appear to be confronted with a difficulty for, while the society pictured is one in which the liberty of thought and discussion is exercised, and to beneficial effect, it does not exemplify the liberal political order he favours. Nor does it exemplify the political order favoured by subsequent liberal philosophers such as Rawls (see especially Rawls 1971/1999).[3] On the contrary, it bears more of a resemblance to the 'totalitarian' state portrayed by Plato in his *Republic* (375 BC/1987) – a state run by expert 'philosopher rulers' and within which the ordinary people get on with their 'own business.' The point is that a defence of the liberal order must explain why a bundle of freedoms which may be loosely categorised under the heading 'free speech' – one of which is, to be sure, 'the liberty of thought and discussion' – should be available to *all* adult members of society, and not only to a few.

'Thought and discussion' and academic freedom within the liberal order

There is no doubt that Mill considered the liberty of thought and discussion to be of supreme importance, so much so that it merited a chapter of *On Liberty* all to itself. Of its 'grounds,' he wrote that, 'when rightly understood [they] are of much wider application than to one division of the subject' and that, 'a thorough consideration of this part of the question [of liberty] will be found the best introduction to the remainder.' In other words, he considered it possible to generalise from those grounds to a wider defence of the liberal order. Against this, it is the upshot of the argument up to this point that the exercise of thought and discussion in the pursuit of truth is a somewhat specialised activity, and that the possibility of generalising to any great extent from an account of its virtues is by no means self-evident. We are therefore faced with the question of what principles or suppositions there might be to, as it were, 'license' such a generalisation.

In fact, Mill could answer the question in a number of ways. Mill's argument for thought and discussion can be construed, in one way, as setting an ideal template to which, in reality, society considered as a whole may conform to a greater of a lesser degree. Where public acts of expression are concerned, there ought to be some resemblance between those situations and an ideal situation in which opinions and hypotheses are advanced for the purposes of discussion, and with a view to gaining greater understanding and knowledge. In this way, though with a certain artificiality, society might be thought of as resembling a vast discussion group within which each citizen is a participant.[4] This would yield a criterion for distinguishing acts of expression which are *merely* offensive, no more than that, from those which embody opinions which are genuinely open to rational debate or empirical test, even though their expression may be offensive to those who do not share them. Acts of 'hate speech' would fall into the former category, and expressions of atheistic opinion – offensive to religious believers – would fall into the latter. This might give you a reason for censoring acts which fall into the former category, but tolerating those which fall into the latter. This interpretation, it could legitimately be held, counts in favour of Mill's argument.

There is rather more to it than that, however, for Mill clearly held, not only that the tendency to engage in thought and discussion was becoming widespread throughout society at the time he was writing – that it was something which distinguished his time from earlier periods – but also that it was a tendency to be encouraged. 'Mankind have outgrown old institutions and old doctrines,' he wrote, and

> Men may not reason better, concerning the great questions in which human nature is interested, but they reason more. Large subjects are discussed more, and longer, and by more minds. Discussion has penetrated deeper into society; and if no greater numbers than before have attained the higher degrees of intelligence, fewer grovel in that state of abject stupidity, which can only co-exist with utter apathy and sluggishness.

That was in an essay entitled, 'The Spirit of the Age' (Mill 1831/1985). Clearly, things had changed since the late eighteenth/early nineteenth century – the time of the French Revolution, Napoleon, Waterloo, and then Peterloo – and one difference which impressed Mill was the way in which the volatile rabble of those times had been replaced by a new upper working/lower middle class. This new class placed a high value upon 'respectability' and conformity, and the threat of revolution (emulating the French 'Terror') had been replaced by that of 'the tyranny of the majority' (or 'the tyranny of the prevailing opinion and feeling [and] the tendency of society to impose, by other means than civil penalties, its own ideas and practices as rules of conduct on those who dissent from them'). So far as Mill was concerned, then, one great virtue of the liberty of thought and discussion lay in the way that, through its exercise, it serves as a bulwark against the latter tyranny.

The argument that the exercise of the liberty of thought and discussion will undermine the tyranny of the majority may well be open to a number of objections. For one thing, it is a consequentialist argument and therefore questionable for reasons mentioned earlier. In addition, there may be a question of whether 'tyranny of the majority' is an expression which can be given a precise definition and, if it can, there is then the further question of why it should be objectionable. In other words, while one may agree with Mill that individuality and 'pagan self-assertion' are admirable traits, and while one may hold that a dull tendency to conform to convention is not especially attractive in a person, one may also feel that it is neither a vice nor a sin. The point here, though, is simply that a high valuation was placed upon such virtues as individuality, non-conformity, and intellectual independence by Mill himself. It is a valuation which shows up throughout *On Liberty* and indeed throughout his work.

Mill's vision of the liberal order is complex and antiquated in certain respects. In this context, its main features are simply as follows: first of all, Mill considered himself to be writing at a time of transition. 'Mankind have outgrown old institutions and doctrines, and have not yet acquired new ones' (Mill, 1831/1985, 170). As a consequence, 'the multitude' was, as he put it, 'without a guide,' and society had become, 'exposed to all the errors and dangers which are to be expected when persons who have never studied any branch of knowledge comprehensively and as a whole attempt to judge for themselves upon particular parts of it' (Mill, 1831/1985, 174–5), there being 'no source of principles, no guide, so authoritative that it deserved to command confidence' (Mill, 1831/1985, 171). Secondly, Mill held that it was in the activity of discussion, diffused throughout society as it had to be, that the remedy lay for this unstable state of affairs. Thirdly, and most saliently, Mill's argument is underpinned by a particular representation of society's fundamental character. Individuals, each pursuing his or her own good in his or her own way – or, at least, what each believes to be that good – are pictured as lacking any over-arching guide. (Earlier generations – Christian believers, for example – might have found guidance in a settled body of doctrine. Such a doctrine was not available, according to Mill [1831/1985], to the individuals of his own time.) It is a picture similar to that which underpins the work of Mill's utilitarian predecessor, Bentham (see especially Bentham [1789/2000]). Although, unlike Mill, Bentham was unconcerned with the development of individuality. He sought only to ensure that happiness, construed as the having of pleasurable sensations, was distributed equitably throughout society. It is true enough, however, that, for both utilitarians, the best that can be hoped for is that the Principle of Utility, according to which 'the greatest good is the greatest happiness of the greatest number,' will assist legislators in what is, in effect, their role as 'traffic policemen' seeking to alleviate any negative effects which might arise from 'collision' between individuals as each follows his or her own trajectory (Bentham, 1789/2000).

What are we to make of this? Certainly, there is a streak of intellectual elitism in Mill's argument which, it is safe to assume, most today would find unacceptable.[5] On the other hand, however, most would agree with his conception of society as comprising a diversity of individuals and, likewise, a diversity of the belief systems to which those individuals subscribe. In the specific context of academic freedom, there are considerations which apply and are similar to those Mill raises in the case of 'discussion.' Thus, it is Mill's argument that the purpose of discussion is not merely to aim at the formulation of acceptable moral and political principles but to ease society through its transitional stage. In other words, he sees it as having a social role to play. Similarly, a true understanding of the nature of academic freedom must involve a recognition of the role played by universities within the wider social context – of their 'appropriate function.'

This is a view which requires a definition of 'academic freedom' which is broader than that implied up to this point. It is a definition which includes the freedom to engage in critical activity with a view to advancing the pursuit of knowledge and understanding, but which treats it as just one component in the array of liberties which ought to be available to universities if they are to function in a manner appropriate to the social context within which they are placed. The university is an arena in which the intellectual habits and the character of younger generations are, to a considerable extent, formed. The freedom to pursue truth and understanding is one component of what 'academic freedom,' construed in a certain way, involves. Of course, it can sometimes happen that freedoms come into collision. For example, students are normally free to form societies, but that freedom can come into question where the society involved is a branch of an extreme right, racist group. It is a freedom whose exercise can obviously come into conflict with the duty of universities to respect the multicultural character of society by creating an environment within which students of any ethnicity can feel free to pursue an education.

Let me bring this chapter to a close with lines drawn from a work in which education is discussed by Mill himself, his 1867 *Inaugural Address, Delivered to the University of St Andrews*. The object of a university, he wrote, 'is not to make skilful lawyers, or physicians, or engineers, but capable and cultivated human beings,' the latter being 'part of what every generation owes to the next, as that on which its civilisation and worth will principally depend' (Mill, 2010 [1867], 2). Clearly, Mill would have agreed that a university's role must involve rather more than the provision of a facility within which thought and discussion can take place. That role may have become more complex since Mill's time, but the requirement remains that universities should be free to perform this wider – and crucial – role.

Notes

1 A full account of how ideas of toleration and freedom of expression developed over time from the seventeenth century onwards would – of course – involve making reference to arguments other than Mill's. Notable examples are to be found in the work of Milton (1644/1974), Locke (1689/1993), and Hume (1752/1953). My purpose here is not to offer such an account; it is rather to analyse one influential argument, Mill's, and to determine what there is to be learnt from that analysis.

For an account of earlier arguments, especially Milton's and Locke's, see Haworth (1998), especially chapters 7, 10, and the appendix.

2 'Holocaust Denial,' strictly speaking, consists of a set of brazenly unsustainable claims – for example, that there were no gas chambers at Auschwitz, that the inmates of concentration camps were, in fact, comfortably housed, and that Hitler knew nothing of the camps. It is not to be confused with attempts by genuine historians to portray the Holocaust accurately. On this subject, see Haworth (2015, 45).

3 For an account of Rawls's arguments for freedom of speech and expression, see Haworth (1998) chapters 8 and 9.

4 The idea of a public sphere, or public 'realm,' has played a significant role in the work of writers other than Mill. See, for example, Arendt (1958/1998). See also Habermas (1962/1989).

5 Mill's suggestion that society is going through a transitional phase betrays a Comtean streak running through his argument. For Mill's debt to Auguste Comte, see Mill (1865/1961).

References

Arendt, H. (1998 [1958]). *The Human Condition*. Chicago and London: University of Chicago Press.

Bentham, J. (2000 [1789]). The Principles of Morals and Legislation. In R. Harrison (ed), *Selected Writings on Utilitarianism* (75–309). Hertfordshire: Wordsworth Editions.

Habermas, J. (1989 [1962]). *The Structural Transformation of the Public Sphere* (T. Burger and F. Lawrence, Trans.). Cambridge: Polity.

Haworth, A. (1998). *Free Speech*. London: Routledge.

Haworth, A. (2015). *Free Speech: All That Matters*. London: Hodder and Stoughton.

Hume, D. (1953 [1752]). Of the Liberty of the Press. In C. W. Hendel (ed), *David Hume's Political Essays* (3–11). Indianapolis: Bobbs-Merrill.

Johnson, J. (2017). *Free Speech in the Liberal University*. GOV.UK. https://www.gov.uk/government/news/jo-johnson-calls-for-free-speech-to-be-protected-on-campus

Locke, J. (1993 [1689]). A Letter Concerning Toleration. In D. Wootton (ed), *John Locke: Political Writings*. London: Penguin.

Mill, J. S. (1961 [1865]). *Auguste Comte and Positivism*. Ann Arbor: University of Michigan Press.

Mill, J. S. (1985 [1831]). The Spirit of the Age. In G. Williams (ed), *John Stuart Mill on Politics and Society* (2nd ed.). London: Fontana.

Mill, J. S. (1991 [1859]). On Liberty. In J. Gray (ed), *John Stuart Mill: On Liberty and Other Essays* (5–128). Oxford: Oxford University Press.

Mill, J. S. (2010 [1867]). *Inaugural Address, Delivered to the University of St Andrews*. London: Longmans.

Milton, J. (1974 [1644]). Areopagitica. In C. A. Patrides (ed), *John Milton: Selected Prose*. London: Penguin.

Plato. (1987 [375 BC]). *The Republic* (D. Lee, Trans.). London: Penguin.

Rawls, J. (1999 [1971]). *A Theory of Justice* (2nd ed.). Harvard: Harvard University Press.

PART II

Academic Freedom

Case Studies from British Higher Education (1945–1990)

4

ACADEMIC FREEDOM, UNIVERSITIES, AND THE LEFT

A case study of British university adult education in the early years of the Cold War[1]

Richard Taylor

Introduction

Since the inception of the modern university, and arguably for many years prior to that, there has been a near-universal, rhetorical commitment to freedom of thought and expression for appropriately qualified (and tenured) academics in Western developed societies (see Chapter 2 by Peter Scott). Of course, in many parts of the world, there are very different cultures and practices in relation to academic freedom. However, even in the liberal democracies of the developed world, there are instances where it can be argued that there was discrimination against those who held and publicly advocated political views which lay outside the parameters of the accepted liberal consensus.

This is a perennial problem, endemic in the very nature of the university *qua* university. It is thus a contemporary, and not only a historical, issue. One recent example is illustrated in a 2023 Policy Exchange survey where a sample of 820 UK academics reported what would seem like a high level of acknowledged bias: '...20% of conservatives evinced a willingness to hire an inferior centrist candidate over a better qualified leftist candidate, while 15% of leftists would hire a less qualified left-winger over a centrist' (Srinivasan, 2023, 6).

The case study which is the focus of this chapter is from the UK and concerns alleged discrimination by university leadership, at both departmental and institutional levels, in the immediate post–World War II period, against academics who were Marxists and/or members of the Communist Party of Great Britain (hereafter, CP).[2] The specific example examined is that of Marxists and/or CP members working in university adult education (hereafter University AE) departments in the early years of the Cold War – that is, the late 1940s and early 1950s.

DOI: 10.4324/9781003363262-6

In order to understand the context within which these controversies took place, it may be helpful, particularly for those not familiar with the particular nature of British University AE, to briefly outline its distinguishing characteristics. The development of such work in Britain stemmed from the extramural culture and practice of the University Extension movement of the late nineteenth century. This evolved, from the 1920s onwards, into the provision by the majority of universities of large and diverse programmes of part-time courses for adult students (and day and weekend schools; day release courses for trade unionists and other occupational groups; high level, 'post experience' and intensive courses for professionals; and full or part-time specialist Masters courses in adult and continuing education). It was quite common for the larger, civic universities to enrol 10,000 to 20,000 part-time adult students per year in their region, equating to several hundred full-time equivalent students.

All such departments employed full-time academic staff with a range of disciplinary specialisms, with the arts, humanities, and social sciences predominating. They also employed, on a 'teaching only' basis, a much larger number of part-time tutors.

Many eminent researchers and scholars were located in, and drew much of their inspiration from, the interdisciplinary environment of such departments, including 'founding fathers' such as E.P. Thompson (pioneer of 'history from below'), Richard Hoggart, and Raymond Williams (cultural studies) – and in the field of adult education research itself, Harold Wiltshire, Sidney Raybould, and Michael Stephens, for example (see Hoggart, 1957; Thompson, 1963; Williams, 1979; and Raybould, 1951; Taylor *et al*, 1985; Steele, 1997). But there was always a particular emphasis upon the teaching of adults (and many University AE staff were not engaged in research, preferring to concentrate upon high-quality teaching). The students who attended such programmes, which were usually 'open entry' (that is, no prior educational qualifications were required), often needed considerable support and pedagogical skill to enable them to cope with, and benefit from, university-level study.

Three final points about the nature of British University AE should be noted. First, these departments operated by definition at the interface between the university and its local and regional community, and they were important 'shop windows' for the university's local and regional image. Second, many of the groups with which these departments interacted – trade unions, social workers, the armed services, and the police, for example – were engaged with inherently sensitive, and often controversial, social and political roles. The often radical, social purpose perspectives of many University AE staff were thus always prone to result in contentious, sometimes high-profile, disputes. Finally, with the growing emphasis in universities in Britain as elsewhere in the second half of the twentieth century upon the importance of research specialisms in recognised disciplinary areas, such departments, with their inter- and multi-disciplinary structures and their emphasis upon teaching, were always vulnerable to accusations of having inappropriately 'low standards.' This was considerably exacerbated, from the 1980s onwards, by the dominance of the 'audit culture' and the associated inspection regimes.

These departments, and the wide-ranging provision that they offered, thrived and expanded greatly throughout the remaining decades of the twentieth century. However, as a result of a series of both macro, social and cultural changes, and specific administrative and funding policy enactments by successive governments, they declined rapidly in the early years of the twenty-first century.

University AE and kindred organisations committed to liberal, social purpose approaches to adult education, such as the Workers' Educational Association (WEA), tended to attract those academics with reforming, left of centre, perspectives (Caute, 1973). A significant minority of such staff has been on the 'far left' and thus might be regarded as 'suspect.'

Many left-wing intellectuals leaving the Armed Forces in 1945–46 saw University AE as a fitting and congenial environment in which to combine their political commitments with serious academic work, bringing the university and its wealth of knowledge and culture to the wider community, thereby contributing to the development of the 'good society.' It is also relevant to note that in this period – from the 1940s to the late 1970s – the proportion of the population who had the opportunity of studying at degree level in UK universities remained very low, under 10% of the standard age cohort. Moreover, very few of the adult population had had such opportunities. University AE departments thus provided a unique chance for adults to gain experience of university-level study.

This case study examines, first, the degree to which discrimination may have been practised in relation to academic staff who were acknowledged to be of such political views; second, the extent to which, if extant, such discrimination was at the time arguably justifiable; and finally, the effects and implications of this debate upon more general issues surrounding the nature and importance of academic freedom.

In this example – and other analogous cases – it could be argued that those espousing such 'extreme' political views were inherently unable (and/or unwilling) to adhere to established academic norms and procedures in their teaching and research. They were, it was argued, necessarily engaged not in 'education,' but rather in some form of 'proselytising' for a particular political ideology. They were, in other words, unable to be objective in their academic and professional roles.

Objectivity in the university context

A preliminary discussion, therefore, for this chapter, is to examine the nature of 'objectivity' in the university context – and to discuss whether such objectivity is desirable or indeed attainable.

In many respects, this is not a contentious issue. All those committed to the accepted academic standards of the modern, liberal university would agree that, in their teaching and research activities, academic staff should adhere to rigorous observance of evidence-based inquiry and logical argument (and debate, on 'Socratic principles'), appropriately researched and referenced. Similarly, few, if any, would dissent from the use of scientific methods in the natural and applied sciences.

But, however conscientiously applied, such practices cannot lead, at a fundamental level, to true objectivity. By definition, all experiences, ideas and socialisation processes, are mediated through the individual and his or her subjective consciousness and life experiences. Thus, total objectivity is impossible for anyone, irrespective of political, ideological beliefs. Recognising these limitations and taking action to counter them as far as possible are the first steps towards addressing this intrinsic subjectivity.

If total objectivity is thus unattainable, what mitigating actions should academics take to move nearer to this ideal? First, in teaching, attempting to argue the case for alternative perspectives from within the 'mind-set' of those who advocate these positions is essential. Second, this has to be supplemented by suggested reading – books and articles, etc. – that runs counter to the tutor's own position. Third, encouragement of open discussion, in which all viewpoints are respected – and subsequently challenged – is, again, essential. However, some perspectives are more securely based than others, in that they are rationally argued, verifiable, and evidence-backed. They are thus more reliable and, in that respect, more objective. The academic's job should be to strain to present conclusions that take into account and explain the strengths and weaknesses of all perspectives whilst acknowledging that we all start from subjective positions.

These have always been matters of concern in University AE and in adult education generally. Albert Mansbridge, the influential founder of the WEA, drew attention to the issue in his 1913 book on 'University Tutorial Classes.' He cites the case of one

> tutor [who] had taken his class for two years in Economic Theory with only one textbook and no books of reference. Such a class, from the tutorial class point of view, is useless. A tutorial class in Economics should have access to the opinions of all economic writers, the orthodox equally with the unorthodox. No class, for example, can afford to disregard either Marshall or Marx.
>
> *(Mansbridge, 1913, 119)*

Such approaches, within the tradition of liberal adult education, have been combined with a democratic mode of study, where adult students and their tutor have a symbiotic, mutual learning relationship (as opposed to the one-way transmission of a body of 'expert knowledge' by the tutor to the students). The educational experience, moreover, is designed not only to enhance individuals' understanding of social, literary, and cultural (or, indeed, scientific) subject matter, but also to provide the necessary knowledge, confidence, and ability to articulate challenges to the perceived inequities and injustices that exist in contemporary societies.

In relation to the questions of objectivity posed at the outset, therefore, the conclusion must be that, whilst wholly objective teaching (and research) is by definition impossible, there are practical, mitigating behaviours which academics would do well to adopt. Equally importantly, true objectivity in the context of liberal adult education is not so much concerned with content as with the method of teaching. Students must be given access to the arguments, which will enable them to make up their own minds. 'Openness of mind' and a readiness to listen attentively to what other people are saying: these are the hallmarks of a good University AE class. The objective must be to equip adult students with the necessary skills and information, through discussion, analysis, and the methodologies of study, to find their own way to reasoned and informed judgments. It is emphatically NOT to 'convert' adult students to any particular ideological belief, whether political, religious, or philosophical.

The question, therefore, in the context of this study, is how far were Marxist and other left-wing academics conforming to, or at the very least attempting to conform to, this approach; or, on the contrary, were the university authorities acting reasonably in arguing that such ideological positions were potentially, and on occasion actually, incompatible with the core values of the modern, liberal university?

The Cold War context and academic freedom in British University AE departments

Whereas during World War II, at least after 1941, the USSR had been seen in the West, including the USA, as an ally and at least a semi-friendly nation, by 1947 the agreement over respective 'spheres of influence' in post-war Europe had begun to disintegrate. A succession of crises in, *inter alia*, Greece, Turkey, and Czechoslovakia culminated in the 'Berlin blockade' in 1948. In Britain, all these tensions were exacerbated by the British Government's decision to manufacture the Atom Bomb (forerunner to the Hydrogen Bomb). By 1948, Communism had become perceived as the major threat to the 'free world' and hence 'the British way of life.' Echoes of American McCarthyism[3] were to be found throughout British society and its institutions. It should be noted that hostility to 'Communism,' and fear of its 'infecting' the British working class, had deep roots in the British Establishment (Miliband, 1982).

These pressures applied with particular force to the University AE/ extramural world (and indeed the WEA) for the reasons alluded to. Two questions arise: first, what was the extent, if any, of clear, proven discrimination against such 'far left' academic staff? and, second, what were the arguments on this issue put forward in the academy by the proponents of the two opposing viewpoints?

There were undoubtedly CP members, and several others who could legitimately be termed 'fellow travellers,' in most of the larger University AE departments in the late 1940s. However, they were always a small minority of the total (Fieldhouse, 1985, chapters 3, 4, and 5). The Oxford University department (or 'Delegacy' as it was known) had the highest proportion of such staff: by 1947, according to Fieldhouse (35), who drew his evidence from the Oxford Delegacy archives, 9 out of a total full-time teaching staff of 30 were CP members, or 'fellow travellers,' including Thomas Hodgkin, the Head of Department, known as Secretary to the Delegacy. (For analysis of the general relationship between Oxford and working-class adult education, see Goldman, 1995.) The appointment of such a large number of self-acknowledged Marxists to the academic staff demonstrates that such commitments were by no means an insuperable barrier to appointment, although, as discussed below, such staff were often, in effect, debarred from 'sensitive' areas of teaching work. It is much harder to determine whether or not other applicants of a Marxist persuasion were not appointed largely or entirely because of their views, rather than their professional suitability or unsuitability for the post in question. It seems beyond doubt that this was the case with other leading academic Marxists, in the wider university context – notably, the Marxist historian and CP member, Eric Hobsbawm (Hobsbawm, 2006; Evans, 2019/2020). After exhaustive analysis, Fieldhouse's conclusion was that, at Oxford, there was 'some evidence...to suggest that there was a latent anti-communism not far below the surface of the liberal tolerance within the Delegacy...and that Lindsay's[4] dominant influence was wielded against the appointment of known communists from time to time...' (Fieldhouse, 1985, 32). Whether or not this was the case – and Fieldhouse provides no concrete, archival evidence on this point – the fact remains that having a full-time staff group where approximately one-third were avowed Marxists or 'fellow travellers' was hardly indicative of pronounced discrimination against those with left-wing views.

Similar concerns about the suitability of Marxist and CP members of staff were also voiced by other Heads of University AE departments: Sidney Raybould at Leeds University and Tom Kelly at Liverpool University, for example. Kelly, in an interview with Roger Fieldhouse, was quite unequivocal in his opposition to the appointment of Marxist, Communist, or other extreme left staff:

> My war-time experience led me to...the conclusion that it is not wrong to deny freedom of speech to those who by their philosophy are seeking to destroy freedom of speech....I have no scruples in saying that I would refuse

a communist as a full-time member of staff in a university and refuse to appoint a communist as a part-time lecturer in a subject in a political field....I don't see why one should commit social and political suicide by allowing these people to take over.

(Fieldhouse, 1985, 18–9)

Raybould did not go this far, though he harboured serious misgivings about appointing committed Communists, because he doubted that they were capable of the required objectivity in their teaching and research. He believed that CP members were committed 'to propagating Communist Party policy to stir up industrial unrest, to spread disaffection in the Armed Forces, to encourage treasonable activities.' It was for this 'reason that there are doubts in adult education quarters, and in academic circles generally, as to whether objective teaching can be expected of Communists' (Raybould, 1950–51, 102–4).

Raybould, of course, did not acknowledge his own subjectivity, in relation to his clear ideological commitment to centrist Labour politics (Raybould, 1951). Nevertheless, he did appoint at least three CP members to his staff, the most prominent being the subsequently famous historian E.P. Thompson (of whom more later). One of Thompson's referees for the Leeds post was Frank Jacques, District Secretary of the Eastern Region of the WEA. Although unstinting in his praise of Thompson in his formal reference, it is significant that, in a private letter to Raybould, he warned the latter about Thompson's Communist affiliations: '*But* he [Thompson] is a member of the CP and a very sincere one, if you know what I mean by that' (Jacques, 17 April 1948, cited in Steele, 1997, 146). It is arguably to Raybould's credit that he nevertheless supported Thompson's appointment: and he continued to recognise Thompson's undoubted abilities. Indeed, when Thompson was offered a Readership at Warwick University in 1965, Raybould was keen to retain Thompson in the Leeds Department. (Thompson did take the Warwick post and remained there until he decided to become a full-time writer and political activist [see Fieldhouse and Taylor, 2013].)

All in all, therefore, University AE Directors acted on what they saw as correct principles, but also pragmatically, in their practice in relation to Marxists and/or CP members on their staff. The most important principle was their commitment to the individual's freedom to hold, and publicly advocate, any political, religious, moral, or other beliefs. This was held by most Directors – but perhaps not by the most vehemently anti-Communist characters, such as Tom Kelly – to be a foundational *a priori* value of Western liberal democracies. Pragmatically, however, Directors operated what was in effect an *ad personam* policy, whereby applicants for posts were judged entirely on professional criteria; and, if appointed, their teaching and research activities were kept well away from 'sensitive' areas, especially trade union and related teaching, where it was clear that the CP had a very particular perspective and political interest.

This might be seen as a typically British example of 'principled pragmatism.' Arguably, it was eminently sensible. Had CP members been engaged on teaching trade unionists, for example, almost certainly (some) trade union officials would have objected and Departments' overall 'suitability' professionally, within the university, might well have been questioned. But it does raise questions of principle. How far should academic freedom be constrained in this way? Surely, the *a priori* freedom of academics, once recognised by their peers, to teach and research as they see fit, should be sacrosanct? These are questions which apply across the whole academy.

Two specific examples of alleged bias

There were two instances in the British context, in University AE departments, in the late 1940s, where concerns over Communist propaganda and bias in teaching were held to be so prevalent that formal complaints and accusations were made. These concerned the trade union classes held from 1947 at the Wedgwood Memorial College, taught largely by Oxford Delegacy academic staff, and organised by J.O.N. Vickers, the College's Warden and a man of explicit and strongly held Marxist views. And, secondly, the Queen's College, Oxford, trade union school, held from 3 to 10 April 1948.

In relation to the former, the North Staffordshire Adult Education Committee (representing the Local Government authorities in the area), in liaison with the Oxford Delegacy, secured a lease on Barlaston Hall and the Wedgwood Memorial College opened there in 1945. Vickers, who had joined the CP in Cambridge before the War, was appointed Warden in June 1946. He was responsible to both bodies – the Local Authority Committee and the Delegacy – but ultimately he, and through him, as Warden, the College's programme, was responsible to the Oxford Delegacy's Tutorial Classes Committee (TCC). There was general agreement that the College should make trade union education a significant part of its programme.

However, there was unease at Vickers's apparent foregrounding of Communist viewpoints in the course programme, both those concerned with industrial and economic matters and those focusing upon political and international affairs. (These concerns were privately expressed by both the WEA Acting District Secretary, C.A. Scrimgeour, and Frank Pickstock of the Oxford Delegacy. [Fieldhouse, 1985, 44].) It was certainly the case that the tutors Vickers used on the programmes were very largely CP members or close 'fellow travellers.' In the 1948–49 session, for example, 'the trade union courses were taught very largely by Vickers and Bridget Sutton' and several other Marxist tutors. But it is equally true that many non-Marxist tutors and lecturers also taught on these trade union courses. It was, Fieldhouse concluded, 'difficult to say' whether there was any 'imbalance' in the overall teaching (Fieldhouse, 1985, 46).

Frank Pickstock's view, as Secretary of the Oxford TCC, at the Delegacy, was that Vickers was 'a superb adult educator' but that he was 'overstepping the mark... [in] the kind of things that were being taught; kind of speakers; kind of students he made a set at...the lefties and the Communist Party' (Pickstock, as cited in Fieldhouse, 1985, 44).

These very public concerns resulted in a series of formal complaints about the alleged Communist bias in the work of the College and thus of the role of the Oxford Delegacy and its staff. A longstanding critic, alleging persistent, widespread, and undue Marxist/CP influence in the Delegacy's teaching, was Ernest Green, District Secretary of the WEA. He had written privately in October 1947 to R.H. Tawney about Thomas Hodgkin: 'I am doubtful about Hodgkin. I do not think he is reliable and I have evidence that he is playing a double game...' (R.H. Tawney Correspondence, WEA National Office, cited in Fieldhouse, 1985, 38)

Similar issues were raised in the context of the trade union residential school held at Queen's College, Oxford, from 3 to 10 April, 1948, where the Trades Union Congress (TUC) General Council also alleged that there had been undue Communist influence in the teaching. Organised by the Oxford TCC and the Workers' Education section of the TUC, the programme was intended both as a 'refresher' course for University AE tutors and as an experiment in trade union education. (It was attended by 21 tutors and 33 trade unionists.) There was a concentration upon industrial and economic policy issues; and there was also wide-ranging debate over contemporary, and contentious, directly political issues, such as steel nationalisation, and the appropriate role of trade unions in a capitalist, mixed economy such as prevailed in the UK.

From the outset, there were tensions, on occasion breaking into open, vociferous conflict, between those espousing a centrist, social democratic position and those taking a Marxist or quasi-Marxist approach. To an extent, however, such tensions reflected the cultural differences between the academics' open-ended, discursive, and dialectical approach and the trade unionists' more pragmatic traditions: the latter were more familiar with the carefully prepared statements of trade union conferences.

That these allegations were taken seriously is evident from the senior membership of the TCC sub-committee that was established in June 1948 to examine the issues involved: the Oxford Vice-Chancellor, John Lowe; the Warden of Nuffield College, Sir Henry Clegg; the Chairman of the Delegacy, A.D. Lindsay (the former Master of Balliol College and the 'grand old man of Oxford adult education' [Fieldhouse, 1985, 30]); and the senior academics, G.D.H. Cole and Lucy Sutherland, the Principal of Lady Margaret Hall. This committee held eight meetings and produced its Report for the TCC on 5 March 1949.

The key conclusion was that, after wide consultations with the parties involved, the Committee felt 'confident that at these courses neither the organisation nor teaching gave undue prominence to the communist point of view.'

Although there were some concerted attempts by some of the students to press the communist perspective, this 'was dealt with quite adequately in free discussion by the majority of the students and tutors and they are convinced that the courses served a very useful purpose' (Green Special Report, 1949). The allegations against the 1948 trade union school were officially declared non-proven.

In relation to the allegations made specifically about the provision at Wedgwood Memorial College, the Committee were critical of Vickers's judgment, albeit emphasising that they found no evidence of undue partiality by the tutors. The main conclusion of the Committee, and the TUC, was thus 'not guilty as charged.' However, it is reasonable to assume that doubts remained over Vickers's professional probity, in terms of his having an appropriately impartial approach to his programme planning and teaching responsibilities. Whether or not this was the case, there is little doubt that the tide of opinion turned against him: and his three-year contract was not renewed on its expiry in August 1949.

Despite strongly expressed dissatisfaction with the conclusions of the Committee, made at the WEA Annual Meeting of the North Staffordshire District, these decisions were ratified. Even Hodgkin did not argue against these recommendations; and nor did he defend publicly Vickers's position.

However, despite the formal rejection of these allegations, some of the McCarthyite mud did stick. In Hodgkin's view, there was 'this cold wind blowing through the Delegacy but it was blowing through the world at the same time. But I think the major force was that we had our own McCarthy movement that had stirred a lot of mud...There was an understood convention from then on that appointments would be carefully watched to ensure that, as far as possible, left wing candidates were not preferred. They had to be outstanding to make it possible for them to be appointed at all...' (Hodgkin, interview with Fieldhouse, cited in Fieldhouse, 1985, 51) As the Cold War atmosphere intensified, CP and Marxist influence declined in the Oxford Delegacy (and, generally, elsewhere in the University AE world).

In the spring of 1949, the staunchly anti-Communist Frank Pickstock was not only Secretary of the TCC, but also in charge, temporarily, of Wedgwood Memorial College. Hodgkin's 'cold wind of the Cold War' was evident in the Delegacy. As Secretary of the Delegacy, he felt both pressurised and increasingly isolated and several Marxist tutors either left the Delegacy or, like Raymond Williams,[5] distanced themselves from the CP and orthodox Marxism. By late 1949, a new Administrative Assistant, Joan Carmichael, who had experience with MI5, had been appointed to the Delegacy, on the recommendation of Lucy Sutherland. Not surprisingly, by the end of 1949, Hodgkin was considering resignation, and turning his attention to writing and analysing (and becoming an activist in) the rapidly developing anti-imperialist movements in Africa. (In the event, he delayed his final decision to resign until 1952.)[6]

University provision in colonial West Africa

In addition to these specific instances, there were two more general and prominent areas of University AE work in this period where there were clearly political sensitivities concerning tutors' ideological perspectives: the rapidly developing extramural work in British colonial states in Africa and the extensive programmes of adult education for the Armed Services. In both cases, there were inherently uneasy relationships between the universities and the governing authorities – the relevant colonial administrators in the one case, and the Services Command structures in the other.

There is considerable evidence, in the colonial context (Young, 1970; Fieldhouse, 1985), that University AE programmes, many of them taught by acknowledged Marxists, concentrated upon subjects which would be useful and relevant to the African nationalist independence movements: economics, politics, and history. In most cases, the syllabuses and approach were tailored to the African context and the perceived needs of the nationalist movements for independence. The cornerstone of the educational approach was, in Hodgkin's words, 'to help Africans to understand how they could develop for themselves a way of thinking about history and society.' Just as adult education in the UK should be geared towards enabling the emancipation of the working class, so, in Africa, adult education should play its part in facilitating the process of nationalists 'moving into power and displacing the colonial regimes...to equip them [the nationalist movements] to govern their own society' (Callaway, 1978, 23–5).

Indeed, it is clear that the Oxford tutors not only involved socialist theory and analysis in their economics, history, and politics classes but also explicitly advocated independence for the West African colonies. This led, in late 1948, to the Colonial Office decision to draw upon universities other than Oxford in its colonial work. Both Sidney Raybould at Leeds University and H.D. Boyden at Durham University – 'safe' social democrats both – developed close links with Nigeria and the Gold Coast (now Ghana). Raybould and later Jim McGregor (from Leeds University, subsequently to become the Leeds Registrar) were seconded for substantial periods to Ibadan University; and Boyden developed similarly close links with Fourah Bay College in Sierra Leone. In this increasingly Cold War vein, although at least three Marxists (and members or former members of the CP) – Dennis Wiseman, John Rex, and (later) Michael Barratt Brown – were appointed to posts in the Gold Coast/Ghana and Sierra Leone, all three had their appointments cancelled by the Colonial Office.

Such apparent discrimination against Marxist tutors is hardly surprising (though this does not of course make it necessarily justifiable): in the general Cold War climate, and given the specific concerns of the British Government about 'Communist infiltration' of nationalist, independence movements in

West Africa, there was good reason for the authorities to counter what they perceived as overtly political interference, under the guise of educational provision, by such tutors. Nevertheless, discrimination it was; moreover, there is no evidence of Communist propaganda or 'indoctrination' by the tutors concerned. Rather, as Hodgkin repeatedly claimed, the educational objective was to instil 'independent thinking' through critical, analytical adult education provision. (The issues underlying these conflicting perspectives are returned to in the Conclusion to this chapter.)

University provision in the armed services

Conflicting Cold War perspectives were even more apparent in the other primary context under consideration: adult education provision for the Armed Services. Although Sir Walter Moberly, Chairman of the Advisory Council for Education in HM Forces, maintained that a *modus vivendi* had been reached between the universities and the Armed Forces on the overall approach and practice of adult education for Services personnel, there were in reality profound differences of perspective.

University adult educators – of all political and ideological perspectives – believed in open and free discussion; critical, analytical, and open-ended analysis of all points of view; and the rigorous practice of academic methods of enquiry. The military authorities, on the other hand, came from a very different culture, and were somewhat suspicious of free discussion of 'controversial' subjects. Rather, they regarded education as being ideally concerned with 'making better soldiers.' The Central Committee for Adult Education in HM Forces (CCAE), formed in 1948, was quite explicit about its perspective on contentious ideological issues. For example, it stated, in November 1949, that 'the propagation of anti-democratic views could not be tolerated; and the topic of conscientious objection to military service must obviously be avoided.' Similarly, it was emphasised that adult education teaching should be carried out 'in such a way as to ensure that it is not prejudicial to training, morale or the maintenance of mutual confidence and goodwill between officers and other ranks' (CCAE Memorandum, 1949, cited in Fieldhouse, 1985, 80).

In addition, by the end of 1949, the CCAE had made it quite clear that, although the universities would have the initial responsibility for the appointment of tutors on the teaching programmes for the Armed Forces, the final decision on their 'suitability' would rest with the Services authorities. Moreover, as Professor Robert Peers, now Chairman of the CCAE, complained in June 1950, the Armed Services authorities were not required to provide any reasons for their debarring certain tutors. In the mounting Cold War climate, this was not perhaps surprising: but the mood of the times is shown by the acceptance by the Tutors' Association that the banning of Communist tutors, and even those suspected of being, or having been, Communists, was legitimate

(E.C. Report, Tutors' Association, 'Principles involved in MI5 intervention in Services Education,' n.d. but probably 1950). At Leeds, for example, the Armed Services authorities refused permission for E.P. Thompson to lecture on the Services programme. Again, this was understandable, perhaps even justifiable, given Thompson's explicit Marxist perspective and active CP membership (at this stage of his career and political development) (Fieldhouse and Taylor, 2013; Taylor, 2020). However, also refused permission to undertake Services lecturing was George Hauger, a staunch Liberal since 1945 and never a member of the CP. (After intervention by the Vice-Chancellor, the decision was reversed and Hauger was added to the 'approved list.')

Services education was thus a fraught, contested arena. Nevertheless, the problems should not be overstated. The programme survived and indeed expanded over the next 20 years or so; a wide range of genuinely liberal adult courses was provided, without undue interference by the Services authorities; and the programmes delivered were regarded by all those involved – the participants, the universities, and the Services authorities – as both appropriate and valuable.

The educational, pedagogic, and ideological issues were complex: whilst there was clearly no authoritarian clampdown on 'deviant,' oppositional perspectives, there was nevertheless, and equally clearly, evidence of unease, at the very least, about those propounding Marxist, and particularly CP, perspectives. The issues were discussed in the columns of 'The Highway,' the WEA Journal, in 1950–51, with prominent contributions from all parts of the ideological spectrum: notably, Thomas Hodgkin, Sidney Raybould, Roy Shaw, and Frank Jacques (Hodgkin et al., 1950–51).

E.P. Thompson and 'university standards'

However, perhaps the most insightful contribution to the debate came from E.P. Thompson, in his paper 'Against University Standards' (Thompson, 1950). This paper was written as a riposte to Raybould's position, in a series of 'Adult Education Papers,' inaugurated by the latter, as Head of Department, in 1950. Raybould's educational philosophy stemmed from his long immersion in the WEA's 'Great Tradition' of liberal adult education. He envisaged the central task of adult education as enabling adult students to gain access to an understanding and appreciation of both the social sciences and economics, and the arts and humanities. There were two crucial underlying assumptions to Raybould's approach: first, he assumed *a priori* that the established, accepted formulations of the disciplines concerned were both 'objective' and largely unchallengeable; and second, he saw his own mainstream social democratic perspective as the embodiment of objectivity. Moreover, he saw such objectivity and the rigorous quality standards that accompanied the adult education programmes (principally, attendance and written work requirements) as essential attributes of 'university standards.' And the attainment of such standards was a *sine qua non* of gaining credibility and esteem across the University for his Department's work and 'status' for his academic staff (Fieldhouse, 2013).

Thompson saw the issues rather differently. Although he readily acknowledged that objectivity and tolerance were highly desirable attributes of adult education pedagogy, they were methods and approaches – essentially mechanisms and by-products – of the educational endeavour, rather than the aims of education *per se*. For Thompson, 'to prescribe an attitude of calmness, or moderation, or tolerance towards a society or social problems is to pre-judge that this attitude is an appropriate one...' (Thompson, 1950, 24–5) and is implicitly giving a strong steer to students' ideological adherence to the (social democratic) established norms. Central to Thompson's approach was his insistence that the tutor's more extensive knowledge of relevant scholarship was not superior to adult students' life experience. Indeed, it was primarily in the dialectics of discussion between tutors and students that the true value of adult education lay.

The symbiosis between 'education' and 'experience' became a continuing theme in Thompson's writing and practice, as can be seen in his 1968 Mansbridge Memorial Lecture of that title (Thompson, 1968). In this lecture, he emphasised that 'universities engage in adult education not only to teach but to learn.'

To what extent were Raybould and other University AE Directors of similar outlook behaving reasonably in voicing their defence of the liberal values of the university and correspondingly expressing caution over the potential lack of impartiality in Marxist/CP tutors such as E.P. Thompson? Or, alternatively, were Thompson and those of like mind articulating perspectives which could be held legitimately to fall within the liberal culture of the academy?

It is a moot point. The overall picture is complex. In one sense, the history of these tensions and disputes can be construed as ultimately the avowal, protection, and renewal of the essentially liberal principles of the academy. The absolute right of the individual academic to hold and to advocate any political, or other ideological, belief system was asserted by (most) Directors of University AE Departments and by the most senior university officers (as was the case, for example, in the 'Green Report' of Oxford University, cited above). A crucial proviso, as has been argued above, was that academic staff espousing such views should abide by the academic standards of the university's mainstream culture. There was no *a priori* reason why Marxists, even if they were active members of the CP, should not be appointed to academic posts: and, indeed, as has been emphasised above, many such appointments were made.

However, as so often in British political culture, it can be argued that the dominant ideological perspective of the politically centrist establishment reasserted itself in this as in other contexts. Those who 'deviated' from this consensual position were thus not directly 'barred' or 'excluded.' There were few instances of direct confrontation and conflict. Rather, University AE Directors and the wider university leadership abided by established academic criteria in appointing a number of such 'extremists' to the university, provided that they undertook their academic duties in accordance with the established parameters of professional activity and provided that they were excluded from politically sensitive areas of work.

Similarly, those with 'extreme' political views were not debarred from senior roles: Thomas Hodgkin, for example, had one of the most senior roles in the field. Nor were they explicitly discriminated against. They were, rather, it could be argued, undermined and, whenever possible, marginalised and isolated.

These processes usually resulted, as in the case of Hodgkin, in resignation or 'withdrawal from the fray.' Universities, like all other social institutions, reflect the predominant values and culture of the societies of which they are a part. It is thus unsurprising that the long-established 'cultural methods' of university establishments in dealing with what is perceived as dangerous or deviant behaviour were arguably in evidence in this context. There was thus a delicate balancing of adherence to liberal principles, with the protection of the foundational ideology and structures of the established system.

Conclusion

Several conclusions, some of them in tension with each other, can be drawn from this case study. Firstly, and perhaps most importantly, the core liberal value of the absolute right of individuals to hold any political or other ideological belief, provided that they practised appropriate professional standards, was maintained. Secondly, there were clearly concerns, on the part of the university establishment, as manifested in our context by University AE Directors and senior university officers (Vice-Chancellors and the like), about the possibility of Marxist and/or CP bias in teaching (and to a lesser extent, research). Thirdly, as a result of these concerns, strategies were adopted to ensure that such influences were kept 'within bounds.' Fourthly, there was consequently a policy of 'containment' of such views, thereby rendering them relatively harmless in the eyes of the university authorities. Finally, it is notable that such radical perspectives survived – and were triumphantly revived and rearticulated through the humanistic perspectives of the ('First') New Left of the post-1956 period. The writings and activism of this movement – not least as they were expressed by the notable adult educators E.P. Thompson, Raymond Williams, and Michael Barratt Brown – had a profound influence upon both the academy and the wider polity in the 1960s and beyond (Taylor, 2020).

There remains, however, at the kernel of this whole episode, a deceptively simple question: how far was it legitimate, or indeed feasible, for university senior officers to acquiesce in the articulation of educational perspectives and practices which they regarded, not entirely unreasonably, as inimical (because anti-democratic and 'propagandist') to their conception of the liberal idea of the university? Thompson, for example, frequently asserted that his purpose in adult education was 'to create revolutionaries' (Shaw, 1996).[7] Even making allowance for Thompson's famous – or notorious – tendency to hyperbolic rhetoric, and his inherent romanticism, this was surely, to say the least, a worrying stance for any Head of Department or Vice-Chancellor.[8] It also poses the implicit question of how far any government, however committed to liberal perspectives in education, could countenance public financial support for the widespread proselytisation of 'revolution' as an educational objective.

This case study, therefore, though dealing with a relatively small, and long ago, element of the academic world, raises generic issues about the nature and extent of academic freedom. Perhaps, in the end, the central practical question is whether or not those holding such 'extreme' political views departed in any significant sense from the established, liberal criteria and practices in their academic teaching and research. Reviewing the evidence in relation to this particular context, it is clear that, with very few (and partial) exceptions, these 'liberal standards' were upheld, both in theory and in practice by those espousing Marxist and/or CP perspectives. (But see Arblaster, 1972, for a useful discussion of the differences and tensions between 'liberal' and 'socialist' values.)

The title of Roger Fieldhouse's study of these issues was thus well chosen: this was a period of liberal values 'under siege.' But it was a siege that was, in the end, largely repulsed. Liberal, social purpose, adult education survived, and for at least several decades it prospered, albeit articulated in rather different forms (Ward and Taylor, 1986/2012).

Discrimination there may have been at the margins: but the core liberal value system of the academy survived, somewhat battered but essentially intact.

Notes

1 This chapter is dedicated to the memory of my longstanding friend and colleague, Roger Fieldhouse, who died in February 2020. Roger's book, *Adult Education and the Cold War. Liberal Values Under Siege 1946-51* (1985), contains much of the original research material upon which this chapter is based.

2 Communism never gained mass support in the UK, in contrast to many other European countries in the post-war period (for example, France and Italy). At its height, in the mid-1940s, membership of the Communist Party of Great Britain was around 60,000. (However, the Party was successful in building support in some important trade unions.)

3 'McCarthyism' was a widely used description, deriving from the notorious activities of Senator Joseph McCarthy and his acolytes in the USA, of those advocating a 'witch-hunt' to identify, denigrate, and, where appropriate, remove from public office anyone who had been a member of, or shown sympathy towards, the CP and the cause of 'international Communism.' McCarthyism led to a widespread denunciation not only of Communists but also of anyone with liberal, progressive views (Fried, 1990).

4 A.D. Lindsay, formerly Master of Balliol College, Oxford University, was one of the most influential and authoritative figures in British adult education in general and in University AE in particular. Although his political sympathies were clearly on the Left, and he had a general respect for Marxist ideas, he was firmly opposed to the CP and to the political ideology of Soviet Communism.

5 Williams, like Thompson, later became a key figure in the post-1956 New Left and one of the most prominent 'cultural studies' academics of the post-war period (Williams, 1958, 1961, 1979).

6 M15 and M16 were, and remain, the two main branches of Britain's security services. The focus of M15 is broadly upon domestic, homeland issues, whilst the concerns of M16 centre upon international security operations.

7 The full quotation from the relevant passage is:

> … although Raybould had expressed general misgivings about communist tutors he never tried to cramp Edward's style, and Edward made no secret of his beliefs and aims. At a meeting in Raybould's room where a small group of us were asked to say what we saw as the aim of teaching our particular subjects, Edward said breezily 'to create revolutionaries'. There was no shock-horror in anyone's reaction, rather admiration tinged with amusement.
>
> *(37)*

8 However, the prosaic reality of predominantly non-revolutionary, and largely non-working class for that matter, adult students in Thompson's classes in the 1940s and 1950s is recorded in his 'class reports' (see Fieldhouse, 2013, 37–43). On the other hand, there was undoubtedly a minority of working-class radicals who attended Thompson's classes: his most famous book, *The Making of the English Working Class* (1963), is dedicated to two of them – Dorothy and Joe Greenald.

References

Arblaster, A. (1972). 'Liberal values and socialist values'. In R. Miliband and J. Saville, (eds) *Socialist Register 1972* (83–104). London: Merlin Press.

Callaway, H. (1978). A conversation with Thomas Hodgkin: The scholar and revolutionary. *Convergence*. 11 (1), 18–27.

Caute, D. (1973). *The Fellow Travellers: A Postscript to the Enlightenment*. London: Weidenfeld and Nicolson.

Evans, R. J. (2019/2020) *Eric Hobsbawm: A Life in History*. London: Little, Brown.

Fieldhouse, R. (1985). *Adult Education and the Cold War: Liberal Values Under Siege 1946-51 (Leeds Studies in Adult and Continuing Education)*. Leeds: University of Leeds.

Fieldhouse, R., and Associates (1996). *A History of Modern British Adult Education*. Leicester: Narional Institute of Adult Continuing Education.

Fieldhouse, R. (2013). Thompson the adult educator. In R. Fieldhouse, and R. Taylor (eds). *E. P. Thompson and English Radicalism*. Manchester: Manchester University Press. 25–47.

Fieldhouse, R., and Taylor, R. (eds). (2013). *E. P. Thompson and English Radicalism*. Manchester: Manchester University Press.

Fried, R. M. (1990). *Nightmare in Red: The McCarthyite Era in Perspective*. Oxford: Oxford University Press.

Gallie, W. B. (1960). *A New University: A.D. Lindsay and the Keele Experiment.* London: Chatto and Windus.

Goldman, L. (1995). *Dons and Workers: Oxford and Adult Education Since 1850.* Oxford: Oxford University Press.

Green, E. (1947, 26 October). Letter to RH Tawney. *RH Tawney Correspondence*; WEA National Office.

Green Special Report. (1949). *Tutorial Class Committee.* Oxford: Oxford University.

Hobsbawm, E. J. (2002/2006) *Interesting Times: A Twentieth Century Life.* London: Allen Lane.

Hodgkin, T. (1950–51). Objectivity, ideologies and the present political situation. *The Highway, 42.*

Hoggart, R. (1957). *The Uses of Literacy.* London: Pelican Books.

Mansbridge, A. (1913). *University Tutorial Classes.* London: Longman, Green and Co.

Miliband, R. (1982). *Capitalist Democracy in Britain.* Oxford: Oxford University Press.

Raybould, S. G. (1950/51). On objectivity and ideologies. *The Highway, 42*, 102–4.

Raybould, S. G. (1951). *The English Universities and Adult Education.* London: WEA.

Shaw, R. (1996). Recalling Raybould's department. In R. Taylor (ed), *Beyond the Walls: 50 Years of Adult Education at the University of Leeds 1946-1996* (31–8). Leeds: University of Leeds.

Srinivasan, A. (2023). Cancelled. *London Review of Books*, 45(13), 6.

Steele, T. (1997). *The Emergence of Cultural Studies 1945-1965. Cultural Politics, Adult Education and the English Question.* London: Lawrence and Wishart.

Taylor, R. (2020). *English Radicalism in the Twentieth Century: A Distinctive Politics?* Manchester: Manchester University Press.

The Highway. (1950–51). *Workers' Educational Association Journal,* 42.

Thompson, E. P. (1950). *Against University Standards.* University of Leeds, Department of Extramural Studies, Adult Education Papers, 1:4 (July), Leeds.

Thompson, E. P. (1963). *The Making of the English Working Class.* London: Gollancz.

Thompson, E. P. (1968). *'Education and Experience',* Albert Mansbridge Memorial Lecture. Leeds: Leeds University Press.

Ward, K., and Taylor, R. (eds). (1986/2012). *Adult Education and the Working Class: Education for the Missing Millions.* Abingdon: Routledge.

Williams, R. (1958). *Culture and Society.* London: Pelican Books.

Williams, R. (1961). *The Long Revolution.* London: Chatto and Windus.

William, R. (1979). *Raymond Williams. Politics and Letters. Interviews with New Left Review.* London: New Left Books.

Young, C. (1970). Decolonization in Africa. In L. Gann and P. Duignan (eds), *Colonialism in Africa 1870-1960.* Cambridge: Cambridge University Press. 450–502.

5

THE UNIVERSITY AS A CONTESTED SPACE

'No Platforming' controversies at British universities, 1968–1990

Evan Smith

Introduction

Over the last decade, there has been an increasing concern about a free speech 'crisis' at British universities, which has manifested in different ways around fears about a lack of freedom of speech and academic freedom on campuses across the UK. This has included anxieties being raised about the 'no platforming' of speakers at universities (Ellery, 2021), about protests against the research and teaching of certain academics (Adams, 2021), about allegedly intolerant academics teaching particular 'woke' views to students (Stringer, 2023), or alternatively intolerant students pressurising academics (Clarence-Smith, 2023), and about certain events being cancelled (BBC, 2022). While a small number of incidents and interested parties grab the headlines and garner attention on social media, research has shown that only a small number of speakers and events are 'cancelled' (for a variety of reasons) (Dickinson, 2022; Parr, 2023). The apparent media and political consensus in Britain that there is a 'crisis' of free speech at universities fits into a wider 'war on woke' that has gathered pace over the last decade under the Conservatives and particularly since Prime Minister Boris Johnson's right populist turn in 2019 (Davies and MacRae, 2023). It can also be described as a 'moral panic' that has been conjured up, with 'woke' students and academics portrayed as 'folk devils' that need to be disciplined (to use terms originally developed by Cohen [2011]). As Hall *et al* explain in their influential work *Policing the Crisis* (1978), a moral panic emerges when:

> the official reaction to a person, groups of persons or series of events is *out of all proportion* to the actual threat offered, when 'experts,' in the form of

DOI: 10.4324/9781003363262-7

police chiefs, the judiciary, politicians and editors *perceive* the threat in all but identical terms, and appear to talk 'with one voice' of rates, diagnoses, prognoses and solutions, when the media representations universally stress 'sudden and dramatic' increases (in numbers involved or events) and 'novelty,' above and beyond that which a sober, realistic appraisal could sustain...

(Hall et al, *1978, 16)*

The heightened media coverage and political discourse surrounding the supposed free speech 'crisis' on university campuses across Britain certainly seems to fit this characterisation of a moral panic.

Since 2019, this moral panic has made the leap from sensationalist media stories to government policy. In 2019 and 2020, the right-wing think tank Policy Exchange produced two reports suggesting that freedom of speech and academic freedom were under threat at British universities (Simpson and Kaufmann, 2019; Adekoya *et al*, 2020). In the first report, Simpson and Kaufmann (2019, 5) stated, 'there is widespread concern that, instead of being places of robust debate and free discovery, they are being stifled by a culture of conformity.' The danger, they suggested, was that 'academic freedom is being significantly violated due, in particular, to forms of political discrimination.' Despite being criticised for its methodology (Portes, 2020), the Policy Exchange reports were influential and the Conservative Government drew on them when unveiling their Higher Education (Freedom of Speech) Bill in February 2021 (Department of Education, 2021).

Within this contemporary moral panic, it has been claimed, on a number of occasions, that a new generation of intolerant and censorious students have hijacked the universities and transformed them from sites of debate and disagreement into factories of conformity (Young, 2018; Linklater, 2021). An image has emerged of the university of the past where students constructively engaged with their critics and did not attempt to shut them down. For example, in *The Critic*, Allison (2023) wrote that one of his memories of this sort of debate was that 'of the South African ambassador... defending apartheid to a Politics Society audience consisting mostly of black students; they gave him a lot of stick, but they turned up and they engaged.' For Allison, conduct at the university in the 1970s was 'at a somewhat higher standard... than it is conducted these days.'

However, this characterisation of the university is arguably something of a 'rose-tinted' view of the past. Since the 1960s, universities have been contested spaces where there has been conflict over who should be allowed a platform on campus. The moral panic that free speech is under threat at British universities has been raised several times over the last six decades, with students often portrayed as an intolerant mob that chooses censorship over the free discussion of ideas.

This chapter will outline how freedom of speech and academic freedom issues generated controversy between the late 1960s and mid-1980s, from the height of the student movement in Britain to the height of the Thatcher era. These decades have become mythologised as a period when students and academics were less inhibited and not shackled by 'political correctness,' wielding free speech and shock value against the traditional conservatism of British society at the time. But a closer look at the history of student activism on campus in these decades shows that there were significant challenges by students and academics to certain speakers and scholars having platforms at various universities. In particular, the 1970s saw the formalisation of the National Union of Students' (NUS) 'no platform' policy, which has remained in place since then. This chapter seeks to historicise contemporary debates about free speech – with associated direct and indirect implications for academic freedom – at universities and looks at the alleged contemporary 'moral panic' through a much longer lens.

Free speech on campus and the '1968' generation

Student radicalism dramatically rose in university campuses in Britain in the mid-to-late 1960s. This coincided with a greater radicalism in British society more broadly as witnessed with the wave of strikes that began in 1966 and the emergence of the anti-Vietnam War movement. As Hoefferle (2013) has shown, the student movement in Britain was a vital part of several social movements, such as the anti-Vietnam War movement, the Anti-Apartheid Movement, and the Women's Liberation Movement, but also challenged the structures of higher education that traditionally existed. The university campus, once largely the preserve of the British upper classes, was being opened up to a more diverse cohort of students, many of whom were the first generation in their family to enter higher education. Within this, students now became more assertive over who should be granted a platform at universities and particularly questioned whether those who expressed racist or imperialist views should be offered the opportunity to address a wider audience.

In 1968, the symbolic year of student upheaval across the globe, there were several incidents where right-wing politicians had their speeches disrupted, in protest at their anti-immigration politics. In the same year, a Member of Parliament, Enoch Powell, made an infamous 'Rivers of Blood' speech; his talks were interrupted by protestors on two occasions, at the University of Essex in February and the University of Exeter in October (Smith, 2020, 69–74). At Essex University, Powell and the local MP who joined him were also harangued by anti-war protestors as they left the university. Justifying the protest, one of the students was quoted as saying:

> By associating themselves with American policies, to us the Powells and the Wilsons of this country come to symbolise these policies. Thus when

Mr Powell, in addressing us blandly talks of 'unavoidable inhumanities,' can he really be surprised that instead of gentlemanly debate he gets shouts of disgust and bitter derision?

(Essex County Standard, *1 March 1968*)

In October, Powell's talk at Exeter University was halted after 15 minutes when a small number of students disrupted proceedings. The *Daily Telegraph* (24 October 1968) reported that '[f]ighting broke out, banners were torn and Mr. Powell was pelted with paper darts and marbles.' In response, and claiming that a new phenomenon was emerging, Powell told the *Daily Express* (24 October 1968), 'I have never had to halt a speech at a university before. But this is a new technique – it is not just me. Over the last few months it has become almost routine for Ministers and other speakers to suffer this sort of behaviour.'

Alongside Powell, another Conservative MP, Patrick Wall, had his speech at Leeds University interrupted in May 1968. Wall belonged to the Monday Club, a right-wing pressure group inside the Conservative Party, which was against decolonisation, was anti-immigration, and supported apartheid in South Africa and Rhodesia (Pitchford, 2007). Giving a talk on Rhodesia and British foreign policy, Wall was, according to the *Daily Telegraph* (4 May 1968), 'constantly heckled' and scuffles broke out as Wall and his wife tried to leave the meeting room. After the protests against Wall and Powell, an editorial in *The Times* (8 May 1968) described the students' action as 'the silencing of opponents by mob action' and lamented that the university was supposedly 'the breeding ground for this form of mindless opposition.' In similar rhetoric to what we find in the 2020s, the editorial further argued that universities were places of 'intellectual liberty, critical inquiry, and free traffic in ideas' and that these places of higher learning failed 'if the young do not acquire..., or if they there unlearn, the habit of tolerating the expression of opinions contrary to their own.' Amidst widespread anxiety about the student movement and militant activists in 1968, the trope of the student radical as censorious and intolerant of other ideas was hatched.

It was not only right-wing politicians that were protested against on campus during the height of the student movement. In 1973, there were two notable incidents where academics had their talks disrupted or prevented from taking place – highlighting the complex interaction between free speech and academic freedom, as discussed elsewhere in this book. The first was Hans Eysenck, who was part of a controversial circle of psychologists that worked in the area of 'race' and IQ. This 'scientific racism,' as criticised by radical scientists in *Socialist Register*, sought to argue that differences in IQ between 'races' was informed by genetics (Rose *et al*, 1973, 235). In May 1973, the Social Science Society at the London School of Economics (LSE) invited Eysenck to speak, an invitation which was opposed by a number of student groups. One of the most vocal was the LSE Afro-Asian Society, which had links to the tiny Maoist Communist Party of England (Marxist-Leninist) (CPE [M-L]). The Afro-Asian Society distributed a leaflet prior to the event, entitled 'Fascist Eysenck has no right to speak,' which declared:

> Today, fascist Eysenck has been sent by his masters, the British imperialists of the London School of Economics to spew out more of his fascist propaganda. This represents not only a brazen attack on the progressive masses of students and staff at LSE but represents another step in the insidious scheme of British imperialism to provide a rationale to unleash fascist and racist attacks on the broad masses of the English people including the various national minorities.
>
> *(LSE Afro-Asian Society flyer, 'Fascist Eysenck Has*
> *No Right to Speak,' n.d., LSE/Student Union/24,*
> *LSE Student Union Papers, LSE Archives, London)*

In the same flyer, the Society called for 'the progressive LSE students and staff ... to exercise their right to oppose the fascist propaganda of H.J. Eysenck,' as well as 'to vigorously develop mass democracy and mass denounciation [sic] to expose the anti-people and anti-science theories of Eysenck.'

On 8 May 1973, Eysenck attempted to speak at LSE, but was constantly heckled by activists in the audience. After a brief pause, Eysenck tried to continue despite the vocal protests, but a small group of protestors allegedly linked to the CPE (M-L) rushed the stage. The President of the London University Conservative Association, who was in attendance, described what happened next for the *Daily Telegraph* (9 May 1973): 'About 15 students from the front two rows jumped over the table and dived in with their fists flying. They were hitting out in all directions.' The newspaper further reported that Eysenck had 'had his spectacles smashed, his nose cut and his hair pulled.'

This action was condemned on all sides, including in the media, by politicians, by the student union, and even by other far-left groups on campus. For example, the Conservative Under-Secretary of State for the Department of Education and Science, Norman St John-Stevas, was quoted in *The Times* (10 May 1973) as saying that disagreements with Eysenck needed to be wielded through 'the weapon of dialogue and rational discourse and not by the fist of the thug.' On the other side of the political spectrum, the Trotskyist International Marxist Group at LSE produced a flyer that asserted that was it was 'not in principle... incorrect to stop Eysenck from speaking,' but 'the physical act to prevent him from speaking is not understood by the mass of students at this stage' and thus tactically ill-thought-out (LSE Red Mole flyer, 'Defend the Union! Defend the Afro-Asian Soc! Defend the CPE (M-L)!,' n.d., LSE/Student Union/24).

The next month, another incident occurred at the University of Sussex when American academic Samuel P. Huntington was refused access to a lecture hall by protesting students. The reason that Huntington came under fire was that he worked with the US Pentagon during the Vietnam War and had argued in the late 1960s for 'forced draft urbanisation' (Huntington, 1968), which critics suggested was 'academic speak' for an intensification of the war in Vietnam and targeting of Vietnamese villagers. Although Huntington had later acknowledged the 'undesirability of the war' (*Daily Telegraph*, 6 June 1973), activists felt that he should have been challenged on this. When it was announced that because Huntington's lecture was not going to be on the Vietnam War, he would not be answering questions on the subject, the students protested and occupied the space where Huntington would be talking (Anon., 1973, 45). Around 500 students protested inside and outside the lecture, with the *Daily Telegraph* (6 June 1973) describing the scene thus: 'The students, waving a red flag and carrying pictures of Chairman Mao and placards declaring that Fascists had no right to speak, crowded into the lecture theatre 20 minutes before Prof. Huntington was due to begin.' Compared with the Eysenck protest, there was no violence at Sussex that day, although the media and the university raised the spectre of possible violence, despite a spokesperson for the student activists telling the press, 'Our objective was to stop the lecture without using violence' (*Daily Telegraph*, 6 June 1973; *The Times*, 6 June 1973).

Coming shortly after the Eysenck protests, at the time the two incidents were twinned in the eyes of many. Inches of column space were dedicated to the spectre of student violence and the apparent end of free speech at British universities. An editorial in the *Daily Telegraph* (5 June 1973) proclaimed, '[r]ecent events suggest that universities are no longer firmly wedded to free speech and free academic inquiry.' Another editorial in the *Guardian* (11 June 1973) posed the question:

> If in face of such threats [to freedom of speech] university authorities and academic staffs generally decide to do nothing, they should not be surprised when Parliament and the public begin to believe that 'academic freedom' is a term which has lost its meaning. If the universities cease to defend it, will anyone else?

As mentioned above, the trope of students as authoritarians seeking to end free inquiry at universities was already in development by the late 1960s and early 1970s, even before the NUS' policy of 'no platform' came into place in 1974.

'No platform' and anti-fascism in the 1970s

Right-wing politicians and controversial academics were not the only concern for students when it came to having a platform on campus. The National Front (NF), a far-right group that came to prominence in the late 1960s, had started making their presence felt at universities, attempting to intimidate protestors at various on-campus demonstrations and forming nationalist student groups. In 1973, a nationwide National Front Student Association was established to try and co-ordinate a fascist opposition to the student movement (Smith, 2020, 90). In wider British politics, the NF also worried the left due its growth in the early 1970s, seeking to attract disaffected Conservatives who opposed the immigration of Ugandan Asians in 1972 and Britain's entry into the European Economic Community (Smith *et al*, 2017). In 1974, the NUS developed its 'no platform' policy to counter the potential fascist creep at British universities.

As Smith (2020, 3) explains, 'no platform' was, as the NUS proposed, a policy that allowed student unions to withhold resources, such as union-run spaces and funds, from fascist and racist organisations and speakers, as well as disinvite these speakers if invited by certain student groups, or encourage protest activities that attempt to prevent these people from speaking on campus, such as pickets. Left-wing groups, such as the International Marxist Group, had started to formulate a strategy of 'no platform' a few years earlier, inspired by the anti-fascist tactics of the 1930s used against Oswald Mosley's British Union of Fascists (*The Red Mole*, 18 September 1972). The Left, primarily the Communists and the Trotskyists, had significant influence in the NUS in the early 1970s, and at the April 1974 conference, the 'no platform' resolution was proposed as part of a wider policy to fight discrimination against international students. The resolution stated:

> Conference recognises the need to refuse assistance (financial or otherwise) to openly racist or fascist organisations or societies ... and to deny them a platform. However conference believes that in order to counter these groups, it is also necessary to prevent any member of these organisations or individuals known to espouse similar views from speaking in colleges **by whatever means necessary** (including disrupting of the meeting).
>
> *(NUS, 1974, 79. Bold in original text)*

The policy was heatedly debated at the conference, and some felt that it was unfairly restricting free speech on campus. In response to this, Steve Parry, NUS General Secretary and Communist Party member, retorted, 'Did reasoned argument stop the fascists led by Mosley in the East End in the 1930s? Of course, it did not' (NUS, 1974, 80).

Anticipating the controversy surrounding the passing of the resolution, the NUS issued a press release to clarify what 'no platform' meant. The press release stated the NUS were 'not going to send round a "heavy squad" to break up meetings' nor were they 'going to try to restrict activities of the Conservative Party,' but instead stated that the NUS intended 'to deny platforms to the apostles of racial hatred,' listed in the original resolution as the Monday

Club, NF, Action Party/Union Movement, and the National Democratic Party (NUS press release, 'NUS Statement on Racism,' 16 April 1974, MSS 280/54/1, NUS papers, Modern Records Centre, University of Warwick; NUS, 1974, 79).

But this did not prevent a strong reaction in the press. The *Guardian*'s John Fairhall described the move as a denial of free speech, voted for by students 'under the spell of Mr Parry's oratory' (the *Guardian*, 9 April 1974). Fairhall predicted that '[t]rouble and violence seem inevitable' and warned, '[s]tudents should perhaps remember that frustration which leads to a denial of the right of one section of society is not something new. It is classic pattern of fascism.' An editorial for the *Times Higher Education Supplement* declared, 'By its very actions, the NUS has become a blunted and tarnished weapon in the fight for civil rights and social justice' (*THES*, 14 June 1974). Questions were also raised in Parliament about the policy, with both Labour and Conservative politicians criticising the NUS. The Labour Government's Education Secretary Reg Prentice argued that the NUS had 'gone down the wrong road' on this issue, but when pushed by Tory MPs to publish a list of student unions who opposed the policy, Prentice said, 'It is for the student unions to run their own affairs' (*Hansard*, 23 July 1974, col. 1283).

While a majority of delegates voted for the 'no platform' policy (and reiterated its policy at a special conference in June 1974), its application continued to be contested. Part of this was a difference between the minimalist and maximalist opinions of the left-wing students that pushed the resolution through the NUS. As Renton (2021) points out, one group, the International Socialists, argued for a narrow application of the policy, for use only against the NF and other explicitly fascist organisations. For the International Socialists, Hans Eysenck and Enoch Powell were figures whose speeches should be picketed, rather than broken up (LSE IS, 1974, 4) On the other hand, the aforementioned International Marxist Group wanted to extend the policy further and saw Eysenck and Powell as possible targets for 'no platforming' actions, because racists like them 'stir[red] up social violence – legal and illegal – against minorities' (IMG, 1974, 16–7). Throughout the 1970s, this would become a point of contention amongst student activists and the left more broadly: how widely or narrowly the principle of 'no platform' should be applied?

At the same time, some activist university scholars also campaigned against the scientific racism espoused by Eysenck and others, arguing against their research, and not just their speaking engagements. For example, in 1974, a group of left-wing educators and psychologists formed the Campaign on Racism, IQ and the Class Society to 'expose the "scientific" racialism behind the theories propoganded [sic] by Professors Eysenck, [Arthur] Jensen and [William] Shockley,' producing pamphlets and running education sessions to combat academic racism and its use in the education system (*Red Weekly*, 29 March 1974). The inaugural meeting of the campaign at the Polytechnic of

Central London in March 1974 was disrupted by figures from the NF, leading to a discussion amongst attendees over whether the gatecrashers should have been allowed to speak (a month before the NUS' 'no platform' policy was adopted).

This kind of activism would continue throughout the 1970s, with the anti-fascist magazine *Searchlight* publishing a pamphlet by social psychologist Michael Billig (1979) titled *Psychology, Racism and Fascism*. The pamphlet outlined how racialised psychology, science, and anthropology was being promoted by academics in Britain, North America, and Europe, coinciding with the rise of fascism in the 1970s. Eysenck would be invited to speak on other campuses later in the decade as well. In February 1977, Eysenck was invited to debate at the University of Leeds, but was faced with 30 to 40 student activists linked to the International Socialists who yelled 'racist bastard' and 'no platform for fascists' every time he tried to speak (*Leeds Student*, 11 February 1977).

By the end of the 1970s, the principle of 'no platform for fascists' had broken out of the confines of the student left and was accepted by a wider section of British society. The reason for this was the emergence of the Anti-Nazi League, a mass movement that existed between 1977 and 1981 and which mobilised people against the NF. Renton (2021, 47) explains:

> The ANL set itself the goal of closing every National Front talk and of disrupting every Front paper sale. The members of the League set out to make it impossible for the Front to grow again. The justification for this incursion on free speech principles was a theory of fascism in which that movement carried the threat of destroying both social democracy and democracy itself.

As long as the threat of the NF was there, many people accepted that the far-right should not be allowed public platforms and that their politics be directly challenged. However, after the NF started to internally combust in the wake of poor election results in the 1979 general election, the Anti-Nazi League and the anti-fascists in the student movement found momentum waning, questioning how the policy of 'no platform' might be applied in the 1980s.

'The new barbarians' in the 1980s

1979 saw the election of Margaret Thatcher and a general rightwards shift in British politics. For anti-racists and anti-fascists in the 1980s, it seemed as though the threat of the far-right had decreased, but the 'authoritarian populism' of the Thatcher government now meant that the racism of the State presented a clear danger to Britain's minorities (Hall, 1979). Members of the Thatcher government were often seen as *persona non grata* on university campuses in the 1980s, which were regarded as one of the bastions of resistance to Thatcherism during the long decade. The government attempted to introduce a wave of reforms to the higher education system, such as the cutting of student grants, which brought it into sharp disagreement with a new generation of student activists. At the same time, the relative success of the anti-fascist/anti-racist movement in Britain in the late 1970s convinced some students and activists that the tactics of the movement, such as 'no platforming,' could be applied to fighting other forms of discrimination, such as sexism and homophobia.

While the NUS 'no platform' policy remained limited at the national level, individual student unions and student groups sought to expand the policy and practice of 'no platform' to stop sexist and homophobic speakers on campus. In January 1981, feminists at LSE argued for a 'no platform for sexists' policy as part of a wider campaign against sexual harassment and violence. As well as calls for support for women's right to self-defence, adequate alarm systems in the halls of residence, and NUS support for the 'Reclaim the Night' demonstrations, a motion was put forward which demanded that the union 'maintain a "no platform" policy for sexist ideas, literature of any kind, etc., as this obviously contributes to the socialisation process which breeds violence against women' ('Agenda for Union General Meeting to be Held on 29.1.81,' LSE/STUDENTS UNION/23, LSE Student Union Papers, LSE). The motion was successfully applied for several months, before it was overturned later in the year (Smith, 2020, 115).

There were also attempts to 'no platform' homophobes during the 1980s: an infamous incident being the protests made against Tory councillor Richard Lewis in Swansea in 1987. Coming at the height of the AIDS crisis in Britain, Lewis had, according to the student newspaper at Swansea University, called the disease a 'gay plague' (*Bad Press*, 3 February 1987). Invited by the Conservative Association at Swansea, Lewis was originally banned from speaking by the student union for the short notice of the invitation, while acknowledging that Lewis's views were 'very dangerous.' In any case, Lewis still attempted to speak at the university, surrounded by protestors (*Bad Press*, 3 February 1987). In the wake of the Lewis incident, the student union implemented a formal 'no platform' policy, with *Bad Press* (24 February 1987) reporting that the union believed that 'positive action against bigots, racists and homophobes must have to be taken as their views [had] no place on a university campus.'

However, the ire of the press and politicians was particularly raised after protests against right-wing politicians speaking on campus. In some instances, student unions attempted to formally use 'no platform' policies to prevent politicians from appearing at universities, while at other times there were more *ad hoc* pickets and episodes of disruption. But both forms of protest were depicted as examples of free speech being under threat at universities.

This wave began with a visit by Home Secretary Leon Brittan, in the wake of the Miners' Strike, to Manchester University in March 1985. The student union had concluded that its 'no platform' policy did not apply to Brittan, but many students descended on Oxford Road outside the venue where the Home Secretary was to speak (Manchester City Council, 1985, 9). To deal with the protest, the Greater Manchester Police's Tactical Aid Group (the anti-riot squad) went into the crowd and attempted to violently disperse the demonstration, resulting in 33 arrests (Pullan and Abendstern, 2013, 201). An independent inquiry by Manchester City Council stated that they were 'left with little doubt that the action of some police officers was unnecessarily forceful' and that while there was some 'physical and violent resistance' to the police by protestors, it did not excuse the conduct of the police, particularly when some of the violence was directed at 'passive demonstrators who offered no resistance' (Manchester City Council, 1985, 14–5).

Following this, the next two years saw increased reporting on protests against Members of Parliament at universities. John Carlisle, a right-wing Tory MP who was known for his support for apartheid South Africa, and Enoch Powell both had extensive campus tours, which provoked protest from students in most places that they visited. In February 1986, Carlisle was rushed by protestors while speaking the University of Bradford and had a speaking engagement at Oxford University cancelled a few days later after the venue was occupied by anti-apartheid protestors (the *Guardian*, 14 February 1986; *Cherwell*, 21 February 1986). Carlisle had planned to visit Leeds Polytechnic, having been invited by the Federation of Conservative Students. However, following the events at Bradford and Oxford, his speaking engagement was cancelled, with the Polytechnic suggesting that there was 'no suitable venue where the meeting could be held in "a safe and orderly manner"' (*Leeds Student*, 21 February 1986).

The following month, Carlisle visited the University of East Anglia (UEA) and Bristol University. At UEA, a vigil of several hundred students, organised by the student union, and a picket by around 50 to 60 people, organised by the Socialist Workers' Student Society, protested against Carlisle's visit (Phoenix, 1 May 1986; 'Confidential Report to the Vice-Chancellor on the Visit of John Carlisle MP to the University of East Anglia on 24th April 1986' [July 1986] appendix 2(i), UEA/GRAY/1/3, UEA archives). Unlike many of his previous attempts to speak at universities, Carlisle was able to address a crowd when he next visited Bristol University, despite significant student protests. *The Times* (26 April 1986) reported that 'more than 100 left-wing students attempted to disrupt a meeting on free speech' and that both MPs faced 'a barrage of screaming, foot stamping and obscenities.' In response to the protests at Bristol, Carlisle, using the trope of the 'red fascist,' said that the reaction by the protesting students reminded him of 'what happened in Nazi Germany in the 1930s' (*Daily Express*, 26 April 1986).

After Carlisle's experiences, Enoch Powell's visits to universities in 1986 gained significant attention. In October of that year, Powell attempted to speak at both the University College Cardiff and Bristol University. Students disrupted Powell from speaking, with a number of protestors yelling 'no free speech for racists' at the politician (*Gair Rhydd*, 15 October 1986). A few days later, Powell spoke at the University of Bristol where he again encountered a protest against his presence. Around 200 students picketed the venue where Powell was speaking on campus, but a smaller group sought to disrupt proceedings. The student newspaper at Bristol, *Bacus* (24 October 1986), blamed anarchists for the disruption, reporting that the alleged anarchists 'blew whistles, let off stink and smoke bombs and at one point threw a ham salad sandwich at him.'

The University of Bristol was also the site of a more complicated protest campaign by students against a professor at the university. However, unlike Hans Eysenck, this professor drew criticism from students not due to his academic research, but his opinion writing for the tabloid press. Seen as part of the 'new right' of the 1980s, Professor John Vincent taught in the history department at Bristol and came under fire for his allegedly racist writing for *The Times* and the *Sun*. One column that he wrote in July 1985 for the *Sun* blamed the death of a black toddler on Lambeth Council's belief in 'separate treatment' for black people. Cited by Paul Gordon (1990, 184–5), 'The anti-racist "mumbo jumbo about black identity"', Vincent wrote, 'had overridden the safety of the child and had led to disaster.'

Protests against Vincent began in 1985 and escalated in 1986, coinciding with the Wapping Strike in which the Murdoch newspapers, such as *The Times* and the *Sun*, moved his printworks and led to a long-running industrial dispute. Students disrupted Vincent's lectures on a regular basis throughout February 1986. This was condemned in the media, with an editorial in *The Times* (28 February 1986) declaring that the disruption of an academic lecture was 'an act of intellectual vandalism as dangerous as any other effort to truncate learning and the exchange of opinion.' Eventually, 19 students were charged with a variety of offences relating to these protests, although 9 were eventually acquitted and only 7 found guilty (*The Times*, 10 May 1986).

The increased reporting on protests at universities caused the Thatcher government concern. Sir Keith Joseph, the Education Secretary, wrote to the President of the NUS calling the student protestors 'the new barbarians' who were not interested in discussion (*Daily Mail*, 16 May 1986). A Green Paper on higher education released in 1985 had included a line that universities had 'a responsibility to protect freedom of speech within the law, even for those with widely unpopular views' (UK Government, 1985, 5), and the protests encouraged the government to take action. In February 1986, Fred Silvester, a backbench Conservative MP, introduced a Private Member's Bill 'to safeguard the right of free speech and institutions of higher education, including student unions, to establish the duties and powers necessary for the enforcement of this right' (*Hansard*, 11 February 1986, col. 793).

The Bill was withdrawn, but subsequently incorporated into a broader Education Bill that was introduced to Parliament in October 1986, a few days after the protests against Enoch Powell at Cardiff and Bristol. The clause in the Bill sought to outlaw 'no platform' policies at universities, with the Under-Secretary for Education, George Walden, explaining its purpose:

> the clause will require authorities to exercise judgment, sometimes as to whether a meeting should proceed at all. It will not prevent them from concluding in the last resort, although they would do well to consult the police before reaching such a conclusion, that a meeting should be cancelled or at least postponed because the threat of a breach of the peace was too substantial. But the clause will be beneficial in requiring them to weigh the situation most carefully before reaching a decision, rather than simply taking the line of least resistance.
>
> *(Hansard, 21 October 1986, col. 1120)*

John Carlisle, adding to the debate, claimed that it sent a message to student unions that 'the British taxpayer will not tolerate no-platform policies,' which 'should not be a part of any university' (*Hansard*, 21 October 1986, col. 1114).

Despite last minute attempts by university leaders to convince the government that universities were capable of dealing with the issue of protests by themselves, the Education (No. 2) Act was passed in November 1986, with section 43 outlining the new duties of universities with regard to free speech:

> Every individual and body of persons concerned in the government of any establishment to which this section applies shall take such steps as are reasonably practicable to ensure that freedom of speech within the law is secured for members, students and employees of the establishment and for visiting speakers.

This was the first time that freedom of speech at British universities had been legislated for, but the new Act still had its critics and those pointing out its limitations. As Cram and Fenwick (2018, 856–8) noted, student unions argued that the new law did not apply to them as they were separate legal entities to universities. Others argued that the universities only had to take reasonable steps to ensure freedom of speech and that if protestors threatened public safety, they could still shut down events as university administrators would err on the side of caution (Smith, 2020, 161). The imperfections of section 43 of the Education (No. 2) Act 1986 would become a sticking point for the British right for the next four decades. For example, the Policy Exchange report in 2020 called for the extension of the 'existing statutory duty to ensure freedom to include student unions' (Adekoya *et al*, 2020, 96). This recommendation was taken up in legislation introduced by a Conservative Government in 2021 – along with a number of other matters relevant to the exercise of free speech and academic freedom, as discussed by Peter Scott in Chapter 3.

Conclusion

The purpose of this chapter has been to highlight the fact that in the first two decades of the twenty-first century the rhetoric from commentators, journalists, and politicians to the effect that British universities have become overrun by 'woke' students, aided by left-wing academics, is fallacious. On the contrary, the history of student protest shows that freedom of speech and academic freedom have always been contested issues.

Since the late 1960s, the ideal of the university as the site of free inquiry without restrictions has been challenged by students questioning why certain speakers should be allowed a platform on campus, and whether their presence inhibited the freedoms of others (such as ethnic minorities, women, or the LGBTQ+ community). Although the NUS instituted a policy of 'no platform' in 1974, this chapter demonstrates that *ad hoc* student protests against external speakers and academics were taking place for several years beforehand.

Furthermore, after the policy was introduced, the implementation of the policy has also been contested by students, in addition to pickets, occupations, and disruptions not sanctioned by student unions. In the 1980s, the Conservative Governments of the time attempted to crack down on these forms of protest at universities, but found there were limitations to this legal approach. Although it is too early to tell, recent legislation passed by the Government under Prime Minister Sunak will also have to deal with a number of competing priorities and it is more than likely that student protests over controversial issues will continue.

References

Adams, R. (2021). Sussex professor resigns after transgender rights row. The *Guardian*. https://www.theguardian.com/world/2021/oct/28/sussex-professor-kathleen-stock-resigns-after-transgender-rights-row (accessed 30 May 2023).

Adekoya, R., Kaufmann, E., and Simpson, T. (2020). *Academic Freedom in the UK: Protecting Viewpoint Diversity*. London: Policy Exchange.

Allison, L. (2023). Free speech: we should try it again. *The Critic*, February, https://thecritic.co.uk/issues/february-2023/free-speech-we-should-try-it-again/ (accessed 30 May 2023).

Anon. (1973). Huntington at Sussex. *Science for the People* (November), *45*.

BBC (2022). 'University of Edinburgh film screening cancelled due to protest', *BBC News*, 15 December,. https://www.bbc.com/news/uk-scotland-edinburgh-east-fife-63986755 (accessed 30 May 2023).

Billig, M. (1979). *Psychology, Racism and Fascism*. Birmingham: Searchlight.

Clarence-Smith, L. (2023). 'Universities are "Dumbing Down Courses" to avoid "Being Cancelled By Intolerant Students". *The Telegraph*, https://www.telegraph.co.uk/news/2023/02/13/universities-dumbing-courses-avoid-cancelled-intolerant-students/ (accessed 30 May, 2023).

Cohen, S. (2011). *Folk Devils and Moral Panics*. London: Routledge.

Cram, I. and Fenwick, H. (2018). Protecting Free Speech and Academic Freedom in Universities. *Modern Law Review*, *81*(5), 825–73.

Davies, H. and MacRae, S. (2023). An anatomy of the British war on woke, *Race and Class*, *65*(2), 3–54. https://journals.sagepub.com/doi/10.1177/03063968231164905.

Department of Education (2021). *Higher Education: Free Speech and Academic Freedom*. London: HMSO.

Dickinson, J. (2022). Growing more and more intolerant over the free speech agenda. *WonkHE*, 14 July, https://wonkhe.com/wonk-corner/growing-more-and-more-intolerant-over-the-free-speech-agenda/ (accessed 30 May 2023).

Ellery, B. (2021). Universities will be fined for "no-platforming" speakers. *The Times*, 14 February, https://www.thetimes.co.uk/article/universities-will-be-fined-for-no-platforming-speakers-26hj0bfj7 (accessed 30 May 2023).

Gordon, P. (1990) 'A Dirty War: The New Right and Local Authority Anti-Racism' in Ball, W. and Solomos, J. (eds) *Race and Local Politics*. Houndmills: Macmillan, 175–190.

Hall, S. et al (1978) *Policing the Crisis: Mugging, the State and Law and Order*. Houndmills: Macmillan.

Hall, S. (1979). The great moving right show. *Marxism Today* (January) 14–20.

Hoefferle, C. (2013). *British Student Activism in the Long Sixties*. London: Routledge.

Huntington, S. (1968). Bases of Accommodation. *Foreign Affairs*, *46*(4) (July) 642–6.

IMG. (1974). *Fascism: Smash It Now!* London: International Marxist Group.

Linklater, M. (2021). Bring back lost days of campus free speech. *The Times*, 24 May, https://www.thetimes.co.uk/article/bring-back-lost-days-of-campus-free-speech-00tk8m8fb (accessed 30 May 2023).

LSE IS. (1974). *The Red Agitator Special: No Platform for Fascists*. London: London School of Economics, International Socialist Group.

Manchester City Council. (1985). *Leon Brittan's Visit to Manchester University Students' Union, 1st March 1985: Report on the Independent Inquiry Panel*. Manchester: Manchester City Council.

NUS. (1974). *NUS, April Conference: Minutes and Summary of Proceedings*. London: National Union of Students.

Parr, C. (2023). Fewer than 1% of English university speakers "cancelled", *Research Professional News*, 25 May, https://www.researchprofessionalnews.com/rr-news-uk-universities-2023-5-fewer-than-1-per-cent-of-english-university-speakers-cancelled/ (accessed 30 May 2023).

Pitchford, M. (2007). *The Conservative Party and the Extreme Right*. Manchester: Manchester University Press.

Portes, J. (2020). The rightwing defence of "academic freedom" masks a McCarthyite agenda. The *Guardian*, 4 August, https://www.theguardian.com/commentisfree/2020/aug/04/rightwing-academic-freedom-policy-exchange-thinktank (accessed 1 June, 2023).

Pullan, B. and Abendstern, M. (2013). *A History of the University of Manchester, 1973–90*. Manchester: Manchester University Press.

Renton, D. (2021). *No Free Speech for Fascists: Exploring 'No Platform' in History, Law and Politics*. London: Routledge.

Rose, S., Hambley, J., and Haywood, J. (1973). Science, Racism and Ideology. In R.Miliband and J. Saville (eds), *Socialist Register*, *10*, 235–60.

Simpson, T. and Kaufmann, E. (2019). *Academic Freedom in the UK*. London: Policy Exchange.

Smith, E. (2017). Exporting fascism across the Commonwealth: The case of the national front of Australia. In N. Copsey and M. Worley (eds), *Tomorrow Belongs to Us: The British Far Right Since 1967* (69–89). London: Routledge.

Smith, E. (2020). *No Platform: A History of Anti-Fascism, Universities and the Limits of Free Speech*. London: Routledge.

Stringer, C. (2023). Half of our universities peddle their woke agenda to students. *Daily Mail*, 16 January, https://www.dailymail.co.uk/news/article-11638389/Half-universities-peddle-woke-agenda-students.html (accessed 30 May 2023).

UK Government. (1985). *The Development of Higher Education into the 1990s*. London: HMSO.

Young, T. (2018). Free speech is officially dead at British universities. *The Spectator Australia*, 17 November, https://www.spectator.com.au/2018/11/free-speech-is-officially-dead-in-british-universities/ (accessed 30 May 2023).

PART III

Academic Freedom

Contrasting International
Experiences

6

ACADEMIC FREEDOM UNDER IDEOLOGICAL ATTACKS IN MEXICO

Wietse de Vries

Introduction

This chapter makes the case that higher education and academics have been under new forms of pressure, amounting to an attack on academic freedom in Mexico under the Government that came to power in 2018. These developments are part of an all-encompassing reform agenda of Mexican politics and policies, a process termed the 4th Transformation, or 4T (Fuentes, 2018). These policies are enacted by a Government that defines itself as left-wing and populist and announced its main task is to 'bury neo-liberalism' (Presidencia de la República, 2019, 9).

According to public policy priorities, higher education needed profound transformation. From this perspective, higher education had succumbed to neo-liberalism over the previous three decades. Policies from the former five governments – from 1988 to 2018 – were criticised as having stressed productivity, efficiency, competition, cooperation with private enterprises, and personal gain. These policies seriously undermined core academic values, which it was argued should contribute to national sovereignty, independence, and self-sustainability, all for the benefit of the population, especially the poor (Álvarez-Buylla Roces, 2022). Since then, Government policies have 'changed the rules of the game,' notably by modifying evaluation and funding criteria but also, as will be discussed in this chapter, by abolishing collegiate bodies and installing loyalists in key positions.

Such approaches run contrary to the principles and practice of academic freedom. They are especially noticeable because, at the very same time, the Government enshrined academic freedom for the first time in a (national) General Law on Higher Education. The new law states that academics should be

DOI: 10.4324/9781003363262-9

able to work 'without suffering any discrimination and without fear of repression from the State or any other entity' (Diario Oficial de la Federación, 2021).

How did things arrive at this point? This chapter reviews how academic freedom has evolved in Mexico since the beginning of the twentieth century, why these recent problems, arguably amounting to attacks, occur, and what the implications are.

A history of academic freedom

No legal definition of academic freedom existed in Mexico for over a century, although the term frequently appeared linked with institutional autonomy. For example, the statutes of the largest public university, the Mexican National Autonomous University (UNAM), observed in 1935 that academic freedom is essential for the university's mission but pointed out that 'professors should comply at any moment with the authorised study plan, addressing the themes it includes' (Rodríguez Gómez, 2022). But save for a few mentions in university statutes, the concept remained undefined until 2021. The new law defines academic freedom as:

> The respect for academic freedom, of teaching and research, understood as the liberty to teach and debate without facing limitations from instituted doctrines, the liberty to carry out research and disseminate and publish the results, the liberty to express opinions about the institution or the system where one works, the freedom from institutional censorship and the freedom to participate in professional bodies or representative academic organizations, according to the normativity of each institution, without suffering any discrimination and without fear of repression from the State or any other entity.
>
> *(Diario Oficial de la Federación, 2021, Art. 8. XVI, author's translation)*

Because the proclamation appears in national law, it applies to all public and private higher education institutions, not just autonomous public universities. However, as Rodriguez (2022) observes, it is unclear how this law will function and to whom academics might turn to demand their rights. Crucially, it misses the operational aspects that appear in similar definitions, like those of UNESCO (UNESCO, 1997) and the European Higher Education Area (EHEA, 2020). For example, EHEA points out that guaranteeing academic freedom has significant political and practical implications. It stresses the importance of the decision-making process regarding recruitment, retention, job security, and the financial support of academic staff. It states, 'Although academic freedom is intrinsic to quality higher education, it is not a value that can be automatically assumed. Rather, the interaction of the different elements and conditions that ensure that academic freedom is operationalised need to be constructed, regularly assessed, protected and promoted' (EHEA, 2020).

This raises questions this chapter will seek to answer. How is academic freedom operationalised in Mexico? What are the conditions in which academic staff work? Who determines what and how to research and publish? Who sets the evaluation criteria, and what are the rewards or punishments? What are the funding criteria? To answer these questions, we need to go back in time.

Institutional autonomy or individual freedom

Since the beginning of the twentieth century, Mexican universities have struggled for autonomy and academic freedom. As the State transformed various religious colleges and schools into public universities, it became the new controlling body. Public universities suffered multiple State interventions. In most cases, these interventions focused on governance, not academic matters, so securing independence from political authorities became the priority, while academic freedom was a lesser concern.

Various authors trace the struggle for autonomy back to the student movement of 1918 at the University of Córdoba, Argentina. They cite the declaration of the *Reforma Universitaria* (University Reform) as the first demand for self-government and democratisation of the (public) universities in Latin America (Albornoz, 1966). Yet the declaration never mentions institutional autonomy or academic freedom. On the contrary, the students claimed more power vis-a-vis their professors in the form of co-government. As Bernasconi points out:

> In fact, so much was Córdoba not about autonomy that the rioting students called upon the Argentine federal Government in Buenos Aires to intervene in the Universidad Nacional de Córdoba to solve the impasse with the university authorities and faculty. Nor was it about academic freedom, at least not for the professoriate, it was a student movement against academics.
> *(Bernasconi, 2021, 58)*

However, the myth stuck and grew over the following decades (De Figueiredo-Cowen, 2002). Autonomy became a widespread demand in Latin America and more so when some countries became governed by undemocratic regimes. However, the call for autonomy became basically a political one, demanding the right to self-government and freedom from political intervention.

As a result, academic freedom remained a secondary issue. According to Bernasconi:

> The core distinction between the US and Latin America is the locus of autonomy, that is, where it resides. In the US, university autonomy is a

consequence of the academic freedom of professors. Autonomy is the academic freedom of the university as a community of scholars. In Latin America, conversely, academic freedom is understood as a consequence of the university's institutional autonomy. The locus of autonomy is the university, and the freedom of the faculty derives from that vested in the university.

(Bernasconi, 2021, 57)

This reversal of roles derives from the academic model that distinguishes Mexican universities from counterparts in other countries. European or North American universities adopted a Humboldtian model, with full-time academics combining teaching and research. Mexican universities began with a tradition of teaching traditional professions (Law, Accountancy, Administration, Medicine, Engineering) with a part-time faculty and little to no research (Bernasconi, 2007). The sciences, philosophy, and the humanities were added much later (after the 1950s) or, in some cases, were never incorporated into the mainstream system. Graduate programmes and research were mainly absent until the 1980s.

Until today, these professional fields enrol most students, and 70% of Mexican academics are part-time, almost exclusively dedicated to teaching alongside their professional or other occupations. For example, in 1910, the UNAM founders looked at North American and European universities as the model to follow, but to be able to do so, they had to bestow honorary Ph.D. degrees on the freshly appointed full-time faculty (Garciadiego Dantán, 2000). Even so, of the 4,766 academics the UNAM employed in 1960, only 470 were full-time (Guevara Niebla, 1986). By 2021, the UNAM registered 41,542 academics, but 32,736 (78%) worked by the hour (UNAM, 2022).

As a result, academic freedom was never a significant issue championed by full-time tenured professors. Tellingly, the most common term in Mexico is *libertad de cátedra*, the freedom to teach, not academic freedom. And while academic staff had considerable freedom to define course content and teaching methods, this resulted more from benign neglect or lack of interest from the authorities than from a struggle for academic freedom (Fuentes Molinar, 1989).

This form of academic freedom was a by-product of the struggle for autonomy. After the repression of student protests in 1968, several public universities became a bulwark for the left-wing parties opposed to right-wing governments. The answer from the Federal Government was one of cautious *détente*. Budgets increased steadily in the 1970s, government intervention was mainly avoided (shifting the financial burden from the local state to the Federal Government), and more academics were hired to cope with increasing student numbers.

During the continuing stand-offs between public universities and the national Government, academic freedom remained a by-product of autonomy, not a right rooted in academic communities. It appeared as a part of a political discourse invoked by university administrators. In the struggle for autonomy, the university's administrators obtained the upper hand, leaving the freedom of individual academics as a second-order priority. With attention focused on autonomy, academic freedom was taken for granted. Most universities discreetly left study plans and course content to each academic, who taught without supervision (Kent, 1986).

The situation changed after the financial crisis of 1982. Academic salaries lost around 50 per cent of their purchasing power between 1982 and 1989 (Kent, 1993). Some public universities kept hiring more full-time faculty, which led to a financial and political crisis in 1989. Even so, by 1989, only 25 per cent of academics had a full-time appointment or tenure, and even fewer had a doctorate. Most academics were employed on a teaching-only basis and were not engaged in research, and the majority had to combine several jobs in various institutions to make ends meet (Gil Antón *et al*, 1994).

As to research and graduate programmes, few existed outside the UNAM. The Federal Government created the National Council for Science and Technology (CONACYT) in 1970. To promote research, CONACYT started to develop research centres outside Mexico City. By 1976, 15 centres were in place; by 2017, there were 26 (CONACYT, 2017). Each centre's budget depends on CONACYT, which appoints each centre's director. All centres focus on research and postgraduate teaching, while most academic staff are full-time. Some public universities started research activities, but generally organised research centres and institutes were separate from the *facultades*, where undergraduate teaching occurs.

In 1984, in the middle of the financial crisis, CONACYT created the National System of Researchers (SNI). The SNI was set up as a temporary programme to avoid the collapse of research during the crisis. The SNI supports researchers with a monthly stipend, additional to their salary, that depends on the result of a peer evaluation every 3 or 5 years. In 1984, 1,396 researchers became members of the SNI; by 1995, there were 5,863.

While teaching remained unregulated, research became increasingly defined by the Federal Government. These policies promoted mainstream science because categories and stipends depended on the number of publications in peer-reviewed journals. Of course, every academic was free to do research, but only a few qualified for the SNI. Since the CONACYT is the only research funding agency, very few had access to funding.

These developments also led to a division of labour in the federal bureaucracy. The Under-secretariat of Higher Education became the authority for undergraduate programmes, while the CONACYT had responsibility for research and graduate programmes.

By the 1990s, nearly all public universities in México had obtained autonomy. This allows public universities to define their internal governance structures by electing their rector and organising the institution's academic work. However, the Federal Government controls the budget and the payroll. At the same time, public institutions created during the last three decades (Technological Institutes and Universities, Polytechnics, and Intercultural Universities) are not autonomous, and in practice the federal bureaucracy makes all academic decisions (hiring, promotions, course contents). These newer institutions are exclusively dedicated to undergraduate teaching.

The rise of neo-liberalism

By 1990, the economic crisis ended (temporarily), federal funding recovered, and the Government implemented novel policies. These new policies embodied two basic tenets: evaluation and conditional funding (De Vries and Álvarez Mendiola, 2005). Furthermore, these policies explicitly stated their objective to insert Mexican higher education into the 'first world'; and international organisations such as the World Bank and the Organisation for Economic Cooperation and Development (OECD) influenced national policies (Kent, 2005).

The Federal Government introduced different types of evaluation, ranging from the systemic to the institutional, programme, and individual levels. All these evaluations were tied to conditional funding: institutions had to submit development plans for additional monies, and programmes would receive extra money if they submitted to external assessment and accreditation. Academics could receive merit pay after submitting proof of their productivity. Remarkably, these policies continued almost unchanged from 1988 to 2018, even when national governments changed every six years, and different parties came to power.

As to academic labour conditions, several initiatives stand out. First, throughout the 1990s, federal governments stressed that higher education in Mexico should live up to the same quality standards as applied in developed countries. It essentially meant that academic staff in public universities should have the same characteristics as the professoriate of a globally leading university such as Harvard (Gil, 2000). Second, the Federal Government started to offer scholarships to promote graduate studies for already appointed teachers in public universities to increase the number of full-time academics with a doctorate and introduced a merit-pay system to reward productive teachers.

These policies created an enormous demand for graduate studies, above all from lecturers who were already employed (usually part-time) because hiring, promotion, and incentives became contingent upon acquiring a graduate degree. Universities rapidly created graduate programmes to respond to the new demand. In 1970, Mexico registered 5,753 graduate students; by 1990, the number had increased to 45,899 (of which 36,990 were in the public sector). By 2010, graduate enrolment reached 208,225; in 2018, there were 240,822. The private institutions registered the largest increase: from a mere

8,909 students in 1990, they jumped to 121,051 in 2018. While private institutions register 30% of undergraduates, they enrol over 50% of graduate students (Secretaría de Educación Pública, 2020a).

The CONACYT introduced a National Register of Quality Graduate Programmes (PNPC) to regulate graduate studies. To qualify, programmes should aim to prepare future researchers and need to submit evidence about their academic staff, curriculum, graduation rates, and publications. Those who are eligible, after peer evaluation, have access to funding, principally to stipends for students. However, participation is not mandatory, and most graduate programmes opted out.

The initiatives merged in 1997 in the Programme for the Improvement of the Professoriate (PROMEP). The PROMEP sought to address a fundamental problem in Mexican higher education. Only 25% of academics had a full-time contract, but even fewer had a graduate degree. According to PROMEP data from 1995, only 5.1% of academics had a Ph.D. degree, and 7.7% had a Masters (De Vries and Álvarez, 1998, 169).

Besides offering support for graduate studies to academics already employed, PROMEP introduced what was termed the 'PROMEP profile' – a description of the ideal academic. This person must be full-time, with a Ph.D., tenured, and dedicated 'in a balanced fashion' to four tasks: teaching, mentoring, collegiate decision-making, and research. In return, academics with a graduate degree and a PROMEP profile would receive a bonus to improve their working conditions and be qualified to participate in the upper echelons of the merit-pay programme for teachers. The programme limits access to these financial incentives to full-time teachers.

The SNI continued to operate in parallel to the teacher merit payments. The SNI expanded from 5,868 in 1995 to 7,466 in 2000, 16,519 in 2010, and over 30,000 in 2020 (Atlas de la Ciencia Mexicana, 2017). It also gradually raised the bar for admission and promotion: potential members must hold a Ph.D. and a permanent full-time contract, and publish in peer-reviewed, indexed journals. Further bonus points were added for supervision of completed dissertations and teaching on graduate programmes included on the national register.

Although both merit-pay programmes operate separately, they have crucial overlaps. Both reward research, teaching, and tutoring and favour full-time academics with a Ph.D. Both mainly reward academics with the recognised PROMEP profile. As a result, the different programmes started to show a 'Matthew effect' (Merton, 1968): those with a Ph.D. and a full-time appointment stood a better chance for promotion and several merit payments, while those without full-time positions were excluded from all rewards.

Unsurprisingly, therefore, a small group of academics profited from these rewards. In the 1990s, less than 25% of academic staff held full-time appointments, and most worked in public universities. Although PROMEP sought to

TABLE 6.1 Academic staff: types of contracts in private and public sector universities in Mexico (2017–18 academic year)

Type of contract	Private sector	%Private	Public sector	%Public	Total	%Total
Full-time	15213	9.7	81134	36.9	96347	25.6
Three quarts	2404	1.5	3515	1.6	5919	1.6
Half-time	6010	3.8	10556	4.8	16566	4.4
Per hour	133468	85	124391	56.6	257859	68.5
Total	157095	100	219596	99.9	376691	100.1

Source: Asociación Nacional de Universidades e Instituciones de Educación Superior (ANUIES, 2018, 76).

increase the number of full-time professors with a Ph.D. in the public sector after 1997, the proportion of full-time staff remained limited (Table 6.1.), and not all obtained a Ph.D. Furthermore, research remained concentrated in public universities and a very small number of private universities.

As a result of these policies, by 2018, the academic profession in Mexico had become highly segmented. With nearly 30,000 members of the SNI, some 22,000 with PROMEP profile (SES-DGESUI, 2021), and a similar number of beneficiaries of teachers, incentives in the public sector, an estimated 15,000 to 20,000 profited from all programmes and saw their full-time income triple or quadruple, earning the equivalent of around 3,000 euros per month. At the same time, 75% of academic staff worked on a part-time contract, without merit pay, at a salary of around 4 euros per hour (Maldonado, 2016). As ANUIES observed: 'the limited wage renumerations cause a not so optimistic dynamic that affects the quality of teaching, as professors need to accumulate many courses to meet their economic necessities, to the detriment of the time dedicated to the preparation of their classes' (ANUIES, 2015, *author's translation*).

The implications for academic freedom were profound. Academics with a part-time contract receive a salary according to the number of hours spent in the classroom. Their contracts do not take into account the time to prepare for their courses or conduct research. Most teach pre-established content. Job stability is minimal; most have no benefits such as pension plans, medical insurance, paid leave, or vacations. Even in the public sector, many are hired at the beginning of the semester, fired at the end, and, if lucky, rehired at the start of the following semester (Canales and Luna, 2003; Gil, 2008; López *et al*, 2016).

Although these policies sought to convert public universities into research universities (Acosta, 2006), the strategy depended wholly on additional funding linked to performance indicators, creating a segmented public higher education system (Rubio Oca, 2006). Universities with more full-time personnel in 1990 had better chances of having more SNI members or PROMEP profiles and receiving additional financing, which, in turn, heightened the possibility of hiring more full-time faculty. Thus, at the institutional level, the 'Matthew effect' led to a situation where, by 2020, some public universities had less than 25% of full-time academic staff, while others had almost 100%. At the same time, most undergraduate courses – on occasion up to 80% – continued to rely heavily on part-timers (de Vries *et al*, 2008), while full-time academics concentrated on research and graduate programmes.

The segmentation also created a generational divide: PROMEP and other policies improved the qualifications and payments of already hired professors, while newcomers, even with a Ph.D., are hired on a part-time, temporary contract, or not at all, due to the saturation of the academic labour market. The apparent problems in the labour market caused the CONACYT to create a particular programme of 'CONACYT chairs.' It offers young researchers who obtained a Ph.D. the opportunity to work at a public university as federal employees (CONACYT, 2022). By 2021, there were 1,076 researchers hired this way, of which 75% were members of the SNI (CONACYT, 2022).

Rectors and government officials tended to boast about the increasing number of professors with a Ph.D., SNI, or PROMEP (Tuirán, 2011). Slowly but surely, it seemed, Mexico was gaining ground in quality research and teaching and closing the gap with developed countries.

Some researchers criticised these policies, highlighting the perverse effects of incentives (Acosta, 2006; Ibarra and Porter, 2007; Moreno, 2014; Buendía *et al*, 2017). Many academics learned to play by the rules to obtain a full-time appointment or increase their income. In response, the SNI and other merit-pay programmes raised the bar: only publications in SCOPUS-indexed journals should count. Even so, the number of beneficiaries increased steadily.

The success of these policies had a critical drawback. By 2014, the incentive system started to show signs of exhaustion for two reasons: the increasing administrative costs of the planning, evaluation, and auditing processes; and the rapidly growing number of beneficiaries (Álvarez and de Vries, 2014). For example, between 2003 and 2016, the SNI budget grew from 1,433 million to 3,070 million Mexican pesos (Rodríguez, 2016). By 2018, financial constraints led the Government to cut back several special funds. These cutbacks continued during the following years under the new Government. As ANUIES observed in a communique in 2021: '...extraordinary funds have suffered such cutbacks that they practically ceased to exist, as they passed from 11,053 million pesos in 2015 to a mere 132 million pesos in 2021' (ANUIES, 2020).

As a result of these policies, academic freedom had been curtailed in several ways by 2018. For most academic workers, the concept simply did not apply. They worked part-time, teaching pre-established courses, with little to no job security. A small group of full-time scholars in the public sector had access to merit-pay programmes, which also provided little stability. The benefits are contingent on annual evaluations in the case of ESDEPED or every three to five years for SNI. And to qualify, they had to meet international publication standards.

Furthermore, after three decades of neo-liberal policies, public higher education became completely dependent on the Federal Government. Although full-time academics participate as (unpaid) peers in various evaluation processes, federal agencies design, operate, and supervise them. Likewise, all funding comes from the Federal Government (even funds allocated by the states). Although academics are not government employees, their wages are regulated and paid for by public subsidies. The Government controls the number of academic appointments in each public institution. All types of merit-pay incentives are federal. Practically all infrastructure and science and technology investments come from national budgets. In this way, the Federal Government established a firm grip on autonomy and academic freedom.

Then, in 2018, a new government came to power and promised a radical transformation.

Changes since 2018

The newly elected Government started with a different higher education agenda. During the political campaign, the Government promised to create 100 small new community-based universities for low-income students, reform the Constitution so that higher education would be tuition-free, and publish a new General Law for Higher Education. As the President's party (MORENA) had obtained a qualified majority in Parliament, it quickly moved to comply with these promises.

The second wave of modifications, not announced during the campaign, proceeded much more slowly. Its basic tenet was to overturn three decades of neo-liberal higher education policies.

Government officials announced that these reforms were integral to the 4T. Once the COVID-19 pandemic arrived, some proposals started circulating at first informally, on social media, and on virtual platforms. It is hard to say whether these reforms were rooted in a clear 'reform agenda' or whether initiatives just 'popped up' along the way.

In 2019, the Under-secretary of Higher Education announced – in an interview – that the merit-pay systems had created an academic elite with serious vices and that those systems had to be abandoned or revised, and that those who did teach, primarily part-timers, should receive additional benefits (Fernández, 2019). Likewise, CONACYT's new director launched ideas to reform the institution and its programmes, such as the SNI. It further floated ideas to abolish the lowest level of the SNI, introduce new evaluation criteria, and bar researchers from private universities from receiving SNI stipends (Sánchez and Morales, 2021). In 2022, it announced that peer reviewers should also assess which SNI members should not receive grants in case of insufficient budgets. At the same time, the President, in his daily news conferences, started to accuse public universities and academics of having succumbed to neo-liberalism for personal gain (Villa y Caña and Morales, 2021). Suddenly, what once had been the 'ideal' academic sought after in government policies was, in effect, labelled as part of an undesirable elite.

With the declared aim of combating corruption, the Federal Government opted to freeze the budgets for higher education. Public universities were not allowed to hire any additional personnel. In 2020, 'rectors complained that from 2015 to 2020, the federal budget increased less than inflation and did not consider the increase in enrolments or the need to hire professors and employees' (Moreno, 2020). CONACYT also restricted its research budget (Riquelme, 2019) and decided to cancel all the research budgets of its research centres.

Some of these initial proposals seemed reasonable answers to critiques from the academic community on past policies. However, the reform agenda gradually became shaped by ideological dogma rather than academic criteria.

The change in ideology can be discerned in various public documents and declarations. Importantly, the Institutional Programme for Science and Technology of the main funding research agency explicitly states:

> The CONACYT aligns itself with and shares the interests of the 4T: it is time to unite. With a concerted effort of all sectors, government, business, academic and scientific communities, and the whole society, we can obtain scientific sovereignty, technological independence, and the level of innovation that the country deserves and requires for the welfare of its population....
>
> *(CONACYT, 2020,* author's translation*)*

CONACYT's presentation, in 2019, of its ten national strategic programmes (*Programas Nacionales Estratégicos, PRONACES*) perhaps best reflects the new ideology. After declaring that the PRONACES represents a paradigmatic shift in research and development, it reviews all that went wrong under previous neo-liberal governments. According to the CONACYT, during the decades of neo-liberalism, the State worked with scientists, entrepreneurs, and private enterprises to innovate and create 'value chains,' making production more efficient and generating capitalist and individual monetary gains. All this went against the interests of the poor and the nation. It points out that:

> The benefits, costs, and risks derived from the model were very unequally distributed, including among the subjects that participated enthusiastically in the model, and there was an accumulation of very grave problems derived from the concentration of economic wealth and political power, among which the deepening of the structural acts of violence that today menace the country because of the tetrad of inequality-racism-sexism-violence.
>
> *(García Barrios, 2021)*

The term 'neo-liberal science' was coined, and defined, as a kind of science that should not receive public support (Saldierna and Méndez, 2022). From this perspective, the objectives of genuine science should contribute to national sovereignty, independence, and self-sustainability, all for the benefit of the population, especially the poor (Álvarez-Buylla Roces, 2022).

For the first time in history, the Mexican Government proclaimed a State ideology that observes that science, technology, and education should contribute to the goals announced in the 4T. Laws and statutes changed accordingly, putting more discretionary power in the hands of the Director of CONACYT. Meetings began 'behind closed doors,' and all proceedings were declared secret. The Government excluded the private sector from all funding and proclaimed collaboration with private enterprises as suspect. The CONACYT's Director went as far as to compare graduate programmes offered by private institutions to junk food (Álvarez-Buylla Roces, 2022).

The ideology has an impact on all aspects of academic work: to be eligible for evaluation for the SNI, graduate programmes seeking inclusion into CONACYT's quality register, or research projects submitted for funding, all need to indicate how their work has contributed, or will add, to these new priorities.

While CONACYT reformed science and graduate programmes, the Subsecretariat for Higher Education (SES) appeared to follow a different path. Initially, the new Under-secretary suggested that the incentives schemes established in the past should be discussed and modified. He pointed out that three decades of neo-liberal policies had created a small academic elite that had learned to profit from the merit-pay programmes to enrich themselves while providing little of value (Fernández, 2019).

In 2019, the SES cut most special funding, which led to protests by rectors (Moreno, 2019). By 2020, amid the pandemic, some special funds reappeared or were renamed (Acosta, 2020a). One programme that continued is the merit payment programme, which, remarkably, continues to operate on the same criteria it had employed for the previous three decades. Incentives benefit full-time tenured professors with a Ph.D. who comply with the PROMEP (now PRODEP) ideal profile. Thus, some policies would appear to have remained unchanged (Acosta, 2020b).

This continuity appears to respond to political considerations. The new National Plan for Education (Secretaría de Educación Pública, 2020b) does not propose any new academic goals nor seek to change or reform the system. Instead, it omits problems that were on the agenda before 2018, concerning issues associated with retirement and pension plans, generational turnover, wages, infrastructure, internationalisation, lifelong learning, adult education, distance education, world-class universities, and competitive research. These topics disappeared from the agenda, but remain unresolved.

However, at the same time, research and development funding has steadily declined, from 0.328 per cent of gross domestic product in 2017 to 0.296 in

2020 (OECD, 2023). As a result, fewer research projects are funded or receive less funding.

The strategies followed since 2018 seem to converge on one common issue: political control. However, the new national plans and laws fail to mention academic goals for reform. The reforms relate to the national agenda of the 4T and consider sovereignty and national independence as the new goals. With this political agenda in mind, government officials seem to have concluded that abolishing all incentives would erode political support and that the combination of evaluation and incentives is a much more effective way to control and steer the behaviour of institutions and individuals. To this end, the main modifications concern who sets the evaluation and funding criteria.

The political logic remains identical to the preceding decades of neo-liberalism but with a twist. The Government continues to offer additional payments to 'an elite' of full-time workers who comply with federal evaluation criteria inherited from neo-liberal times. However, researchers must now accept and adopt the new State ideology of the 4T to receive incentives. As a result, researchers need to demonstrate not only high productivity measured by international standards, but also how they contributed to national sovereignty and improved living conditions for the poor and minorities.

The academic community is increasingly excluded from decision-making, while government officials appear to make unilateral decisions about who to admit to the SNI or fund – by expecting all to support the 4T, in effect, it means that all criticisms are in danger of being defined as neo-liberal, conservative, or, even potentially, treasonous. Public universities – and their professors – are accused of succumbing to neo-liberalism and corruption, while private universities are deemed not deserving of public funding. As a result, the debate about the desirable future of higher education is not an academic one. Instead, the discussion, as evidenced above, tends to revolve around issues such as plagiarism, with, as mentioned above, 'junk food' analogies, and the battle against neo-liberalism.

Conclusions

The changes in policies since 2018 have severe consequences for academic freedom in Mexico. The effects are perhaps even worse than previous right-wing attacks because the 'left-leaning' Government tried to impose a specific ideology on academic work. Funding appeared to be based more on political loyalty and support of the 4T policies, instead of peer review of research and teaching. This way, political perceptions, beliefs, and dogmas replaced neo-liberal performance indicators such as productivity, efficiency, or quality.

The State has defined academic freedom through legislation and announced that it would promote it. But, at the same time, it in reality reduced academic freedom by declaring what traditions or rules are valid, what counts as good work or products, what will be rewarded or punished, and what the Government will fund.

The new law defines academic freedom as a right that protects academics from prosecution by the State and State ideology. However, the case that is made in this chapter, is that this is precisely what the Government has been doing: the academic community is thus under pressure in numerous ways from political and ideological points of view.

For many, labour conditions and job security have declined even further. Academics continue to have inadequate, or even worse, working conditions, and salaries have risen by less than inflation. Most continue as part-timers, and new appointments and promotions have reached a standstill in both the public and the private sectors. The different merit-pay programmes have come under scrutiny. Evaluation criteria remain focused on productivity but include new factors requiring additional evidence of compliance with the new ideology. The Government has decreased and reoriented funding for higher education and scientific research. There have been constant attacks on researchers, intellectuals, journalists, and anyone opposed to the Government.

By demanding proof of compliance with the national 4T strategy, the Government attempts to limit academics in what they should think and how they should think. Unless this approach is radically changed, and the problems it has produced are rectified, there is a real danger that independent thinking, research autonomy, and academic freedom itself will all be severely restricted in Mexico.

References

Acosta, A. (2006). Señales cruzadas: Una interpretación sobre las políticas de formación de cuerpos académicos en México. *Revista de la Educación Superior*, 35(139), 81–92.

Acosta, A. (2020a). La educación en la era de la 4T. In R. Becerra and J. Woldenberg (eds), *Balance temprano. Desde la izquierda democrática* (205–26). México: Grano de Sal. https://www.researchgate.net/publication/346927064_La_educacion_superior_en_la_era_de_la_4T

Acosta, A. (2020b). Agenda universitaria en México: novedades y rutinas. *Pensamiento Universitario*, (19), 131–5. http://www.pensamientouniversitario.com.ar/index.php/2020/09/22/agenda-universitaria-en-mexico-novedades-y-rutinas/

Albornoz, O. (1966). Academic freedom and higher education in Latin America. *Comparative Education Review*, 10(2), 250–6. http://www.jstor.org/stable/1186219

Álvarez, G., and de Vries, W. (2014). Un modelo agotado de relación entre el estado y las instituciones de educación superior. In H. Muñoz (ed), *La Universidad Pública en México. Análisis, reflexiones y perspectivas* (37–54). México: UNAM/Porrúa.

Álvarez-Buylla Roces, M. E. (2022, January 15). La indispensable reforma del posgrado. *La Jornada*. https://www.jornada.com.mx/2022/01/15/opinion/013a2pol

ANUIES (2015). *Los profesores de tiempo parcial en las universidades públicas mexicanas. Elementos para un diagnóstico.* México: Asociación Nacional de Universidades e Instituciones de Educación Superior.

ANUIES. (2018). *Visión y Acción 2030. Propuesta de la ANUIES para renovar la educación superior en México.* México: Asociación Nacional de Universidades e Instituciones de Educación Superior. https://visionyaccion2030.anuies.mx/Vision_accion2030.pdf

ANUIES. (2020, November 12). *Comunicado Consejo Nacional.* http://www.anuies.mx/media/docs/avisos/pdf/201112172624Comunicado+Consejo+Nacional+42020.pdf

Atlas de la Ciencia Mexicana. (2017). *Sistema Nacional de Investigadores: Gráficas y mapas.* http://atlasdelacienciamexicana.org/es/sni.html

Bernasconi, A. (2007). Is there a Latin American model of the university? *Comparative Education Review, 52*(1), 27–52.

Bernasconi, A. (2021). University autonomy and academic freedom: Contrasting Latin American and US perspectives. *Higher Education Governance and Policy, 2*(1), 56–67. https://dergipark.org.tr/en/download/article-file/1786735

Buendía, A., García, S., Grediaga, R., Landesman, M., Rodríguez, R., Rondero, N., and Vera, H. (2017). Queríamos evaluar y terminamos contando: Alternativass para la valorización del trabajo académico. *Perfiles educativos, 39*(157), 200–19. https://doi.org/10.22201/iisue.24486167e.2017.157.58464

Canales, A., and Luna, E. (2003). ¿Cuál política para la docencia? *Revista de la Educación Superior, 32*(127), 45–52.

CONACYT. (2017). *Reorganización del sistema de centros públicos de investigación del Consejo Nacional de Ciencia y Tecnología.* México: CONACYT.

CONACYT. (2020). Programa Institucional 2020-2024 del Consejo Nacional de Ciencia y Tecnología, *Diario Oficial de la Federación.*

CONACYT. (2022). *Cátedras CONACYT.* https://conacyt.mx/conacyt/areas-del-conacyt/desarrollo-cientifico/catedras-conacyt/

De Figueiredo-Cowen, M. (2002). Latin American universities, academic freedom and autonomy: a long-term myth? *Comparative Education, 38*(4), 471–84. https://doi.org/10.1080/0305006022000030702

De Vries, W., and Álvarez, G. (1998). El PROMEP: ¿Posible, razonable y deseable? *Sociológica,* (36), 165–86. https://www.researchgate.net/publication/313602253_El_PROMEP_Posible_razonable_y_deseable

De Vries, W., and Álvarez Mendiola, G. (2005). Acerca de las políticas, la política y otras complicaciones en la educación superior mexicana. *Revista de la Educación Superior, 34*(134), 81–105. http://www.scielo.org.mx/scielo.php?pid=S0185-27602005000200081andscript=sci_arttext

de Vries, W., González, G., León, P., and Hernández, I. (2008). Políticas públicas y desempeño académico, o cómo el tamaño si importa. *CPU-e,* (7), 2–32. https://www.uv.mx/cpue/num7/inves/completos/de_vries_politicas_publicas.pdf

Diario Oficial de la Federación. (2021, April 20). Ley General de Educación Superior. *Diario Oficial de la Federación.*

EHEA. (2020). *Statement on Academic Freedom. Rome Ministerial Communiqué ANNEX I.* Rome: European Higher Education Area. http://www.ehea.info/Upload/Rome_Ministerial_Communique_Annex_I.pdf

Fernández, A. (2019, June 18). Existe un desconocimiento de las nuevas políticas para las IES: Concheiro Bórquez. *La Jornada de Oriente*.

Fuentes, Y. (2018, October 4). AMLO presidente: ¿qué es la "Cuarta Transformación" que propone Andrés Manuel López Obrador para México? *BBC News Mundo*. https://www.bbc.com/mundo/noticias-america-latina-45712329

Fuentes Molinar, O. (1989). La educación superior en México y los escenarios de su desarrollo futuro. *Universidad Futura*, *3*, 2–11.

García Barrios, R. (2021). *¿Qué son los PRONACES?* https://conacyt.mx/que-son-los-pronaces/

Garciadiego Dantán, J. (2000). *Rudos contra científicos: la Universidad Nacional durante la revolución mexicana*. México: El Colegio de México/Universidad Nacional Autónoma de México.

Gil, M. (2000). Un siglo buscando doctores. *Revista de la Educación Superior*, *29*(113), 23–42. https://www.researchgate.net/publication/312538800_Un_siglo_buscando_doctores

Gil, M. (2008). Los académicos en instituciones privadas que captan demanda. Una aproximación a otros actores hoy en la sombra. *Revista de la Educación Superior*, *37*(145), 115–21. https://www.researchgate.net/publication/237037165_Los_Academicos_en_instituciones_privadas_que_captan_demanda_Una_aproximacion_a_otros_actores_hoy_en_la_sombra

Gil Antón, M., *et al*. (1994). *Los rasgos de la diversidad. Un estudio sobre los académicos mexicanos*. México: Universidad Autónoma Metropolitana-Azcapotzalco.

Guevara Niebla, G. (1986). Masificación y profesión académica en la Universidad Autónoma de México. *Revista de la Educación Superior*, *15*(58), 1–15. http://publicaciones.anuies.mx/pdfs/revista/Revista58_S1A3ES.pdf

Ibarra, E., and Porter, L. (2007). El debate sobre la evaluación: del homo academicus al homo economicus. *Reencuentro*, *18*(48), 34–9.

Kent, R. (1986). ¿Quiénes son los profesores universitarios? Las vicisitudes de una azarosa profesionalización. *Crítica*, *86*(28), 17–32.

Kent, R. (1993). Higher education in México: From unregulated expansion to evaluation. *Higher Education*, *25*(1), 73–83.

Kent, R. (2005). La dialéctica de la esperanza y la desilusión en políticas de educación superior en México. *Revista de la Educación Superior*, *34*(134), 63–79.

López, A. I., García, O., Pérez, R., Montero, V., and Rojas, E. L. (2016). Los Profesores de Tiempo Parcial en las universidades públicas estatales: una profesionalización inconclusa. *Revista de la Educación Superior*, *45*(180), 23–39. https://doi.org/10.1016/j.resu.2016.06.007

Maldonado Maldonado, A. (2016). Pérdida de poder adquisitivo y limitada competitividad internacional: indicios sobre los salarios de académicos mexicanos a partir de una comparación internacional. *Revista Iberoamericana de Educación Superior*, *7*(20), 3–20. http://www.scielo.org.mx/scielo.php?script=sci_arttext&pid=S2007-28722016000300003&lng=es&tlng=es.

Merton, R. K. (1968). The Matthew Effect in Science. The reward and communication systems of science are considered. *Science*, *159*(3810), 56–63.

Moreno, C. I. (2014). *Políticas, incentivos y cambio organizacional en la educación superior en México*. Guadalajara: Universidad de Guadalajara-Universidad Nacional Autónoma de México.

Moreno, T. (2019, July 20). ANUIES: Tienen crisis financiera 9 instituciones. En riesgo el pago de nómina para empleados de 9 universidades públicas. *El Universal.* https://www.eluniversal.com.mx/nacion/sociedad/anuies-tienen-crisis-financiera-9-instituciones

Moreno, T. (2020, November 13). Preocupa a ANUIES recorte de presupuesto de 2021. Rectores de universidades ven deterioro en la educación superior. *El Universal.* https://www.eluniversal.com.mx/nacion/preocupa-anuies-recorte-depresupuesto-de-2021#google_vignette

OECD (Organisation for Economic Co-operation and Development). (2023). *Gross Domestic Spending on R&D.* https://data.oecd.org/rd/gross-domestic-spending-on-r-d.htm

Presidencia de la Republica. (2019). *Plan Nacional de Desarrollo.* https://presidente.gob.mx/wp-content/uploads/2019/05/PLAN-NACIONAL-DE-DESAR-ROLLO-2019-2024-1.pdf

Riquelme, R. (2019, July 14). Se redujo la inversión en tecnología durante el primer semestre del 2019: PwC México. *El Economista.* https://www.eleconomista.com.mx/tecnologia/Se-redujo-la-inversion-en-tecnologia-durante-el-primer-semestre-del-2019-PwC-Mexico-20190714-0001.html#

Rodríguez, C. E. (2016). *El Sistema Nacional De Investigadores En Números.* México: Foro Consultivo Científico y Tecnológico. http://www.foroconsultivo.org.mx/libros_editados/SNI_en_numeros.pdf

Rodríguez Gómez, R. (2022, January 20). Libertad de cátedra ¿para quién? *Campus Milenio.* https://suplementocampus.com/libertad-de-catedra-para-quien/

Rubio Oca, J. (2006). *La Política Educativa y La Educación superior En México 1995-2006. Un Balance.* Ciudad de México: Secretaría de Educación Pública/Fondo de Cultura Económica.

Saldierna, G., and Méndez, E. (2022, August 5). Álvarez-Buylla: dio Conacyt 45 mil mdp a la IP de 2001 a 2018. *La Jornada.* https://www.jornada.com.mx/notas/2022/08/05/politica/alvarez-buylla-dio-conacyt-45-mil-mdp-a-la-ip-de-2001-a-2018/

Sánchez, I., and Morales, F. (2021, February 12). Temen investigadores nuevo golpe al SNI. *Reforma.* https://www.reforma.com/aplicacioneslibre/preacceso/articulo/default.aspx?__rval=1andurlredirect=https://www.reforma.com/temeninvestiga-dores-nuevo-golpe-al-sni/ar2124213?referer=-7d616165662f3a3a6262623b727a7a7279703b767a783a—

Secretaría de Educación Pública. (2020a). *Principales cifras del sistema educativo nacional 2019-2020.* México: SEP.

Secretaría de Educación Pública. (2020b, July 6). *Programa Sectorial de Educación 2020-2024.* Diario Oficial de la Federación. https://www.gob.mx/cms/uploads/attachment/file/562380/Programa_Sectorial_de_Educaci_n_2020-2024.pdf

SES-DGESUI. (2021, December 1). *Subsecretaria de Educación Superior.* Programa para el Desarrollo Profesional Docente para el Tipo Superior S247 (PRODEP). https://dgesui.ses.sep.gob.mx/programas/programa-para-el-desarrollo-profesional-docente-para-el-tipo-superior-s247-prodep

Tuirán, R. (2011). *La educación superior en México: avances, rezagos y retos.* Secretaría de Educación Pública. https://www.academia.edu/23975720

UNAM. (2022, January 15). *Universidad Nacional Autónoma de México.* Portal de Estadística Universitaria. https://www.estadistica.unam.mx/series_inst/xls/c16%20persaca.xls

UNESCO. (1997). *Recommendation Concerning the Status of Higher-Education Teaching Personnel, Adopted by the General Conference at Its Twenty-Ninth Session.* United Nations Educational, Scientific and Cultural Organization. Paris: UNESCO. https://unesdoc.unesco.org/ark:/48223/pf0000113234.page=2

Villa y Caña, P., and Morales, A. (2021, October 21). La UNAM se volvió individualista y defensora de proyectos neoliberales: AMLO. *El Universal.* https://www.eluniversal.com.mx/nacion/amlo-la-unam-se-volvio-individualista-y-defensora-de-proyectos-neoliberales

7

BEYOND WESTERN IDEALS

Academic freedom, capabilities, and social knowledge

Liz Jackson

Introduction

In 2020–2021, global associations for academic freedom including Varieties of Democracy (V-Dem, Sweden), the Global Public Policy Institute (GPPI, Germany), and Scholars at Risk (SAR, United States) reported the decline of academic freedom in Hong Kong. While linking the change to the passing of the National Security Law in 2020 and the subsequent arrests of academics and students for their involvement in anti-government protests (Lam, 2021), these organisations draw a broader portrait of Hong Kong being enveloped in the past few decades by the People's Republic of China, which they also judge as 'poor' with regard to academic freedom, in contrast with Western countries (Scholars at Risk, 2019). Indeed, Hong Kong and China were given 'D' and 'E' statuses, respectively, for academic freedom by GPPI in 2021, while nearly all Western countries were assessed as 'A' status (Kinzelbach *et al*, 2021).

In this chapter, I do not focus on the national-level policy issues at play in Hong Kong and China related to academic freedom. Instead, I take this international context as a starting point to explore cultural issues undergirding so-called global definitions and conceptualisations of academic freedom. More specifically, I aim to flesh out a sense of idealism and individualism underpinning mainstream Western ideas of academic freedom, which I trace to their roots in liberal philosophy. Then I will elaborate on a more socially based understanding of academic freedom, as a kind of capability held in relation to others and the ways in which knowledge is valued within a particular community.

Using this alternative understanding of academic freedom, I consider how scholars may, or may not, be challenged in relation to academic freedom regardless of the country in which they work and its laws. I draw here on my

DOI: 10.4324/9781003363262-10

knowledge of the United States, China, and Hong Kong, as I am a United States citizen who has lived and worked in Hong Kong (and occasionally in China) for over ten years, with in-depth knowledge of these societies' working conditions, academic cultures, and legal systems. Through this comparative analysis, I hope to shed light on some issues related to academic freedom that may go under the radar in Western contexts.

Defining freedom: A Western rights-based view

As discussed in the three chapters in Part I of this book, Western liberal philosophy provides a foundation for understanding contemporary international discourse about academic freedom. The individual and their rights loom large in this framing (Jackson, 2021a; 2022). While various thinkers have discussed and defended a case for academic freedom, Immanuel Kant's views are particularly relevant here. For Kant, one must be free from external influences and barriers in order to engage in and express a more independent form of thought and judgment (Jackson, 2007; 2021a). Kant strongly defended the principle that a person should 'act so that you treat humanity, whether in thine own person or in that of any other, in every case as an end withal, never as a means' (Kant, 1898, 47). In other words, one should allow others to pursue their own interests and never use others to achieve one's own interests. Thus, by protecting others' freedom to think and exercise and express their own judgment, one can also protect their own freedom and capacity to engage in critical thought and reasoning.

In 'What is Enlightenment?' Kant extends these ideas into the political domain. Kant states people are not enlightened, because they are ruled by emotions and overly influenced by others. In this case, he promotes a gradual granting of freedom, and notes that an enlightened scholar 'is completely free as well as obliged to impart to the public all his carefully considered, well-intentioned thoughts' (Kant, 1970a, 56). Kant saw each person's freedom as necessary to develop a kind of public knowledge constructed by people collectively (Jackson, 2007). In this context, one cannot take on their duty to contribute to the greater good unless they are free to speak and think independently. Each person has something to offer to the collective, and without freedom at an individual level, society as a whole will suffer from dogma and corruption. As he writes, the 'existence of reason depends upon this freedom; for the voice of reason is not that of a dictatorial and despotic power, it is rather like the vote of citizens of a free state' (Kant, 1993).

There are two important things to note here. First, freedom at the individual level is key. To say a group should have the right to freedom of speech or academic freedom (for example, Raz, 1986) would not make sense here, because each person's individual right, ability, and perspective counts. That each can contribute as an individual to the whole necessitates freedom at the individual level.

Second, Kant's articulation of intellectual freedom is idealistic. Kant acknowledges that most people are not enlightened. Additionally, he often contrasts in his work his ambitions for enlightenment and what can be achieved. For instance, in discussing his own and others' philosophical pursuit of reason, he writes of a tower which would reach to heaven, versus a reality that is much more modest:

> We have found, indeed, that, although we had proposed to build for ourselves a tower which should reach to heaven, the supply of materials sufficed merely for a habitation, which was spacious enough for all terrestrial purposes, and high enough to enable us to survey the level plain of experience, but that the bold undertaking designed necessarily failed for want of materials... while, at the same time, we cannot give up the intention of erecting a secure abode, we must proportion our design to the material which is presented to us, and which is, at the same time, sufficient for all our wants.
>
> *(Kant, 1993)*

Practically, Kant desires more enlightenment in society and the development of humankind's potential. However, in reality he recognises that men are not 'free' in thinking and expressing themselves simply because they are not in physical or legal chains (Kant, 1970a). Yet as progress depends on the human pursuit of knowledge, he still hopes for positive intellectual development in the future (Kant, 1970b).

This idealism and individualism can be seen underneath the surface of more contemporary Western-oriented discussions of academic freedom (for example, Kleinig, 1982). As Cain (2012) shows, academics have emphasised the need for individual freedom in research and teaching throughout United States history, while there has often been a gap in reality between the freedom and autonomy desired and that attained.

V-Dem, which develops the methodology underpinning the GPPI's Academic Freedom Index, similarly uses an individualistic and idealistic understanding of academic freedom. V-Dem conceptualises academic freedom firstly in relation to international rights law, citing 'Article 15 of the International Covenant on Economic, Social and Cultural Rights of 1966, which states in paragraph 3: "The States Parties to the present Covenant undertake to respect the freedom indispensable for scientific research and creative activity"' (Spannagel *et al*, 2020, 4). Additionally, it cites the 1997 UNESCO Recommendation Concerning the Status of Higher-Education Teaching Personnel, which defines academic freedom as

> the right...without constriction by prescribed doctrine, to freedom of teaching and discussion, freedom in carrying out research and disseminating and publishing the results thereof, freedom to express freely their opinion about

the institution or system in which they work, freedom from institutional censorship and freedom to participate in professional or representative academic bodies.

To develop the index, V-Dem relies upon country experts to give views on: (a) freedom to research and teach and engage in academic exchange and dissemination, (b) the autonomy of universities, (c) campus integrity, and (d) freedom of expression (Spannagel *et al*, 2020). In relation to this, V-Dem clarifies that interference with academic freedom is only judged as undue when performed by 'non-academic' actors, while 'we do not consider restrictions that are set by the academic community itself as interference...regarding research priorities, ethical and quality standards in research and publication, or standardized curricula' (Spannagel *et al*, 2020, 7–8). Additionally, V-Dem uses countries' legal frameworks and 'international legal commitment' in their index.

There are a few noteworthy aspects of how academic freedom is conceptualised by V-Dem. First, as Robeyns (2006) points out, a focus on legal frameworks for measuring rights protections is idealistic, because there is a difference between what is on paper and what happens in reality – hence, the need for other kinds of measurement. Thus, comparing societies in terms of their expressed legal rights frameworks and legal commitments freedom is somewhat conceptual and formal, as the legal frameworks do not necessarily correlate with experiences and practices within countries. A State can have ideal policies and laws but fail to uphold them; there are many examples of this in rights discourse (Robeyns, 2006). Alternatively, one can imagine (while it may not be common) a country not bothering with elaborate rights discourses but nonetheless having a cultural context where rights are normally well ensured.

Second, that V-Dem considers interference undue based on whether it comes from non-academic versus academic actors is not as straightforward as might be hoped. One initial question here is what count as interference. For instance, in Hong Kong, the situation of non-academic actors influencing higher education has not formally changed. As one recent report shows, it has always been standard practice for the Chief Executive of the region to preside as Chancellor over public universities and engage in related responsibilities. This is often regarded as problematic in relation to academic freedom, but in the past, it was not considered such an issue in Hong Kong. In this context, changes in perceptions relate to a subjective impression that external actors are now participating or interfering 'differently' (Scholars at Risk, 2019). As Scholars at Risk (2019, 56) puts it:

Previously, under British colonial rule, the governor of Hong Kong was named the chancellor of all public universities, while the heads of those universities served as vice-chancellors. While the governor technically had significant powers in this role, in practice the title was primarily ceremonial, with governors declining to play an active role in university governance.

Following the 1997 transition – and especially since the Occupy movement – the territory's chief executive (the equivalent of a colonial-era governor) has adopted a more active role in university affairs, including exercising varying degrees of power to appoint council members at Hong Kong's universities. This has been described as an unusual development in Hong Kong and has furthered debate over the role of government in university administration.

Third, the academic community is taken as non-interfering – or as not interfering in an undue way – with academic freedom. This means that individual experiences within academia are not meaningfully engaged after all as the 'academic community' is a social construct in this context (Cain, 2012; McLaughlin, 2021). It is represented, particularly when 'experts' are used as research informants, by influential and powerful members of the so-called community (deans, full professors, presidents, etc.). Meanwhile, such studies rarely include those at the lower rungs of the academic 'food chain': temporary and contract workers, untenured staff, and those whose research is unpopular or seen as non-strategic by their institutional leaders or other influential and powerful academic actors (see Jackson, 2018 and Chapter 10 by Maria Slowey). Academic freedom in this analysis thus remains as an individualistic ideal. It is not being measured or assessed at the individual level across diverse academic actors.

Furthermore, in this framing of the academic community, there is no analysis of the nature of the community or its social, cultural, and interpersonal characteristics. While one might hope that reference to 'campus integrity' in the V-Dem index would relate to such factors, integrity is understood as 'politically motivated on-campus or digital surveillance, presence of intelligence or security forces, presence of student militias, and violent attacks by third parties…to repress academic life on campus' (Spannagel *et al*, 2020, 9). Ironically, in Hong Kong, pro-democracy and anti-government rallies on campuses could lead to a downgrading of its academic freedom ranking – while subsequent political repression could be framed as providing a freer environment (as government proponents claim). These are subjective indicators indeed. There are therefore useful alternative ways to think about academic freedom that focus more effectively on diverse experiences.

Freedom as a relational capability

In contrast with rights-based discourse, Robeyns (2006) argues for a capabilities approach wherein what people are able to do counts more than what they are officially allowed or permitted to do. In this framework (Sen, 1992; Nussbaum, 2000), one needs to consider what people can do and what is needed so that people can actually do it. As Sen (1992, 8) notes, this perspective observes how 'two persons holding the same bundle of primary goods can have very different freedoms…giving priority to the means of freedom over any assessment of the extents of freedom…can be a drawback.'

This view of freedom goes beyond what has been called a 'negative' view of freedom as described previously in relation to Kant's work, which only considers whether one has been interfered with clearly and unduly (Berlin, 1969). It aims to understand more deeply whether various members of a community truly have the means to exercise their freedoms. This view is also inherently relational, because it considers how people have different experiences that take place in relationships with each other within institutions. Additionally, this orientation implies that it is the responsibility of communities to provide for diverse members to develop and exercise their capacities to think and express themselves (Alford, 2005). It is not enough to say, 'I did not interfere,' as people may be thwarted without any official interference if what they need to exercise their freedom is not provided.

This view complicates the understanding of academic freedom by recognising how people's autonomy and agency is connected to how they are treated by others. Once we favour a capabilities approach wherein not everyone in a group (such as an academic community) actually is able to exercise their rights in the same way, a relational philosophy helps articulate at an experiential level how people exercise or are thwarted in exercising their academic freedom. While Kant recognised that people impact upon each other's experiences interpersonally – and thus required that people commit to not interfering with one another to enable freedom for all – this implication tends to be neglected by groups like V-Dem, who do not seem to consider that interference with academic freedom could come from within the academic community.

There are additional sources to draw upon to understand why interpersonal relations count. Existentialists provide powerful articulations of how people experience entrapment in the world, as they are perceived by other people differently from the way in which they perceive themselves (De Beauvoir, 1949; Jackson, 2022). They thus become alienated through engagement with others from their understanding of reality and their self (Heidegger, 1962; Roberts, 2016). Taylor's (1992) related work on the politics of recognition highlights the implications of these insights. Following Fanon (1967), Taylor shows how humans are impacted by each other, and the sense of meaning and self-actualisation one can receive from seeing oneself represented by others sensibly, rather than in an alien way. In this context, not all people are free to contribute to a broader sense of reality when they are a minority, differing in their perspective from mainstream viewpoints. More generally, often minorities' senses of the world and their selves are discounted by mainstream members of society. To have one's self and view of reality accepted by others is thus a vexing, maybe impossible, task for those who are cast as 'other' in a community (Jackson, 2022).

More broadly, none of us is entirely free from expectations related to prevailing norms, while norms negatively impact some more than others. While, for Kant, one should simply rise above dogmatic acceptance of external rules and standards, in reality many cannot turn against norms, even if they are not right. From this perspective, liberal thinkers often depend upon abstract ideals about personal freedom, which are perhaps only accessible to a privileged few, while others must struggle to live up to their view.

Put into an academic context, not all views are recognised equally, and many experience demeaning views of themselves and their perspectives in higher education as elsewhere. This challenges diverse scholars as thinkers, writers, and speakers. Observations about the sociology of knowledge production and higher education back up these perspectives. Kuhn's notion of normal science highlights how much of science involves making prevailing paradigms more reliable and useful in different contexts (Kuhn, 1962). In this case, scientists 'force nature into the preformed and relatively inflexible box' and discard or ignore counter evidence, which is regarded as an unhelpful anomaly. Kuhn thus sees science as a series of paradigm shifts; from a historical view, it is 'ridden by dogma,' as those who call attention to anomalies are ignored or dismissed, until their arguments and data create a crisis about what is the norm and a shift in the dominant orientation.

Across societies, scholarship has historically been conducted in homogeneous environments, dominated by men (in Western societies, White men). While diversity is praised for providing new perspectives and greater creativity, at the interpersonal level academics whose identities and experiences vary from norms, or who hold unpopular scholarly views (meritorious or not), can experience various unofficial and official forms of silencing, through academic processes commonly held by those in privileged positions as basically fair and reasonable. At the very least, they face heightened pressures to conform or defend views which vary from norms.

Among academics, most decisions about performance reviews, employment offers and extensions, and promotions are norms-based within the community. To succeed is to develop what is regarded by one's peers as an excellent career. Gaining the kind of influential academic voice required here means, for example, earning a doctorate from a reputable university and sharing research in sanctioned venues (namely, high-profile international journals and conferences). These tasks in turn require that one's work – that is, their views and expressions, and their articulation and observations about the world – is regularly, continually recognised as meritorious and authoritative by colleagues, professors, advisors/supervisors, and varied other committees of peers throughout their career (from a doctoral committee to journal and conference review boards and hiring committees). Typically, the task also involves learning how to respond with an appropriate degree of patience, generosity, and flexibility in relation to receiving these reviews.

Some subjectivity is built into these systems. Anyone who has worked with a doctoral committee or received journal reviews knows that each scholar has a distinctive view about what counts as excellent, publishable, or problematic. What is appreciated by one professor as novel, original, and important may be dismissed by another as insignificant and banal. Those leading these systems and institutions seek to address this subjectivity through various quality assurance processes and reforms (for example, the use of double-anonymous peer reviewing, or ensuring that members of minority groups sit on hiring or promotion committees). They thus see them as basically fair and transparent and well-intended. However, for those coming from minority positions, these processes and systems can appear almost 'cult-like,' partisan, and opaque – or worse: biased, close-minded, and hierarchical (Jackson *et al*, 2018; Jackson, 2021a).

Historically, the work of Black scholars on racial bias in the United States, such as W. E. B. De Bois, was dismissed by many colleagues, who refused to accept the findings, observations, approaches, and methods. Regarding the V-Dem academic freedom index, no one would argue that De Bois had his academic freedom formally infringed upon in an undue way here: that is, by non-academic sources of interference. However, in contexts of difference and inequity, a more subjective experience of bullying by academic peers should also be seen as a potential source of infringement upon one's academic freedom. Consider Martin and colleagues' (2019) comments here:

> Although nonblack scholars are relatively free to select the topics they research and teach with limited interventions from others, the same is not necessarily the case for black professors, especially black professors who study race, who must calculate the benefits and risks of research in virtually every decision they make in the academy. The scholars themselves are viewed as inferior because of their race, and their scholarship is also viewed as inferior because of its focus on race…
>
> [T]he fundamental reality of bullying is as a form of relation, of proximity, of closeness, of contact. But, more than this, it is a form of locked relation; bullying requires a binding, a tether, a connection that, when broken, denies the bully its power and offers the possibility of reprieve for the bullied. Escape seems to be the answer.
>
> *(Martin et al, 2019, 8, 10)*

Many minority academics when faced with such experiences, particularly as doctoral students or would-be students or untenured assistant professors, face a choice between conforming to others' expectations or leaving. Arguably, all academics experience this, when we think about the tasks of doctoral students and those seeking to publish in journals for the first time. However, for minority scholars, this can be an impossible choice, as their sense of reality may be denied by colleagues who take for granted their own sense of things.

Those who carry on with their work in this context do not later 'win', but they can still experience being treated as problematic and irritating by their peers. Peers can reject them in unofficial and casual ways – not banning their work at an official level, but simply ignoring them and excluding them over time. In other words, they can face shunning, which can be impossible to resolve, apart from leaving the workplace, as Lester (1988) writes:

> Shunning is an action which appears benign. It is an action which can be denied... Thus, if the object of shunning chooses to leave the group, it does not appear to the outsider that he or she was forced out. I have been asked: Why didn't you choose to stay and fight? The question reveals an absence of understanding of the psychological impact of shunning. One does not fight shunning. You either capitulate to the group or you leave. You do not fight silence: you break it by giving in, or appeasing...
>
> *(Lester, 1988, 24)*

Related forms of subtle bias can hinder the careers of anyone who differs from the norms around them (Jackson, 2018; 2019a; 2018a). Women scholars experience pressures related to harassment, including sexual harassment, which can also lead to their leaving academic sites, such as their institutions, as well as conferences, where publishing and employment opportunities particularly arise for new scholars (Jackson, 2019a). Women of colour face intersecting challenges related to gender and race (Jackson, 2017).

None of this meets the stringent criteria of non-academics violating academic freedom. No one is overtly codifying or oppressing the speech of others, in any sense that can be technically proven in terms recognised as valid by academics in authoritative positions. These accounts thus reveal a great deal that is left out of the picture when academic freedom is treated as an idealistic binary, of freedom or its absence. More broadly, from a capabilities view, we should question why academia remains quite unequal around the world with regard to gender, race, and social class. Arguably the dynamics considered here related to interpersonal recognition have implications for the cultivation of diverse students in schools, postgraduate scholars, and those desiring good jobs (where they can share their research) but cannot get their foot in the door (Jackson, 2018a). The next section gives examples related to the arguments here based on my experiences (and others) in the United States, Hong Kong, and China.

Academic freedom in the United States, Hong Kong, and China

A common (Western) assumption is that the traditional, negative form of academic freedom exists in Western higher education and is absent in China. It follows that Hong Kong is losing its academic freedom as it is becoming enmeshed within China (Jackson, 2021b). However, there are some limitations to this argument.

Free versus 'disruptive' speech

First, academic freedom in Western societies is never absolute (Griffin, 2013; Jackson, 2021b; 2022). As stated by V-Dem in relation to campus integrity, speech or acts that are understood to be repressive or inspiring harm are seen to counter academic freedom. In the contemporary academic context, when racist or sexist comments are made, the issue arises as to whether or not the principle of academic freedom should apply (Williams, 2016; Ben-Porath, 2017). The case hinges on how harmful the speech is held to be, by powerful social actors, in relation to a host of other institutional and legal considerations (Jackson, 2021b). Such decisions often go beyond assessments of the content of speech, to also consider the context and quality of speech and who is speaking (Zerilli, 2014; Ben-Porath, 2017). This is true in the case of academic speech of scholars as well as students (see discussions in Chapter 5 by Evan Smith; also, Applebaum, 2003; Jackson, 2008; 2021a).

Academic freedom is clearly constrained in China. Professors have been fired, and their books have been banned, for writing critical essays; they have been arrested and detained for advocacy work (Ruth and Yu, 2019). Where academics' writings are held by State authorities as damaging to society and/ or the State (for example, Zha, 2010), this has ripple down effects on various practices as Crowley (2019) notes:

> In China, aspects such as obtaining research grants require the applicant to consider carefully the ramification of their research on wider national discussions… Naturally, any work that criticises the Chinese state is likely to be rejected and could even be subject to sanctions. Thus, while in western countries there is a degree of freedom to which scholars can be critical of the government, it is worth noting that this tends to be an area that is off-limits within China, particularly if it is critical…
>
> *(Crowley, 2010, webpage)*

However, in the United States, academics have also been sacked for criticising the practices of their institutions, with their speech in such cases framed not as a matter of academic freedom, but instead as unhelpful and harmful complaints about their duties (Squires, 2015). In one case, Salaita (2019) was offered a job at the University of Illinois at Urbana-Champaign and then had the offer rescinded, after he wrote a series of political Twitter posts about Israel. The tone of the tweets was a particular concern; Salaita's standing as a lead researcher of Palestine spurred the university to employ him in the first place. Notably, it was fellow academics who formally made the decision here. The American Association of University Professors and the Illinois state court held the university to be in violation of Salaita's academic free speech.

In Hong Kong, whether there is academic freedom is a controversial issue. Recently, Associate Professor Benny Tai claimed his dismissal from the

University of Hong Kong, due to his leadership in the Umbrella Movement/ Occupy Central with Peace and Love in 2014, marked the death of academic freedom in Hong Kong (Power *et al*, 2020). However, others do not feel their free speech as scholars is curtailed. So-called taboo issues, such as Hong Kong's national status and identity, are discussed in seminars across universities. In this context, Tang (2020) writes:

> The national security law specifically states that Hong Kong people's freedom of speech will be protected... Hong Kong has more academic freedom than the United States, where I spent most of my academic career. In the US, I learned very quickly that professors should avoid advocating their political views because their authority in a classroom can put pressure on students who disagree with them. Academic research is mostly free, but not if your research is to justify [to historically explain] the rise of Nazi Germany...
>
> *(Tang, 2020)*

> Fear is a powerful and effective tool to change people's attitude and behaviour. ...[It] can be detrimental to academic freedom [in] that it will also make people in the Hong Kong scholarly community self-censor what they teach and how they pick their research topics...
>
> *(Tang, 2020)*

My own experience reflects that my academic freedom depends not only on what I say, but also on how I say it. In China, my work on protests in Hong Kong (Jackson, 2019c) has been met with enthusiasm. So long as the point is not (perceived to be) political criticism, and is politely put forward, such speech is welcomed. In contrast, I faced more challenges defending my doctoral dissertation in the US (coincidentally earned at the University of Illinois). In that context, I sometimes had to 'tone down' my rhetoric to appease committee members, who would take offence, for example, if I compared Islamophobia to racism. I was also once admonished in an examination for sounding 'nonchalant.' I was surprised by this (formally given) criticism; I did not mean to be (or feel) nonchalant. Furthermore, I doubt that male students would be likely to be judged for this 'sin.' In any case, these experiences taught me, as many others, that I needed to play the right language games to flourish in academia.

Today, critical race theory (CRT) in the United States and Great Britain has come under attack by political actors and politically conservative scholars as disruptive. In this context, scholars who have been trained in and study CRT must think twice about what they say in classrooms and meetings, lest their work be misconstrued by others for political purposes (Sawchuk, 2021). In contrast, discussing protests and academic freedom in Hong Kong is treated as free speech, rather than a source of disruption.

Capabilities and supporting structures

Neem (2019) writes that the most serious issue facing academic freedom in the United States is the decline of tenure and shared governance, and whether and how academics are given a say in relation to their universities and the scholarship they support. As tenure guarantees and securities are decreasing and being dismantled across a range of societies, the ability for academics to speak out has weakened, even for those with tenure. Tenure decisions are not only made in relation to one's performance, but the establishment of posts and the topics and subjects which scholars are to focus on are also subject to political debates and influences among university (academic) actors. As Salaita (2019) points out, studies of Israel are 'the subject of endowed professorships across the globe,' while few jobs exist anywhere to promote scholarship about Palestine, Pakistan, or Nigeria, for example. The apparent importance of different fields according to key (academic) experts within institutions thus has a strong influence on who gets hired and promoted and under what terms, in relation to an institution's strategic plan.

Additionally, around the world, research capabilities – that is, the ability to focus on one's areas of expertise and interest – are increasingly tied to grant funding, as highlighted, for example, in the case of Mexico as discussed by Wietse de Vries in Chapter 6. In different countries, *who* sets the parameters may be different. But commonly the processes of grant application and funding are influenced and shaped by processes of peer review. This means that an academic's ability to undertake research in their preferred area is impacted by the decisions of colleagues within the relevant field. As Crowley (2019) notes:

> [Across] countries, the argument concerning the ability of authors to publish could be linked to the level of financial support that they receive. In China, unlike the UK, very few sources in the private sector are available... In this respect, funds for researchers will come from...government. Since much of these funds are based on the level of perceived interest and impact... In many respects, it may lead to a decision between writing about what interests you (and maybe not get any money) or force you to target your research towards the topics that are of interest to the education ministry... When this situation is expressed in this blunt fashion, it doesn't appear to be wholly different from many other academic systems in the west!
>
> *(Crowley, 2019)*

In this context, speaking personally, I have been far more able to conduct funded research in my areas of expertise in Hong Kong (and China) than in the United States. In Hong Kong, I can apply for substantial public funding to do work in my area of expertise. Meanwhile, most of my peers in Western societies (particularly the United States and the United Kingdom) are strongly encouraged to change their topics and methods to increase their likelihood of winning grants due to (mostly private) providers' interests – and then, of course, to work on these projects, rather than engaging in their speciality. The latest grant I received was to study education for and about ethnic minorities in China. There are few more political and sensitive subjects in this region (Jackson, 2022).

Freedom and interpersonal recognition

In Western contexts, difficulties around recognition in academia are particularly faced by women and people of colour. These challenges reveal tensions found within the broader society, which are reflected in personal difficulties diverse scholars face within higher education. Salaita (2010) writes of his experience with Illinois, there is a sense that scholars with minority identities and perspectives should 'know their place' in the academy (see also Ahmed, 2012).

Such dynamics also exist in Hong Kong and China. In my experience, being cast as foreign and as an ethnic minority (as white) has been both a blessing and a curse. Foreigners and ethnic minorities in China and Hong Kong can experience at once a sense of freedom from the fear that some local academics experience related to political persecution, alongside a sense of invalidation, as they are continually cast as 'others' without genuine knowledge (see Chow, 2002). I feel freer in some contexts than local colleagues to express academic views on controversial issues. In this regard, I have had some colleagues thank me for undertaking critical work as they perceive that I am in a better position to articulate issues more confidently, based on my international identity. At the same time, I am sometimes dismissed in Hong Kong and China as a 'know-nothing' foreigner, in grant proposals and peer reviews.

Fear about academic free speech, however, is a major challenge in Hong Kong. And it intermingles with a different issue relating to academic bullying. The kind of bullying and shunning experienced by Black academics in Western contexts can also happen to those who write on political topics regarded as 'too edgy' in Hong Kong. To take a specific example: during and after the Umbrella Movement, I edited a special journal issue on the movement. Authors involved with the special issue came mostly from Hong Kong, and many were nervous about contributing. One wrote an article with the condition that they could publish it under a pseudonym, concerned that their involvement could harm their reputation or result in future professional penalties (Jackson and O'Leary, 2019). I also began to receive strange comments from peers. Some said they believed the point of the special issue was to make political claims; another group described my research as a matter of me giving biased opinions, lacking an appropriate methodology in their eyes.

This experience left me feeling falsely typecast, as though colleagues were putting words in my mouth and treating me in ways not related to my own sense of self (Jackson, 2021b). There was no sense in defending myself, as their minds had been made up – and their views about me seemed unconnected with anything I had previously expressed. It appeared that I had two choices, both undesirable: to stop doing that kind of research or be dismissed and mildly harassed as a radical. I have since become warier about 'causing trouble,' for example by discussing sexual harassment and discriminatory international student treatment on campus, which I also did at HKU (Jackson, 2019a; 2019d; Jackson and Muñoz-García, 2019). As Ahmed (2012) writes, such work is not always treated with appreciation by universities, despite lip service to diversity. Thus, exercising the capacity to write, share, and critique can come with hidden costs. Academic freedom is not a binary in real life. Instead, it depends on who you are and where, and how you are recognised in dynamic political environments.

Conclusion

In this chapter, I have argued for a reconsideration of what is essential to academic freedom, to go beyond a binary view wherein one simply has or does not have it. While a binary view may be useful to measure and compare societies at a large scale, it may also reflect cultural biases while obscuring some commonalities that can also be found around the world. From a liberal view, academics have academic freedom (or perhaps, societies have academic freedom) if scholars are not interfered with by non-academic actors. Yet from a capabilities view, academics must actualise certain capacities to exercise academic freedom. And for many, despite there being no obvious, overt hindrances to their freedom, they nonetheless are not free to develop and share their scholarly views. In any case, access to such freedom is not equal.

From a relational view, academic experiences and abilities are significantly shaped by peers, and this does not always happen in a fair or reasonable way. The history of academia shows that exclusion of diverse perspectives has often been a norm; today, minority scholars continue to face challenges across societies related to discussing minority views or conducting research on controversial topics. Thus, even if one is not formally deprived of academic freedom, many do not have the means to exercise any so-called rights.

I have not intended here to give a defence of the situation of Hong Kong or China when it comes to academic freedom. Instead, I have used examples from these contexts to complicate mainstream assessments about global levels of academic freedom and highlight complexity that is treated in mainstream assessments as 'white noise' or minor details. Through providing a complicated picture, I have aimed to indicate how academic freedom can be a fragile capability of scholars across borders, regardless of who is a winner or loser in global rankings.

References

Ahmed, S. (2012). *On Being Included: Racism and Diversity in Institutional Life.* Durham: Duke University Press.

Alford, C. F. (2005). *Rethinking Freedom: Why Freedom Has Lost Its Meaning and What Can Be Done to Save It.* London: Palgrave Macmillan.

Applebaum, B. (2003). Social justice, democratic education and the silencing of words that wound. *Journal of Moral Education, 32*(2), 151–62. https://doi.org/10.1080/0305724032000072924

Ben-Porath, S. (2017). *Free Speech on Campus.* Philadelphia: University of Pennsylvania Press.

Berlin, I. (1969). *Four Essays on Liberty.* London: Oxford University Press.

Cain, T. R. (2012). *Establishing Academic Freedom: Politics, Principles, and the Development of Core Values.* New York: Palgrave Macmillan.

Chow, R. (2002). *The Protestant Ethnic and the Spirit of Capitalism.* New York: Columbia University Press.

Crowley, M. (2019). *The debate about academic freedom in China.* Jobs.ac.uk. https://www.jobs.ac.uk/careers-advice/working-in-higher-education/3428/the-debate-about-academic-freedom-in-china

De Beauvoir, S. (1949/1984). *The Second Sex* (H. M. Pashley, Trans.). Harmondsworth: Penguin.

Fanon, F. (1967). *Black Skin, White Masks.* New York: Grove Press.

Griffin, O. R. (2013). Academic freedom and professorial speech in the post-Garcetti world. *Seattle University Law Review, 37*(1), 1–54.

Heidegger, M. (1962). *Being and Time* (J. Macquarrie and E. Robinson, Trans.). Oxford: Blackwell.

Jackson, L. (2007). The individualist? The autonomy of reason in Kant's philosophy and educational views. *Studies in Philosophy and Education, 26*(4), 335–44.

Jackson, L. (2008). Silence, words that wound and sexual identity: a conversation with Applebaum. *Journal of Moral Education, 37*(2), 225–38. https://doi.org/10.1080/03057240801996891

Jackson, L. (2017). Leaning out of higher education: a structural, postcolonial perspective. *Policy Futures in Education, 15*(3), 295–308.

Jackson, L. (2018a). Becoming classy: in search of class theory in philosophy of education. *Philosophy of Education, 2018*(1), 315–28.

Jackson, L. (2018b). Reconsidering vulnerability in higher education. *Tertiary Education and Management, 24*(3), 232–41.

Jackson, L. (2019a). The smiling philosopher: emotional labor, gender, and harassment in conference spaces. *Educational Philosophy and Theory, 51*(7), 684–92.

Jackson, L. (2019c). *Questioning Allegiance: Resituating Civic Education.* London: Routledge.

Jackson, L. (2019d). University of Hong Kong, the world's most international tertiary institution, can still do more to support diversity. *South China Morning Post*, March 28.

Jackson, L. (2021a). Academic freedom of students. *Educational Philosophy and Theory, 53*(11), 1108–15.

Jackson, L. (2021b). Free speech, false polarization, and the paradox of tolerance. *Philosophy of Education, 77*(3), 139.

Jackson, L. (2022). Academic freedom as experience, relation, and capability: a view from Hong Kong. In M. Olssen, R. Watermeyer, and R. Raaper (eds), *Handbook on Academic Freedom* (pp. 226–42). Cheltenham: Edward Elgar.

Jackson, L., and Muñoz-García, A. L. (2019). Reaction is not enough: decreasing gendered harassment in academic contexts in Chile, Hong Kong, and the United States. *Educational Theory, 69*(1), 17–34.

Jackson, L., and O'Leary, T. (2019). Education and the Hong Kong umbrella movement. *Educational Philosophy and Theory, 51*(2), 157–62.

Jackson, L., Peters, M. A., Benade, L., Devine, N., Arndt, S., Forster, D., and Ozoliņš, J. (2018). Is peer review in academic publishing still working? *Open Review of Educational Research, 5*(1), 95–112. https://doi.org/10.1080/23265507.2018.1479139

Kant, I. (1993). *Critique of Pure Reason* (J. M. D. Meiklejohn, Trans.). London: Everyman.

Kant, I. (1898). *Kant's Critique of Practical Reason and Other Works on the Theory of Ethics* (T. K. Abbott, Trans.) (5th ed., Rev.). London: Longmans, Green, and Co.

Kant, I. (1970a). An answer to the question: "What is enlightenment?" In: H. S. Reiss (ed), *Kant: Political Writings* (H. B. Nisbet, Trans., 54–60). Cambridge: Cambridge University Press.

Kant, I. (1970b). *The contest of the faculties.* In H. S. Reiss (ed), *Kant: Political Writings.* (H. B. Nisbet, Trans., 176–90). Cambridge: Cambridge University Press. (Original work published 1798)

Kinzelbach, K., Saliba, I., Spannagel, J., and Quinn, R. (2021). *Free Universities: Putting the Academic Freedom Index into Action.* Gotheburg: Global Public Policy Institute.

Kleinig, J. (1982). Academic freedom. *Educational Philosophy and Theory, 14*(1), 15–25.

Kuhn, T. (1962). *The Structure of Scientific Revolutions.* Chicago: University of Chicago Press.

Lam, O. (2021, March 30). How Hong Kong lost its academic freedom in 2020. *Global Voices.* https://globalvoices.org/2021/03/30/how-hong-kong-lost-its-academic-freedom-in-2020/

Lester, J. (1988). Academic freedom and the black intellectual. *The Black Scholar, 19*(6), 16–26.

Martin, L. L., Mandela Gray, B., and Finley, S. C. (2019). Endangered and vulnerable: the black professoriate, bullying, and the limits of academic freedom. *AAUP Journal of Academic Freedom, 10*, 1–21.

McLaughlin, T. (2021). How academic freedom ends. *The Atlantic*, June 6.

Neem, J. (2019). The subtle erosion of academic freedom. *Inside Higher Education.* April 16.

Nussbaum, M. C. (2000). *Women and Human Development: A Capabilities Approach.* Cambridge: Cambridge University Press.

Power, J., Lam, J., and Cheung, E. (2020). National security law: for Hong Kong scholars, a fear of the unknown. *South China Morning Post*, August 8.

Raz, J. (1986). *The Morality of Freedom.* London: Clarendon.

Roberts, P. (2016). *Happiness, Hope, and Despair: Rethinking the Role of Education.* New York: Peter Lang.

Robeyns, I. (2006). Three models of education: rights, capabilities, and human capital. *Theory and Research in Education, 4*(1), 69–83.

Ruth, J., and Yu, X. (2019). Academic freedom and China. *American Association of University Professors*, Fall.

Salaita, S. (2019). The inhumanity of academic freedom: a transcript of the 2019 TB Davie Memorial Lecture at the University of Cape Town, delivered August 7, 2019. *SteveSalaita.com*, August 7.

Sawchuk, S. (2021). What is critical race theory, and why is it under attack? *Education Week*, May 18.

Scholars at Risk (SAR) (2019). *Obstacles to Excellence: Academic Freedom and China's Quest for World-Class Universities*. New York: Scholars at Risk.

Sen, A. (1992). *Inequality Reexamined*. Cambridge: Harvard University Press.

Spannagel, J., Kinzelbach, K., and Saliba, I. (2020). *The Academic Freedom Index and Other New Indicators Relating to Academic Space: An Introduction*. Gotheburg: V-Dem Institute.

Squires, A. (2015). Garcetti and Salaita: revisiting academic freedom. *American Association of University Professors Journal of Academic Freedom*, 6, 1–18.

Tang, W. (2020). National security law: Hong Kong's academic freedom is safe, but the fear of losing it is harmful. *South China Morning Post*, August 19. https://www.scmp.com/comment/opinion/article/3097823/national-security-law-hong-kongs-academic-freedom-perfectly-safe

Taylor, C. (1992). *Multiculturalism and the Politics of Recognition*. Princeton: Princeton University Press.

Williams, J. (2016). *Academic Freedom in an Age of Conformity*. London: Palgrave Macmillan.

Zerilli, L. M. G. (2014). Against civility: A feminist perspective. In A. Sarat (ed), *Civility, Legality, and Justice in America* (pp. 107–31). Cambridge: Cambridge University Press.

Zha, Q. (2010). Academic freedom and public intellectuals in China. *International Higher Education*, (58), 16–9. https://doi.org/10.6017/ihe.2010.58.8469

8

SELECTIVE ACADEMIC FREEDOM

The case of Hungary[1]

Rebeka Bakos and Andrea Pető

Introduction

'I am glad to see you, I wish you good luck!' – these were the words of Viktor Orbán, the Hungarian Prime Minister, greeting a woman fleeing Ukraine with her family in early March 2022 and widely reported by both pro-government and independent news sources (for example, hvg.hu, 2022; Mandiner, 2022). His supportive stance came as something of a surprise to those familiar with the Orbán Government's strongly anti-refugee rhetoric and actions. In 2015, the Hungarian Government introduced a set of policies against immigrants trying to enter the European Union (EU) through Hungarian borders, and since then the Government has, in effect, dismantled the asylum system. Still, in addition to the Prime Minister, the Minister of Foreign Affairs, Péter Szijjártó, and the recently inaugurated President of Hungary, Katalin Novák, have also made several visits to the Hungarian-Ukrainian border to welcome refugees fleeing the Russian invasion of Ukraine[2] and to assure them of Hungary's support during the war (Nagy, 2016; Novák, 2022; Szabó, 2022). Their sudden change of attitude raises questions. Were these welcoming gestures only part of the pre-election campaign of the ruling political party FIDESZ (Hungarian Civic Alliance) or did they indicate a shift in the fourth time re-elected Orbán Government's refugee politics? Is this hospitality reserved only for Ukrainian refugees, or will it affect the way Hungary approaches other asylum seekers? Or, to put it differently, what kinds of refugees are welcome in Hungary?

The aim of the *Selective Academic Freedom* project is to map from a critical and comparative perspective how scholars in exile are currently being integrated into the academic research infrastructure in the EU in general and in Hungary, Romania, and the United Kingdom in particular. This chapter

DOI: 10.4324/9781003363262-11

examines what treatment refugee scholars receive in Hungary, a country led by a government widely criticised for its restrictive approach towards academic freedom (hvg.hu 2018; Central European University 2022). To investigate these issues, all relevant policies and regulations of the Hungarian refugee system were surveyed, and in-depth interviews were conducted with experts, whose consent was recorded together with the interview. We also explored the extent to which the policies were functional in practice: that is, whether they serve the needs of academics at risk wanting to enter Hungary and whether the system is ready to accommodate individuals' different circumstances. The chapter also offers a short overview of the current state of the Hungarian academic and higher education system and examines in what way it supports the integration of academics at risk into the Hungarian academy. It concentrates on the period between 2015, when the number of refugees crossing Hungary's borders reached its peak (Kallius *et al*, 2016), and August 2022, by which date more than one million people fleeing from the war in Ukraine had crossed the Hungarian-Ukrainian border (UNHCR, n.d.). As will be apparent from our chapter, the Hungarian Government's response to these two events could hardly be more different.

Conceptual and methodological considerations

In the CIVICA research project, an 'academic at risk' was defined as a third-country citizen who was active as a junior or senior researcher and/or scholar in their country of origin, which they eventually had to flee due to security threats. To map the situation of academics at risk in Hungary, we studied the relevant Hungarian and EU legal frameworks, reviewed the literature, and attempted to collect all accessible data about academics at risk who had entered Hungary in the previous seven years. The use of the word 'attempted' is deliberate here, as we encountered a number of obstacles during data collection: several public institutions and universities failed to provide the data we requested or simply did not respond to our queries. This might be due to a lack of data or possibly a climate of distrust, exacerbated by the fact that the researchers came from the Central European University (CEU), which had been forced into exile (Pásztor, 2020). The semi-structured interviews conducted with key position holders represented another source of information, although fewer interviews were made than planned, as the representatives of some Hungarian state institutions specialising in refugee issues declined to contribute. The fact that illiberal states strictly control the apparatus, and its freedom of expression, poses methodological and ethical questions to researchers.

The role of non-governmental organisations (NGOs) working on refugee matters in Hungary cannot be overestimated. Although they have been exposed to increasing governmental pressure and scrutiny during the past decade, the NGOs have gradually taken over many functions that the government had previously undertaken, such as refugee services.[3] Thanks to Vivien Vadasi, a legal adviser working for the largest Hungarian refugee organisation 'Menedék'[4] (Hungarian for 'refuge'), we gained access to invaluable insider knowledge about policy implementation and refugee services 'on the ground.' Another important contribution came from the Director of the Institute of Political and International Studies,[5] Balázs Majtényi, professor of the Department of Human Rights and Politics of the Eötvös Loránd University, Budapest, who in his interview willingly engaged with the details of our research questions. Reflecting on the recent science policies of the Hungarian Government, Majtényi highlighted the fact that Hungarian scholars have already, and may again in the future, become academics at risk themselves:

> Until recently, it has never occurred to me that Hungarian researchers one day may also fit into such a category as academics at risk. [...] We might also have to save those who are already here, because [...] the system tightens.
> *(Majtényi, 2022)*

The following short overview of the evolution of the current political situation in Hungary, and the specific position of Hungarian higher education within it, aims to contribute to a deeper understanding of what is at stake in this statement. It explores whether indeed there is evidence to support Professor Majtényi's assertions in relation to the present situation for academics at risk in Hungary.

Hungary's political trajectory

As soon as Viktor Orbán came to power in 2010, the Government began transforming state institutions, marking 2010 as a turning point in post-1989 Hungarian politics (Juhász *et al*, 2015, 15). The Government first reduced the authority of the Constitutional Court and then changed the laws regulating judges' appointment (16). Further contributing to the strengthening of FIDESZ's power was the appointment of Péter Polt, a long time FIDESZ party member, as the General Prosecutor of Hungary in 2010 (17). Although in principle the President of the Republic has a 'check and balance' role in the system, during the past decade each President of the Republic was a FIDESZ-loyal politician who signed any bill submitted by a FIDESZ loyalist (Sarkadi, 2022). Weronika Grzebalska and Andrea Pető termed the governmental structure Orbán introduced an *illiberal polypore state*, because it acts as 'a parasitic organism that feeds on its host's vital resources while also contributing to its decay, producing only a fully dependent state structure in return' (Grzebalska and Pető, 2021, 463). According to them, the polypore state is built through the gradual creation of more and more polypore institutions, which rely on previous institutions' 'resources and networks, but evolve into a parallel system surrendered to the interests of the government. Thus, the Hungarian polypore state replaced many state institutions with an alternative, government-founded institution, which is subservient to the ruling party' (461–2).

Furthermore, as the Hungarian illiberal polypore state's evolution also entailed the tailoring of the election system to the ruling party's needs, a 'clientele system' was built through which FIDESZ maintained a strong grip on the Hungarian economy. Meanwhile, 'western values' – associated with the EU, liberal values, and socially progressive perspectives, for example on gender matters – have been argued by some critics to be inextricably linked to views on refugees. Moreover, as so often the 'other' – in this case refugees – have been depicted as the source of all contemporary social problems (Juhász *et al*, 2015).

Hungarian refugee politics

In 2015, the Hungarian governmental discourse rapidly dropped the term 'refugee' (menekült) and introduced the word 'migrant' (migráns) to describe those arriving through the southern borders of the country. While the word 'refugee' connotes someone seeking safety, 'migrant' suggests the voluntary transition from one country to another, that is, the switch of words entails a switch of perception. With the support of media, much of which took a pro-government stance, the term swiftly became part of mainstream colloquial language reflecting an image of the 'migrant' who arrives in Hungary not in search of shelter, but to 'take away' the prosperity of Hungarians (Bíró-Nagy, 2022). The Hungarian government was thus, we suggest, able to introduce its anti-immigrant measures and policies with broader societal support.

The implementation of stricter refugee policies since 2010 was integrally associated with what many perceived as an illiberal political framework: however, after 2015, when 177,000 people, primarily from Afghanistan and Syria, asked for refugee status in Hungary within months, the refugee question became the focus of government campaigns (Nagy, 2016). To stop the influx of immigrants, the Hungarian government decided to build a four-metre high razor wire fence, officially termed a 'temporary security border closure' on the southern border of the country.[6] The 2017 Hungarian asylum law introduced further measures: from this time on, asylum seekers were detained in makeshift transit zones set up at the borders for the entire asylum-requesting procedure.[7] In 2020, the Court of Justice of the European Union ruled the detention of refugees in Hungary to be unlawful (Court of Justice of the European Union, 2020b).

In her interview, the legal adviser of 'Menedék,' Vivien Vadasi, states that it has been almost impossible to enter Hungary as a refugee since 2020, when the illegal detention zones were shut down according to the EU's decision:

The European institutions considered that a new common European asylum system would be necessary after 2015, [...] but no new system was created. Hungary went against EU standards, and after the EU court's decision it has become practically impossible for someone to apply for asylum in Hungary. Anyone found without papers in the country is forced by the police to cross the southern border [that is, leave to Serbia] without being able to apply for asylum in Hungary. [...] Since 2018, there has been no EU money used in Hungary for supporting the integration of refugees.

(Vadasi, 2022)

The Hungarian Government's subsequent approach to Ukrainian war refugees has been in stark contrast. On 24 February 2022, when Russia began the invasion of Ukraine, the Hungarian Government immediately published Decree 56/2022 (II.24) in the Official Gazette of Hungary (Magyar Közlöny), replaced after 4 March 2022, when the EU invoked Temporary Protection based on the EU Council's 2022/382 Implementing Decision (Menedék - Hungarian Association for Migrants, 2022).[8] This summarises the minimum standards for providing temporary protection in the event of a mass influx of displaced persons and on measures ensuring a fairer balance across Member States in taking responsibility for refugees and their subsequent support (Council of the European Union, 2001). On 7 March 2022, the Hungarian government implemented the EU Council's decision about providing temporary protection to those fleeing the war in Ukraine: that is, it replaced the previous Hungarian refugee regulation from 24 February, but only for Ukrainian citizens and Ukrainian residents, who are entitled to protection for up to one year under the rules of EU Temporary Protection – or as long as the grounds for temporary protection (war) continue to apply.[9] Beneficiaries of the temporary protection in Hungary have the right to a residence permit, working without a work permit, healthcare, Hungarian language lessons, a monthly subsistence allowance of HUF 28,500 (€70), and financial support in case they permanently leave Hungary (Hungarian Government, 2022c). Third-country citizens who lawfully resided in Ukraine at the breakout of the war may apply for a Hungarian residence permit (National Directorate-General for Aliens Policing, 2022). Importantly, third-country citizens who lawfully resided in Ukraine can only receive a Hungarian residence permit if they arrive in the country with a clearly stated aim, for example, to study or work, and they have sufficient proof of the feasibility of their plan – that is, an acceptance letter from a university or a job contract.[10]

In short, while in recent years the Government has been working to reduce and almost eliminate the support and opportunities offered by the refugee system, since March 2022 it appears to have been positively 'discriminating' in favour of Ukrainian citizens, according to the refugee organisation's legal adviser. In her words,

[I]t's great what they are doing for the refugees from Ukraine, but there are others here as well. [...] It can be seen that both the EU and Hungary have suddenly changed their attitude. The Hungarian government started talking about refugees. This word has not been used by officials since 2015.

(Vadasi, 2022)

Policy in relation to refugee academics

As noted above, the implication of these developments suggests that Hungary implements what is in effect a double standard towards refugees of different origins. As the CEU's expulsion from Hungary shows, the country also implements a double standard towards universities of different origins.

Over the past 12 years, the Hungarian government has introduced several policies to limit the scope of academic freedom. As part of the centralisation of science, a number of accredited study programmes and research institutions were shut down. The legitimacy of scientific fields was undermined, and the majority of Hungarian higher education institutions were speedily given greater levels of autonomy – but regarded by some as having been 'privatised' without consultation – as previously existing quality assurance systems were also dismantled.[11] These policies aimed at centralising and monopolising academic authority, so that it could be used for the legitimisation of the State's actions and decisions (Pető, 2021).

As part of this process, the Hungarian government, in 2017, forced the Budapest-based CEU, a university accredited both in the US and in Hungary, to leave the country. To prepare the grounds for the university's 'ousting,' Orbán publicly accused George Soros, the founder of the CEU, of serving foreign interests with the aim of settling migrants on 'Hungarian soil' (Gőbl, 2018). Ultimately, an amendment to the Hungarian Higher Education Act,[12] known in public discourse as 'Lex CEU,'[13] served as the tool to force the university out of Hungary (Pető, 2020, 9–24). After almost two years of uncertainty, the CEU left the country in 2019 (CEU, 2018; Corbett and Gordon, 2018). One year later, the European Court of Justice has ruled that Hungary had broken EU law when it forced the CEU to continue its academic work in another country (Court of Justice, 2020a).

Paradoxically, during the same period, namely in 2018, the Hungarian government signed an agreement with the Chinese Fudan University for its first European university campus to be built in Budapest.[14] Although the plans for the gigantic, $1.8 billion Hungarian public investment at the time of writing (2023) has not been finalised, the Hungarian government has already declared that the signing of the agreement is a 'great success of science diplomacy.'[15]

Legal hurdles: Visa options for academics at risk in Hungary

Although Hungary is part of the Schengen visa system, there is no unified EU policy concerning visas issued for academics: as a result, every country has its own visa routes and regulations. Academics who wish to work in Hungary can apply for three types of visas or 'permits': (a) *Short-term Mobility Certificate of Researchers*, which is valid for a period not exceeding six months; (b) *Long-term Mobility Certificate of Researchers* for a period of between six months and a year; (c) *Residence Permit for the Purpose of Research* valid for between one and two years. Notably, the latter is not available for refugee academics or academics in exile (National Directorate-General for Aliens Policing, n.d.-a). Academics arriving in Hungary can also apply for an EU Blue Card (EU, n.d.) available for highly qualified individuals, including academics, who arrive with a work contract or job offer from an EU employer. The EU Blue Card is a work visa that can be suitable for academics at risk only as long as they have not been granted refugee status and if they do not possess any other type of researcher visa.

To obtain a Short-term Mobility Certificate, an individual must supply a statement from their host institution confirming the activity they will undertake; the researcher's short-term mobility plan, also indicating the planned duration and dates of the mobility; and a copy of a valid residence permit issued for the purpose of research by the first Member State (National Directorate-General for Aliens Policing, n.d.). Furthermore, the applicant must provide a valid address as their place of accommodation during their stay, proof of sufficient means of subsistence and financial resources, and proof of medical insurance coverage. For the Long-Term Mobility Certificate of Researchers, the mandatory prerequisites are the same. In order to obtain a Residence Permit for the Purpose of Research, in addition to the above conditions, the applicant must prove that they have a passport valid until the end of their stay and a valid departure ticket or sufficient funds to return to their country of origin. In Hungary, the price range of the researcher visas is between €60 and €110, which is like Romania, where the costs of researcher visas are between €80 and €120 (Ministry of Foreign Affairs of Romania, n.d.), whereas in the UK the fees range from €305 (£259) to €1675 (£1,423) together with an additional UK health surcharge, which is usually €735 (£624) per year (Government of the United Kingdom, n.d.). These visas were clearly meant for individuals who only plan to stay for a pre-determined period of time: however, they may represent a possibility for academics at risk to 'buy time' and get acquainted with the academic environment in a new, safer setting. Comparing the three visa regimes, we found that the prerequisites for visa application are very similar in Hungary and in Romania, and although in the UK there are more kinds of visas available for researchers, the baseline requirements are close to identical.

It is important to note that obtaining the necessary documentation for a visa application can be challenging if one is in imminent danger, which is why refugees or exiled academics often do not have access to some of the documentary evidence needed. We put the question to the National Directorate-General for Aliens Policing as to whether there is a protocol in place in Hungary for such situations: that is, what will happen to an academic at risk who cannot supply all documents necessary for visa application: however, unfortunately, we did not receive an answer.

Besides missing or incomplete documentation, the research/work contract may cause further problems, as our legal adviser interviewee, Vivien Vadasi, stated:

> During the previous years, the biggest obstacle to obtaining researcher residence permits was the requirement of a preliminary research contract with the future salary and costs clearly stated. Besides that the employing university or institute had to guarantee that they would cover all potential additional costs of the researcher. Such research contracts are offered by universities for short-term projects, but for longer periods not many universities are able to afford it.
>
> *(Vadasi, 2022)*

In order to have a grasp of the number and constitution of researchers applying for the above-mentioned permits in Hungary, in May 2022 we submitted a data request to the official body (the Hungarian National Directorate-General for Aliens Policing) in which we asked for data on research visa applications from 2015 to 30 April 2022. The data provided[16] showed the number of successful and unsuccessful applications, the gender and the country of origin of the applicant, and the year of application. We found it remarkable that from the 988 applications submitted throughout the eight years in focus (from 2015 to 2022), only six aimed to obtain the *Long-term Mobility Certificate of Researchers*, of which just three were approved. According to these numbers, there are far fewer researchers interested in staying in Hungary for longer periods, and of those applying for long-term visas, proportionally fewer are approved to stay than among those who apply for short or mid-term visas.

Although Vadasi expressed her concern in this regard – *'I'm afraid that Hungary is not a very attractive country for researchers around the world'* – the numbers tell a different story. While in 2015 there were only 60 applications for short-term research visas, in 2018–2019 their number exceeded 200. By July 2022, the authorities had accepted 55 applications. In relation to gender, on average one-third of applicants were women. The largest proportion of applicants arrived in Hungary from China and India.

Despite our efforts, it was not possible to obtain detailed information on the number of researchers with refugee status currently residing in Hungary, as neither the state authorities nor the universities appear to possess relevant aggregated data.

Integration: Recognition of degrees and informal networks

After a refugee researcher has successfully obtained a research visa and arrived in Hungary, the recognition of their academic degrees and diplomas is essential for their further academic and career progress in the country or in any other EU member state.

The recognition of diplomas in the EU is regulated by the Lisbon Recognition Convention from 1997, and by national laws, such as the Act on the Recognition of Foreign Diplomas from 2001,[17] and the Act CCIV/2011 on National Higher Education (Hungarian Government, 2011). In Hungary, the recognition of doctoral degrees lies with Hungarian higher education institutions entitled to award doctoral degrees in the relevant discipline (Hungarian Parliament, 2001). As the supervising institution of Hungarian doctoral schools, the Hungarian Doctoral Council has access to cumulative data about the recognition process. The data show that most foreign researchers who apply for the recognition of their diplomas in Hungary work in the field of the natural sciences: a pattern which needs to be understood in the context of the Hungarian labour market (Hungarian Doctoral Council, n.d.).

Hungary actively aims to attract those working in the natural sciences: according to a new regulation implemented on 28 March 2022,[18] third-country Ukrainian refugees who have fled to Hungary can study only in specific academic disciplines, such as economics, engineering, computer science and information technology, natural science, agricultural science, and medical and health science (Stipendium Hungaricum, n.d.).

In our interpretation, this is due to labour market problems in Hungary, where many professions are struggling with a shortage of professionals because of a 'brain drain.' This phenomenon strongly affects many East European countries, including Hungary, where a significant number of qualified, mostly young professionals leave every year for Western Europe because of better living and working conditions (Kovács, 2020). The 'brain drain' in Hungary particularly affects the research and development sector, and the chronically underpaid public education and public health sectors.[19] These facts may explain why Hungary is more receptive towards third-country nationals studying natural sciences.

Academics in Hungary who can also be defined to be 'at risk' are notoriously underpaid; in addition, the State controls the higher education market.[20] There are thus some key problems. Besides the recognition of their degree, it may be also essential for academics at risk when attempting to settle in a new, foreign environment to find professional but also informal circles consisting of people with a similar educational or cultural background.[21] Concerning this question, Vadasi noted:

> Although we have not met any researcher coming from Ukraine yet, generally those who have connections with their diaspora, or have informal connections with university-scientific circles, go after them. [...] We have seen [...] informal lists circulating, not only Hungarian, but also European and American universities have offered help, but it is possible that the fleeing

researchers did not use these lists either, rather they contacted the people they already knew from academic circles.

(Vadasi, 2022)

The list, which was compiled by a Hungarian researcher, is still available online[22] and mainly offers scholarships and opportunities for undergraduate and masters students coming from Ukraine. According to the list, which certainly does not include all the possibilities, the Semmelweis University in Budapest and the Centre for Economic and Regional Studies offered teaching or research positions during the spring for those fleeing the Ukrainian war. Semmelweis University has offered several researcher and lecturer positions, but the call did not specify whether these are short-term or long-term opportunities for scholarships (Semmelweis University, 2022). The Centre for Economic and Regional Studies has offered two fully funded, but short-term, researcher positions to Ukrainian scientists (Centre for Economic and Regional Studies, 2022).

The Director of the Institute of Political and International Studies, Balázs Majtényi, who has considerable experience in international university relations, says Hungarian universities face an entirely new situation now with the arrival of Ukrainian refugees. Comparing the present situation to that of 2015, when the influx of primarily Middle Eastern immigrants reached its peak in Hungary, he stated:

> Obviously, we organized conferences on the refugee crisis even at that time [in 2015], but no student requested to continue their studies with us. Yet, the government established the Christian Refugee Program *[called Hungary Helps]*[23] that is open to students, and each year we have an entrance exam for those many students who apply through this program, still, they do not receive the scholarship, although most of them fall into the refugee category.
>
> *(Majtényi, 2022)*

The interview also revealed that Hungarian universities not only had never dealt with many refugees seeking university positions before, but they did not have a policy on the admission of eventual refugee researchers either. As Majtényi put it:

> The Ukrainian refugees just appeared in Hungary, and they knocked on our door [to show that] that they were here. And no, we [the university] had no applicable procedure or policy. What we have now was born from the fact that the university started receiving these letters from those fleeing the war in Ukraine [...] so I said let's try to give some sort of institutional answer. Since we are a higher educational institution, we don't have research

positions, but we advertised two lecturer positions. [...] We actually operate like a large civil society organization. If there is something socially useful, we try to do it.

(Majtényi, 2022)

Universities seem to be rather left on their own in this process, but as the above example shows, some faculties can use this measure of autonomy for taking independent action in an otherwise strictly controlled higher education system. Besides the Faculty of Social Science of ELTE, the Centre for Social Sciences (TK)[24] also uses its autonomy to provide help for the Ukrainian researchers, as the professor stated:

Although it was domesticated by the NER [National Cooperation Scheme],[25] the Centre for Social Sciences, which works under the aegis of the Hungarian Academy of Science,[26] retained its autonomy, and jobs were assigned to Ukrainian researchers. This only works where there is some level of autonomy.

(Majtényi, 2022)

Although there is no broader institutional framework for accepting and integrating academics at risk in Hungary, after the breakout of the Ukrainian war the Hungarian government created several scholarship opportunities primarily for Ukrainian citizens. Some of these may be also suitable for third-country academics at risk, including junior researchers and even university lecturers. The final section of this chapter will discuss these opportunities.

Opportunities for academics at risk in Hungary

All Hungarian national scholarship programmes for foreign students and lecturers, such as CEEPUS, Stipendium Hungaricum, Bridge for Transcarpathia, etc., are coordinated by the government-founded Tempus Public Foundation,[27] except for the Hungary Helps Program, which is under direct government coordination. From among these, the Stipendium Hungaricum has a subprogram, called Students at Risk, which focuses on students fleeing the war in Ukraine. In the framework of Stipendium Hungaricum – Students at Risk, refugee Ph.D. candidates from Ukraine, regardless of their nationality, receive the same monthly scholarship as their Hungarian counterparts, together with dormitory accommodation or housing allowance, and health insurance. It is certainly to be welcomed that the support is available to every Ukrainian refugee Ph.D. candidate; however, given the limited number of places available in university dormitories and the very high rental prices in University towns, it is questionable whether these newly arriving Ph.D. candidates will be actually able to support themselves from the scholarship offered by the Hungarian state.[28]

The only programme so far that focuses not only on students but also more on senior academics at risk is the 'Bridge for Transcarpathia' (in Hungarian: *Híd Kárpátaljáért*) initiated by the Tempus Public Foundation. The FIDESZ government invested considerable public money in supporting the 150,000 Hungarian nationals living in the Transcarpathian region. The programme 'Bridge for Transcarpathia' supports lecturers who had an active working status in any higher education institution in Ukraine on 24 February 2022.[29] Their programme offers teaching opportunities in the Hungarian higher education system, but their website unfortunately offers no more information, and nor did they respond to our email queries.

Conclusions

Knowing the Orbán Government's recent anti-refugee policies and illiberal restrictive approach towards academic freedom, the fact that Hungary has no protocol for the aid and integration of academics at risk hardly came as a surprise. As our research revealed, neither state-funded refugee services nor the Hungarian higher education and research institutions were prepared to accommodate academics at risk – although we learned that Hungary is an attractive destination for third-country researchers, especially in the natural sciences. Yet when the war broke out in Ukraine, refugee services as well as universities managed to react rather quickly to the newly rising situation by creating some opportunities for scholars with Ukrainian citizenship to flee to Hungary.

The Ukrainian refugee crisis has a potential effect on the Hungarian higher education system. On the one hand, as already mentioned, the crisis could result in an increase in students in natural sciences, which offers indirect economic benefits for Hungary. More importantly, however, institutions of higher education could potentially benefit from making better use of the level of autonomy they have. As our interviewees explained, some faculties used their autonomy to take independent action during the first months of the war, which could result in more advanced procedures for hosting refugee researchers, which could serve as an example for other Hungarian higher education institutions in the future.

Yet based on the events in the period we have described here, we should emphasise that the Hungarian government's general attitude towards refugees did not appear to have changed. Apart from those fleeing from Ukraine, the policy has seemed to remain negative to all other refugees – and academics at risk are no exception. So, perhaps the 'good luck' wishes by PM Orbán are very much needed for academics who want to find refuge in Hungary.

Acknowledgement

We acknowledge the input from expert interviewees, who have kindly given us permission to quote from these discussions. In the text, these quotations are included in *italics*.

Vadasi, V. (2022, May). Interview with Vivien Vadasi, legal adviser of "Menedék" Hungarian refugee organization.

Majtényi, B. (2022, June). Interview with Balázs Majtényi, professor in the Department of Human Rights and Politics, Eötvös Loránd University, Budapest.

Notes

1 The chapter was prepared in the framework of Protecting Academics at Risk: A Survey of European and EU Practice, CIVICA Research Grant 2022. For more information, see Central European University (2022).
2 For more details, see Novák (2022).
3 Related articles include: Szigeti (2017); Josa and Fedas (2018); and Amnesty International (2021).
4 For the official website, see Menedék - Hungarian Association for Migrants (n.d.).
5 For the official website, see ELTE Institute of Political and International Studies (n.d.).
6 For the Hungarian government resolution, see Hungarian Government resolution 1401/2015 (VI.17) 'on certain measures necessitated by the exceptional immigration pressure' (2015).
7 For the 2017 Hungarian asylum law, see Act XX of 2017 'law amendments relating to the tightening of procedures in the border surveillance area' (Hungarian Parliament, 2017a).
8 For the EU Council's Implementing Decision, see Council Implementing Decision (EU) 2022/382 of 4 March 2022.
9 For more information, see Government decree 86/2022 (III.7), implementing the EU Council's Decision (EU) 2022/382 (Hungarian Government, 2022c; Hungarian Government, 2022a, March 15).
10 For detailed information, see National Directorate-General for Aliens Policing (n.d.-a).
11 The Eötvös Loránd University, the University of Theatre and Film Arts, and the Academy of Sciences were affected as well. For detailed information, see lefteast.org (2018) and Human Rights Watch (2020).
12 For the HEA, see Act XXV of 2017 amending the CCIV 2011 HEA (Hungarian Parliament, 2017b).
13 For more details, see Heinrich-Böll-Stiftung (2017).
14 See Act CIX of 2018 on the proclamation of the Agreement between Hungary and the People's Republic of China on Supporting the Higher Education Activities of Fudan University in Hungary (Hungarian Parliament, 2018).
15 For more details, see Hungarian Government (2021).
16 The data included in the text are summaries of data obtained from the Legal Department of the Hungarian National Directorate-General for Aliens' Policing.
17 See Act C of 2001 on the recognition of foreign certificates and degrees (European Commission, 2001).
18 For the regulation, see 1186/2022 (III. 28) Korm. határozat a Stipendium Hungaricum program keretében a "Students at Risk" alprogram bevezetéséről és az ehhez szükséges finanszírozás biztosításáról (Hungarian Government, 2022b).
19 For more information see, szakszervezetek.hu (2021).
20 For more information, see Heinrich-Böll-Stiftung (2021).
21 This statement is based on other interviews we conducted in the framework of the *Selective Academic Freedom* project.
22 For the list, see Academic opportunities for displaced Ukrainians and third-country nationals fleeing Ukraine (2022).

23 Hungary Helps is a government funded Christian refugee support program. The programme offers opportunity for Christian youth suffering from religious discrimination and/or living in humanitarian crisis zones to study in Hungary. Persons with a granted refugee status/temporary protection/ subsidiary or humanitarian protection status cannot apply to the scholarship, so it is not available to those fleeing the war in Ukraine. See https://hungaryhelps.gov.hu/hungary-helps-program-main-page/ Retrieved 25 August 2022.

24 See The Centre for Social Sciences (n.d.).

25 See Office of the National Assembly and Hungarian Government (2010). After Orbán's election victory in 2010, he announced the creation of the NER, a social contract based on the cooperation of a wide range of voters to implement administrative, social, and economic reforms. Hungarian oppositionists use this term to refer to the elite close to FIDESZ, who got rich and came to power under the Orbán governments. According to the oppositionist interpretation, the NER elite consists of the most influential members of FIDESZ and the top circle of influential people associated with Orbán.

26 See Abbott (2019).

27 See Tempus Public Foundation - Tempus Közalapítvány (n.d.).

28 Through the Students at Risk program, refugee Ph.D. candidates will receive a monthly scholarship: €350 for the first two years of their studies, and €455 during the last two years of their Ph.D. program. See Stipendium Hungaricum (n.d.).

29 See Tempus Public Foundation (2022).

References

Abbott, A. (2019). Hungarian Government takes control of research institutes despite outcry. *Nature*. https://doi.org/10.1038/d41586-019-02107-4

Academic opportunities for displaced Ukrainians and third-country nationals fleeing Ukraine [Data set]. (2022, March 3). https://docs.google.com/spreadsheets/d/1ybcrWZVV7YYELBSt6v57d0sxs7pAqj5K/edit?

Amnesty International. (2021). Hungary: LexNGO finally repealed but a new threat is on the horizon [Press release]. https://www.amnesty.org/en/latest/press-%20%20%20release/2021/05/hungary-lexngo-finally-repealed-but-a-new-threat-is-on-the-horizon/

Bíró-Nagy, A. (2022). Orbán's political jackpot: migration and the Hungarian electorate. *Journal of Ethnic and Migration Studies, 48*(2), 405–24. https://doi.org/10.1080/1369183X.2020.1853905

Central European University. (2018, December 3). CEU forced out of Budapest: to launch U.S. degree programs in Vienna in September 2019. https://www.ceu.edu/article/2018-12-03/ceu-forced-out-budapest-launch-us-degree-programs-vienna-september-2019

Central European University. (2022, March 2). Prof. Pető is co-lead of one of six winners of CIVICA's Research Call 2022. https://gender.ceu.edu/article/2022-03-02/prof-peto-co-lead-one-six-winners-civicas-research-call-2022

Centre for Economic and Regional Studies. (2022). In solidarity with Ukraine – offering fully-funded guest researcher positions. https://krtk.hu/en/2022/03/in-solidarity-with-ukraine/

Corbett, A., and Gordon, C. (2018). Academic freedom in Europe: The Central European University affair and the wider lessons. *History of Education Quarterly, 58*(3), 467–74. https://doi.org/10.1017/heq.2018.25

Council Implementing Decision (EU) (2022/382 of 4 March 2022). Official journal of the European Union (2022). https://eur-lex.europa.eu/legal-content/EN/TXT/?uri=celex:32022D0382

Council of the European Union (2001). Council directive 2001/55/EC of 20 July 2001 on minimum standards for giving temporary protection in the event of a mass influx of displaced persons and on measures promoting a balance of efforts between member States in receiving such persons and bearing the consequences thereof. *Official Journal L 212*, 07/08/2001, P. 0012–0023. http://data.europa.eu/eli/dir/2001/55/oj

Court of Justice of the European Union. (2020a). Judgment in Case C-66/18 Commission v Hungary. https://curia.europa.eu/juris/liste.jsf?nat=or&mat=or&pcs=Oor&jur=C%2CT%2CF&num=C-66%252F18&for=&jge=&dates=&language=en&pro=&cit=none%252CC%252CCJ%252CR%252C2008E%252C%252C%252C%252C%252C%252C%252C%252C%252C%252Ctrue%252Cfalse%252Cfalse&oqp=&td=%3BALL&avg=&lgrec=hu&lg=&page=1&cid=

Court of Justice of the European Union. (2020b). Judgment in Case C-808/18 Press and Information Commission v Hungary. https://curia.europa.eu/juris/liste.jsf?nat=or&mat=or&pcs=Oor&jur=C%2CT%2CF&num=C-808%252F18&for=&jge=&dates=&language=en&pro=&cit=none%252CC%252CCJ%252CR%252C2008E%252C%252C%252C%252C%252C%252C%252C%252C%252C%252Ctrue%252Cfalse%252Cfalse&oqp=&td=%3BALL&avg=&lgrec=hu&lg=&page=1&cid=3577520

ELTE Institute of Political and International Studies. (n.d.). Retrieved May 18, 2023, from https://polir.elte.hu

EU Blue Card. (n.d.). Retrieved May 21, 2023, from http://www.bmbah.hu/index.php?option=com_k2&view=item&layout=item&id=2238&Itemid=2463&lang=en

European Commission. (2001). Act C of 2001 on the recognition of foreign certificates and degrees. https://ec.europa.eu/migrant-integration/library-document/act-c-2001-recognition-foreign-certificates-and-degrees-0_en

Gőbl, G. (2018). Democracy is out of order: CEU forced to leave hungary. *Heinrich-Böll-Stiftung.* https://www.boell.de/en/2018/12/05/democracy-out-order-central-european-university-forced-leave-hungary

Government of the United Kingdom. (n.d.). Work in the UK as a researcher or academic leader (Global Talent visa). Retrieved May 19, 2023, from https://www.gov.uk/global-talent-researcher-academic

Government resolution 1401/2015 (VI.17) 'on certain measures necessitated by the exceptional immigration pressure.' Magyar Közlöny (2015, June 17). http://www.kozlonyok.hu/nkonline/MKPDF/hiteles/mk15083.pdf

Grzebalska, W., and Pető, A. (2021). Corrigendum to "The gendered modus operandi of the illiberal transformation in Hungary and Poland" [Women's Studies International Forum, 68(2018), 164–172]. *Women's Studies International Forum, 85*, 102453. https://doi.org/10.1016/j.wsif.2021.102453

Heinrich-Böll-Stiftung. (2017). Feature: Lex CEU - Orbán's attack on academic freedom in Europe. https://www.boell.de/en/feature-lex-ceu-orbans-attack-academic-freedom

Heinrich-Böll-Stiftung. (2021). The shift in governance models for Hungarian universities. https://cz.boell.org/en/2021/06/14/shift-governance-models-hungarian-universities

Human Rights Watch. (2020). Hungary continues attacks on academic freedom. https://www.hrw.org/news/2020/09/03/hungary-continues-attacks-academic-freedom

Hungarian Doctoral Council. (n.d.). Recognised foreign diplomas. Retrieved May 18, 2023, from https://doktori.hu/index.php?menuid=623&lang=EN

Hungarian Government. (2011). 2011. évi CCIV. törvény a nemzeti felsőoktatásról. https://net.jogtar.hu/jogszabaly?docid=a1100204.tv

Hungarian Government. (2021). Stratégiai megállapodást kötött a kormány a Fudan Egyetemmel. https://kormany.hu/hirek/strategiai-megallapodast-kotott-a-kormany-a-fudan-egyetemmel

Hungarian Government. (2022a, March 15). Új rendelet a menedékesek könnyített státuszáról: a menedékes fogalma. https://jogaszvilag.hu/szakma/uj-rendelet-a-menedekesek-konnyitett-statuszarol-a-menedekes-fogalma/?hilite=menedékes± fogalma

Hungarian Government. (2022b). 1186/2022. (III. 28.) Korm. határozat a Stipendium Hungaricum program keretében a „Students at Risk" alprogram bevezetéséről és az ehhez szükséges finanszírozás biztosításáról [Government Decree 1186/2022 (III. 28.) on the introduction of the "Students at Risk" subprogram within the Stipendium Hungaricum program and the necessary financing]. https://net.jogtar. hu/jogszabaly?docid=a22h1186.kor

Hungarian Government. (2022c). Government decree 86/2022 (III.7.), implementing the EU Council's Decision (EU) 2022/382). https://net.jogtar.hu/jogszabaly? docid=a2200086.kor

Hungarian Parliament. (2001). 2001. évi C. törvény a külföldi bizonyítványok és oklevelek elismeréséről. https://net.jogtar.hu/jogszabaly?docid=a0100100.tv

Hungarian Parliament. (2017a). Act XX of 2017 'law amendments relating to the tightening of procedures in the border surveillance area. https://mkogy.jogtar.hu/ jogszabaly?docid=A1700020.TV

Hungarian Parliament. (2017b). Act XXV. of 2017 amending the CCIV. 2011 HEA. https://mkogy.jogtar.hu/jogszabaly?docid=A1700025.TV

Hungarian Parliament. (2018). Act CIX. of 2018 on the proclamation of the Agreement between Hungary and the People's Republic of China on Supporting the Higher Education Activities of Fudan University in Hungary. https://net.jogtar. hu/jogszabaly?docid=A1800109.TV

hvg.hu. (2018). Diktátum jellegű rendelettel tiltják be a gender szakot Magyarországon. https://hvg.hu/itthon20180809_Diktatum_jellegu_rendelettel_tiltjak_be_a_gen-derszakot_Magyarorszagon

hvg.hu. (2022). Orbán a menekülteknek: "Örülök, hogy látom, sok sikert kívánok maguknak". https://hvg.hu/itthon/20220317_orban_viktor_csengersima_ukran_ menekultek

Josa, B., and Fedas, A. (2018, November 5). NGOs in Hungary learn to adapt under pressure. *New Eastern Europe*, Issue 6 2018: 1918 – The year of independence. https://neweasterneurope.eu/2018/11/05/ngos-hungary-learn-adapt-pressure/

Juhász, A., László, R., and Zgut, E. (2015). Egy illiberális vízió eddigi következményei. *Friedrich-Ebert-Stiftung Budapest.* https://library.fes.de/pdf-files/bueros/ budapest/12523.pdf

Kallius, A., Monterescu, D., and Rajaram, P. K. (2016). Immobilizing mobility: border ethnography, illiberal democracy, and the politics of the 'refugee crisis' in Hungary. *American Ethnologist, 43*(1), 25–37. https://doi.org/10.1111/amet.12260

Kovács, I. (2020). A magyar kivándorlók zöme köszöni, de inkább maradna, ahol van. *HVG.HU.* https://hvg.hu/gazdasag/20201023_kivandorlas_demografia_ munkavallalas lefteast.org (2018). Gender studies in Hungary are now being linked to broader struggles: interview with Anikó Gregor. https://lefteast.org/gender-studies-in-hungary/

Mandiner. (2022). Orbán Viktor dokumentumokkal látott el egy menekült családot. Mandiner. https://mandiner.hu/cikk/20220317_orban_viktor_dokumentumokkal_latott_el_egy_menekult_csaladot

Menedék Hungarian Association for Migrants. (n.d.). Retrieved May 18, 2023, from https://menedek.hu/en

Menedék Hungarian Association for Migrants. (2022, February 25). What will happen to people fleeing Ukraine? https://menedek.hu/en/news/what-will-happen-people-fleeing-ukraine-last-update-10052022

Ministry of Foreign Affairs of Romania. (n.d.). Visa processing fees. Retrieved May 19, 2023, from https://www.mae.ro/en/node/2061

Nagy, B. (2016). Hungarian asylum law and policy in 2015–2016: securitization instead of loyal cooperation. *German Law Journal*, *17*(6), 1033–82. https://doi.org/10.1017/s2071832200021581

National Directorate-General for Aliens Policing. (n.d.). A Kutatás Célú Tartózkodási Engedély. Retrieved March 13, 2024, from http://www.bmbah.hu/index.php?option=com_k2&view=item&layout=item&id=2212&Itemid=2436&lang=hu

National Directorate-General for Aliens Policing. (2022). Tájékoztató az Ukrajnából menekülő nem ukránállampolgárok részére és a fegyveres konfliktus kitörésé megelőzően Magyarországra érkezett ukránállampolgárok részére. http://www.oif.gov.hu/index.php?option=com_k2&view=item&layout=item&id=1763&Itemid=2127&lang=hu

Novák, K. (2022, February 22). Magyarország szerepet vállal a humanitárius katasztrófa enyhítésében. Hungarian Government. https://kormany.hu/hirek/szijjarto-peter-magyarorszag-szerepet-vallal-a-humanitarius-katasztrofa-enyhiteseben

Office of the National Assembly and Hungarian Government. (2010). The Programme of National Cooperation. https://www.parlament.hu/irom39/00047/00047_e.pdf

Pásztor, E. (2020). Money Pits and Public Duty: How Orbán's Government Fails to Restore Hungarian Public's Trust. *Heinrich Böll Stiftung*. https://cz.boell.org/en/2020/12/16/money-pits-and-public-duty-how-orbans-government-fails-restore-hungarian-publics-trust

Pető, A. (2020). Academic freedom and gender studies: An alliance forged in fire. *Gender and Sexuality Journal*, *15*, 9–24.

Pető, A. (2021). Current comment: the illiberal academic authority. An oxymoron? *Berichte zur Wissenschaftsgeschichte*, *44*(4), 461–9. https://doi.org/10.1002/bewi.202100013

Radio Free Europe. (2017, June 13). Hungary Passes Controversial Law On Foreign-Funded NGOs. *Radio Free Europe*. https://www.rferl.org/a/hungary-foreign-ngo-law-passed-orban/28546616.html

Sarkadi, Z. (2022). Fül, szív és száj akart lenni, aláíró kéz lett. *Telex.Hu*. https://telex.hu/belfold/2022/08/21/novak-katalin-100-nap-koztarsasagi-elnok

Semmelweis University. (2022). Semmelweis students help refugees at the Ukrainian border. https://semmelweis.hu/english/2023/01/semmelweis-students-help-refugees-at-the-ukrainian-border/

Stipendium Hungaricum. (n.d.). Call for applications: Students at Risk Subprogramme of the Stipendium Hungaricum Scholarship Programme for third-country students fleeing the war in Ukraine 2022. Retrieved August 19, 2022, from https://stipendiumhungaricum.hu/uploads/2020/03/StaR_Call_for_Applications_third_country_citizens.pdf

Szabó, R. Z. (2022). A magyarok 750 millió forintot gyűjtöttek az ukrajnai menekültek megsegítésére. *Magyar Nemzet*. https://magyarnemzet.hu/belfold/2022/03/novak-katalin-a-magyarok-750-millio-forintot-gyujtottek-az-ukrajnai-menekultek-megsegitesere

szakszervezetek.hu. (2021). Katasztrofális munkaerőhiány sújtja az oktatást és az egészségügyet. https://szakszervezetek.hu/hirek/28283-katasztrofalis-munkaerohiany-sujtja-az-oktatast-es-az-egeszsegugyet

Tempus Public Foundation. (2022, March 8). Bridge for Transcarpathia [News release]. https://tka.hu/new/16255/bridge-for-transcarpathia

Tempus Public Foundation - Tempus Közalapítvány. (n.d.). Retrieved May 19, 2023, from https://www.tka.hu/english

The Centre for Social Sciences. (n.d.). Retrieved May 18, 2023, from https://tk.hu/en

UNHCR. (n.d.). Ukraine refugee situation. Retrieved May 19, 2023, from https://data.unhcr.org/en/situations/ukraine

PART IV

Academic Freedom

Contemporary Themes and Concluding Reflections

9

EPISTEMIC SILENCES

The academic 'precariat' and academic freedom

Maria Slowey

Introduction

Academic freedom, as a social construct, is inevitably subject to ongoing debate and reinterpretation conceptually and in practice. Its importance lies in the fact that the right to academic freedom in teaching and research underpins the very definition of what it means to be an academic in a university in western liberal democracies.[1] It is a right which – unlike its wider counterpart, free speech – is not automatic for all citizens, but is one which, as we discussed in Chapter 1, must be earned through lengthy and rigorous assessment processes. The ways in which these processes work change over time and between different countries, but they are broadly associated with educational achievement, scholarship, and research as defined and recognised by peers in relevant disciplines.

> Academic freedom is historically a specific freedom that refers to the collective rights of those engaged in the dangerous pursuit of knowledge production – dangerous because it challenges established authority, whether of the sciences or the state. This is a freedom granted in principle by the state to scholars (usually within educational institutions: schools, colleges, and universities) because their dangerous activity has nonetheless been considered vital to the public good and because it is a self-regulated activity committed to processes of relentless questioning that require disciplined forms of reading and reasoning.
> *(Scott, 2022, 2)*

The most obvious threats to the exercise of academic freedom come from attempts at influence, or even interference, by external vested interests such as those emanating from the State, religious authorities, commercial market

DOI: 10.4324/9781003363262-13

forces, lobbying pressure groups, and students (particularly in their guise as 'consumers'). Furthermore, not only do universities comprise individuals with their own vested interests – disciplinary hierarchies, inequalities of sex, race and social class, and the like – but also, according to Pierre Bourdieu's analysis, the societal and economic power base of academics is relatively weak.

> As authorities, whose position in social space depends principally on the possession of cultural capital, a subordinate form of capital, university professors are situated rather on the side of the subordinate pole in the field of power and are clearly opposed in this respect to the managers of industry and business.
>
> *(Bourdieu, 1988, 36)*

What are the implications for the defence, let alone the fostering, of academic freedom if the power position of academics is relatively weak – in Bourdieu's terms, based on a 'subordinate' form of capital?

Burton Clark, in his classic work, *The Higher Education System* (1983), outlines a model for the organisational analysis of higher education institutions and systems based on the concepts of knowledge, beliefs, and authority, involving a dynamic interaction in the exercise of power between three forces: the State, the market, and the 'academic oligarchy.' The latter term implies a powerful elite group, which, *inter alia*, work to protect their own interests. Put this way, the term has a rather negative ring to it, implying a high degree of self-interest.

However, individuals across the academic community are evidently *not* equal. In addition, for example, to inequalities based on sex, social class, and race, obvious hierarchical distinctions exist between those at early career stages and senior professors. Decades of expansion in higher education systems has partly been achieved by the establishment of new types of higher education institutions or the redesignation of existing institutions (for example, the polytechnics in the UK). Additionally, and most importantly from the perspective of this chapter, much of this expansion has been achieved by a significant – disproportionate – growth in the number of academic staff who are non-permanent (non-tenured) on part-time, temporary, or contingent contracts. Evidently not part of any 'academic oligarchy,' to what extent do core university values and practices associated with the right to academic freedom apply to them? If their status is marginal, constrained to teaching curricula and/or research on projects which are largely predetermined, what are the implications for the individuals involved, and for knowledge creation, if a large part of the 'membership' of the academy is effectively constrained to a form of epistemic silence?

In this chapter, I draw on Swedberg's (2018) approach to the building of an 'ideal type' in which he adds to Weber's (1978) original parameters, an emphasis on the meaning which members of a group share or the meaning into which a new member of a group is socialised. Here, the concept of academic freedom is explored through the views of experts, who bring to the discussion a unique, dual perspective: firstly, as university academics from a range of disciplinary backgrounds, primarily in the social sciences; and secondly, as international authorities and researchers in the field of higher education.

Building on respondents' conceptions of academic freedom, and associated safeguards and threats, the overall purpose is to try to gain a deeper understanding of the implications for the growing proportion of academic staff who are, in Bruneau's terms, part of *le précariat*: a 'sessional, adjunct, disposable teaching force' (2019, 192). Despite such appointments accounting for around half of the teaching hours 'delivered' in higher education in the United States and Canada, members of this *précariat* play almost no part in university governance. Being marginal to the ideal of the community of scholars, they have little or no power – or even influence – over teaching and research, general policy, or collegial discussions on curricular development and the like.

> The connection between governance and the real work of the university has thus become more and more tenuous. It is all too easy to make an attack on a colleague's academic freedom when she is on a nine-month sessional contract, is not a member of the faculty association or union, and has no vote in the affairs of her department and faculty. Under these circumstances, shared governance has proven to be a weak reed.
>
> *(Bruneau, 2019, 192)*

The focus of this chapter is on the condition of this 'weak reed' which brings together two areas of contemporary concern: academic freedom and the changing shape of the academic profession. The discussion draws on original qualitative material obtained from written responses and interviews conducted over Spring 2023 with 16 experts in the field of higher education from 11 countries: 8 from Europe (Denmark, Germany, Italy, Ireland, Slovenia, Sweden, Switzerland, and the United Kingdom); Japan; South Africa; and the United States. Quotations from respondents are distinguished by the country in which they are primarily working. While it is necessary to be cautious about drawing broader conclusions, the wealth of knowledge of these experts suggests the analysis is likely to have resonance beyond its empirical base.

The remainder of the chapter is divided into five parts. It begins with a discussion of the wider context of academic freedom and the implications of recent and current developments in higher education for the changing shape of the academic profession. The following three parts analyse the outcomes of the expert consultation. First, respondents' conceptions of academic freedom are explored. This is followed by discussion of respondents' perceptions of, on the one hand, the safeguards and, on the other, the threats to academic freedom. These provide the context for analysis of their views about temporary and/or part-time staff in relation to the exercise of academic freedom. The final part of the chapter returns to the question of whether academic freedom is a right for *all* members of the academy: or just for some? And, if the latter, what are the implications not only for the academy but also for wider society, if many academics (teachers and/or researchers) are, in practice, excluded from full participation in the opportunities to generate new knowledge and corralled into a liminal space of effective epistemic silence?

Academic freedom and the changing shape of the academic profession

As several chapters in this book show, there is a considerable literature debating the concept of academic freedom at different historical periods and in particular national contexts. The power of the concept becomes most visible when it is placed under extreme threat, as highlighted by the work of bodies such as Scholars at Risk (SAR) and Chapter 8 in this book in relation to case of Hungary (Rebeka Bakos and Andrea Pető).

However, even in Western liberal democracies, the combined impact of three contemporary trends poses a threat: the financial impact of neo-liberal policies and declining public investment; the effect of 'policy steering'; and the rise of populism and neo-nationalism. A recent review of developments in Europe identifies several factors as underlying the *de facto* erosion of academic freedom across European Union member states, including the growing socio-economic importance of knowledge and its link to innovation, with an emphasis on features such as the governance, funding, and organisation of higher education and research which, as a result, largely neglects basic values and principles, including academic freedom (Maassen *et al*, 2023). An additional factor, which bridges the interface between academic freedom and free speech, is the prominence given in much of the media to the rise of so-called 'cancel culture' – as discussed by Evan Smith (Chapter 5).

Furthermore, as noted above, beyond these generic constraints, the blunt fact remains that academics are *not* all equal. While this can be to some extent associated with the prevailing hierarchy of disciplines – as suggested by Bourdieu – perhaps even more importantly, as is argued in this chapter, it is to do with structural changes and diversification in the positions which academics hold in universities. Because of the varied nature of who is included in categories such as part-time, temporary, and contingent faculty, it is not easy to obtain comparative statistics. However, Figure 9.1 reports on the results of a comprehensive survey administered to chief academic officers of universities in the USA (AAUP, 2022). This shows the percentage of different types of universities which replaced tenure roles with contingent appointments over a five-year period. Overall, more than half (53.5%) had replaced permanent positions with contingent appointments over the previous five years. The proportion was higher for public universities (c. 62%) than private (c. 49%), and for medium-sized institutions (61%) than either larger (c. 53%) or smaller (c. 49%) institutions. The survey was likely to be an underestimate as it did not address, for example,

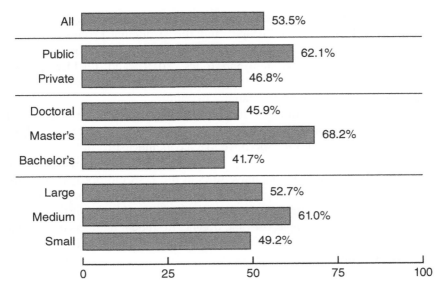

FIGURE 9.1 American universities that replaced tenure lines with contingent appointments (previous five years). Adapted from AAUP (2022).

how many fixed-term positions had been added or how many tenure lines had been replaced, but rather only of whether *any* tenure line had been replaced at the institution (AAUP, 2022, 7).

What are the implications for the future of the hard won, and highly valued, concept of academic freedom when a large – and probably growing – percentage of academic staff do not enjoy the protection of holding permanent positions in the academy? Clearly, the ways in which the concept of academic freedom has developed and the ways in which it is exercised in practice in Western countries are shaped both by the historical development of universities and by the specific policy, political, social, economic, and cultural environments in which they are located. These result in important differences about levels of institutional autonomy and academic freedom between countries and also, in some cases, between different types of higher education institutions in the same country depending on the degree of institutional differentiation and stratification. While it is important therefore not to overemphasise the strength of the trend towards what John Meyer and colleagues (Frank and Meyer, 2020) have termed isomorphism, undoubtedly a high degree of 'policy borrowing' across the Western world can be discerned, along with the increasingly 'steering' role played by bodies such as the Organisation for Economic Co-operation and Development (OECD) (Zapp and Ramirez, 2019; Clancy, 2021).

Over the last three decades or so, a body of comparative empirical research investigating the academic profession has been built up in large-scale international and comparative surveys on the impact of such developments across, in particular, OECD states, including: the 'Changing Academic Profession,' the 'Academic Profession in Europe,' and the 'Academic Profession in the Knowledge-Based Society' – as reported, for example, in Altbach (1996), Teichler *et al* (2013), Finkelstein and Jones (2019), and Teichler (2022). While not directly focused on contingent appointments these surveys show continuities, but also significant changes, over time.

In pragmatic terms, from an institutional perspective, there can be potential benefits in a shift towards employing a higher proportion of part-time and/or temporary academic staff. One incentive may lie in anticipated financial savings on employment costs of permanent positions – although a longitudinal study (2003–14) of a section of public universities in the USA did not find evidence to support this hypothesis (Hearn and Burns, 2021). Another practical consideration is that such appointments can facilitate flexibility, allowing institutions to respond rapidly to, for example, rises and declines in student numbers in different disciplinary areas, the emergence of new curricular topics, and short-term research funding opportunities. In the latter case, the significant focus on securing research grants is a result of a combination of factors including higher education's growing role in the knowledge society and the focus on research in international rankings (as discussed in the chapters by Peter Scott [Chapter 2] and Ellen Hazelkorn [Chapter 10]). The expanding numbers of staff who are employed on such projects generally sit outside 'mainstream' permanent/tenure tracks.

As in many other areas of employment, this has led to the development of patterns which go beyond a traditional pyramid structure, from early career appointments to senior and permanent roles. Beyond these practical considerations, some commentators (Herbert and Tienari, 2013; Swidler, 2017) have even suggested that some higher education administrators may purposefully build job insecurity into faculty structures.

This theme of 'new governance principles' or new public management (NPM) is one which indeed underpins many of the observations of those involved in the expert consultation. These are considered in the next three parts which summarise key themes in relation to: first, respondents' conceptions of academic freedom; second, their perceptions of contemporary safeguards and threats to the exercise academic freedom; and third, the core focus of this chapter, the implications for temporary, part-time, and contingent academic staff.

Expert consultation: definitions of academic freedom

As discussed in Chapter 1 and alluded to above, there are differences in interpretation and emphasis in what is meant by academic freedom, both conceptually and in practice. Many analysts, including contributors to this volume, observe that it is frequently only when the principle of academic freedom is felt to be under threat that it becomes a matter of some urgency to clarify what is actually meant by the concept.

In the consultation with experts reported in this chapter, while there was a good deal of overlap in the ways in which the respondents defined academic freedom, differences could be discerned in the degree of emphasis they placed broadly along a continuum from narrower to wider interpretations. At the narrower end of this continuum, the primary emphasis was on legal definitions; in the middle area of the continuum, the main emphasis was on 'classic' notions of academic freedom as a right earned through the acquisition of disciplinary knowledge and recognition through academic status within autonomous universities; responses at the wider end of the continuum considered academics' role in contributing to the public good and an associated right, indeed, a responsibility, for them to engage beyond the confines of their disciplines.

These are considered in turn below: quotations from respondents are indented and distinguished by the country where the expert is mainly based.

Legalistic definitions

At national levels, there is no shortage of interaction between the academy and legislative issues: in the case of the UK, for example, the standard reference source runs to over 1,000 pages (Farrington and Palfreyman, 2021). Respondents concentrating on this end of the continuum located their definitions of academic freedom exclusively within national legislative frameworks.

In Germany, one respondent referred straightforwardly to the legal definition enshrined in the German constitution (Article 5, Section 3)

> Kunst und Wissenschaft, Forschung und Lehre sind frei. (The arts and the sciences, research and academic teaching are free).
>
> *(Germany1)*

Right to 'profess' a discipline

Most respondents, however, referred to academic freedom in a somewhat wider way, as a right earned on the basis of: (a) disciplinary knowledge and (b) recognised status as an academic (professor, lecturer) in a university – formally recognised through some appropriate form of, often international, peer assessment.

> I am following a tradition of continental Europe by seeing a beginning of academic freedom in Wilhelm von Humboldt's contribution. According to this academic freedom has been a privilege and a cornerstone for the Academy at least in central Europe, and later in the USA. Academic freedom implemented at the Berlin university established in 1810 included three tasks: freedom of research as a main task of a professor; teaching based on research; and students' freedom to choose what to study and to choose a professor to follow.
>
> *(Sweden1)*

I define academic freedom as the liberty in higher education to discuss complex and complicated subjects without fear or favour, and the ability for students to learn from one another and their teachers in an open environment. Somewhat akin to free speech in liberal democracies, although that is now quickly being eroded....

(UK3)

Academic freedom is a cornerstone in mainly the western European university tradition. It's not part of human rights, but it's a customary cornerstone so I would say it's a moral concept. Researchers and teachers in academia should be able to pursue, without hindrance, any knowledge, or investigate any practice that they would like to.

(Denmark1)

The individual professor has the right to academic freedom: however, in practice this is exercised within the context of an institution of higher education. As highlighted by other respondents, such institutions require high degrees of autonomy if the right to academic freedom is to be protected.

Academic freedom is protection of the right of faculty to their professional responsibilities and rights, and competence. This includes the freedom to teach and determine the content of what is taught, the freedom of enquiry and to pursue and disseminate their research, and the right to undertake professional activities outside of academic employment. In the European context, and the European Higher Education Area, there is also an explicit freedom for students to study what they choose and similar rights of enquiry and research.

(USA1)

Academic freedom, I define, as the right to conduct and publish research based on the academic interests of those who conduct research. In many cases researchers who work for universities or other academic institutions can enjoy this right.

(Japan1)

The freedom to be involved unfettered in all activities involved in knowledge production, including speaking truth to power.

(UK2)

The interrelationship of research and teaching also brings in the important question of how students might be considered as part of the – ideal – concept of collegiality.

The freedom of teaching, the freedom of learning, the freedom of research, but finally the unity of it all. The freedom of teachers and students to teach,

study, and pursue knowledge and research without unreasonable interference or restriction from law, institutional regulations, or public pressure. The
freedom of teachers to inquire into any subject that evokes their intellectual
concern; to present their findings to their students, colleagues, and others;
to publish their data and conclusions without control or censorship; and to
teach in the manner they consider professionally appropriate. For students,
the basic elements include the freedom to study subjects that concern them
and to form conclusions for themselves and express their opinions.

(Germany3)

To reiterate, the commonality shared by respondents in this grouping lies in
this emphasis on academic freedom as a right which has to be earned through
the process of becoming recognised an expert in a discipline.

Academic freedom is about being able to study whatever the researcher finds
interesting and report on based on evidence. It has to be ethical, legal and
empirical – not ideological. In a democracy, scholars should respect legal
boundaries. But it is about empirical evidence not ideological arguments.

(Italy1)

Civic engagement and the public good

In contrast to such conceptions of academic freedom, based on the Humboldt
and Newman traditions, a wider definition was articulated in the early stages of
the twentieth century in the USA in the 1915 American Association of University Professors (AAUP). Regardless of legal frameworks, this wider interpretation was reflected in a number of responses from the experts consulted – that
is, academics not only have a right but even a duty to engage with, and 'speak
out' on, matters of wider societal concern – regardless of their disciplinary base.

Academic freedom has intellectual, moral and political dimensions. A liberal
tradition has been a theory of limits of politics as well as political rights. I am
influenced by Hannah Arendt's notion of freedom as only relevant when you
act in public. Therefore it's a political issue – the public space is constituted
through action and deliberation that is through politics. Freedom to act, to
change takes courage. Freedom is not so much about the individual but a community of equals within which an individual lives as a political being. This implies that opting out or disengaging as an academic is not an option. The very
nature of academic work is political; it's about engagement with the world.

(South Africa1)

I think maybe academics forget that they are granted tenure in the same
way that judges are granted tenure: in order that they can speak their
minds freely without any possible threats to their positions, so that is really

important. Universities are elite institutions: there's a lot of resources go-ing into them, there's a lot of expertise, there's a lot of knowledge and they have an opportunity to speak from that knowledge about a whole range of issues...and I think it's critically important that they do.

(Ireland2)

However, even within this wider conception, responsibilities accompany rights.

I am reminded of debates on 'rights' and their relative privileging or ig-noring of responsibilities. AF is not an absolute, not an anarchic 'I can do whatever I choose': but [it is] rather being granted professional autonomy to teach and research and engage with students in a respectful, delibera-tive and open-ended manner that challenges received wisdom and cultural orthodoxies, to enhance insight and understanding with potential to alter behaviours for the better, creating a more equal and just society for all.

(Ireland1)

Furthermore:

Academic freedom is a condition for the advancement of knowledge and thus civilization. It is not possible if external influences, pressures, demands, prohibitions, etc. are tolerated from, for example, political, economic, academic or public sources. However, the realization of the principle of academic freedom also requires unforgiving criticism within the wider aca-demic profession, as well as responsiveness to questions or criticisms com-ing from external actors.

(Slovenia1)

The above three broad grouping of views on academic freedom – narrower legalistic, disciplinary based, and wider social engagement/public intellectual – expressed by these respondents, to a considerable extent reflect the range re-ported by Altbach (2001) writing on the topic of academic freedom some two decades previously.

Expert consultation: perceptions of safeguards for academic freedom

In one sense, safeguards and threats represent two sides of the same coin. Re-spondents were asked two separate questions on these issues: first, they were asked about the safeguards they saw; then, second, the threats. There are, however, nuances in the way they interpreted the two, so these are considered separately in the discussion below.

The safeguards are well summarised by a respondent who highlighted three dimensions –national, governance, and institutional culture.

> There are different spheres of policy and behaviours: first is the larger political and largely national order and environment that determines general civil liberties, including freedom of speech, and that recognizes the special role of academic freedom that can be manifested to some degree in legislation or precedent; second is the governance structure for universities that provides assurances or guarantees and some form of definition of academic freedom; and third is the internal culture and behaviours of institutions themselves which regulate and should provide mechanisms for assuring academic freedom and paths for discourse and judgement, with possible penalties, on specific cases of real or alleged violation of academic freedom within an institution.
>
> *(USA1)*

These spheres of 'safeguards' to academic freedom were reflected to varying degrees by other respondents who tended to place a greater or lesser emphasis on one of the two dimensions identified below.

> I believe that there are two main safeguards for academic freedom in democratic societies:
>
> - national legislation (and international: conventions, resolutions, etc. documents)
> - an autonomous university or other forms of organization of institutions in which academic work takes place.
>
> *(Slovenia1)*

In considering the wider environment – and the need for continuing vigilance – respondents emphasised national frameworks as well as wider political and social culture.

> ...in an Irish context, the Universities Act (1997) is frequently lauded as being strong in terms of academic freedom, legislation alone is not sufficient to continue to deliberate on what AF is and how it is practised, protected and promoted in a rapidly changing higher education landscape in an increasingly unstable and less predictable world. Arguably, therefore, notwithstanding the significance of legislation, ongoing debate, keeping AF under review, is the most important necessity in keeping the concerns and issues that it calls into question, in mind.
>
> *(Ireland1)*

Safeguards to academic freedom are closely tied to the broader socio-political-economic contexts. [They are] also tied to the institutional cultures and social purposes of the university which recognise and acknowledge the intellectual, moral and political roles and responsibilities of universities to engage with, contribute to and lead towards socio-ecological well-being of the broader communities. These broad orientations would then influence the ways that academics' roles and responsibilities are perceived and affirmed.

(South Africa1)

But, of course, governance structures and university culture are important in interpreting, and defending in practice, the exercise of academic freedom. Safeguards here are highlighted at institutional levels.

Independent academic bodies, such as academic senates; tenure of academic researchers and teachers (professors); the right to publish the results of academic research.

(Germany1)

Academic freedom is safeguarded, if the modes of steering higher education (governance and management, financial and career incentives, evaluation, rankings and other kinds of assessment) are diverse and are soft.

(Germany2)

An associated, but slightly different, view emphasises especially the 'classic' notion of a community of scholars and collegiality.

The main safeguards to academic freedom are 1) protection of the academic position even if the researchers' opinions are against the government or central administration of the universities, and 2) due process of internal decision making.

(Japan1)

Collegiality consists of a shared decision-making process and a set of attitudes which cause individuals to regard the members of the various constituencies of the university as responsible for the success of the academic enterprise. Fundamental to this concept is the understanding that a university is a community of scholars who, out of mutual respect for the expertise and contributions of their colleagues, agree that shared decision-making in areas of recognized primary responsibility constitutes the means whereby a university best preserves its academic integrity and most effectively attains its educational mission.

(Germany3)

Tenured/permanent positions. Being able to undertake fundamental research. Obtaining research funding for topics that are not on the political agenda. Hiring professors from different social and ethnic backgrounds.

(Swizerland1)

Overall, governance structures are important in managing the sensitive balance of the autonomy of individual academics – human, and therefore less than perfect – and the ideal of academic freedom.

Guidelines emanating from HEIs alongside self-policing while recognising that institutions cannot rely on individuals' moral compass.

(UK2)

How do we defend against bias? Here I go back to Weber – value neutrality. Max Weber talks about striving for neutrality and scientific endeavour: this is implicit in what academic freedom means.

(Italy1)

Expert consultation: perceptions of threats to academic freedom

As mentioned previously, and elsewhere in this book, considerations of threats to academic freedom are gaining increasing attention not only from academic researchers and university networks with a specialist interest, but also from wider civic society – for example, at national (Adekoya *et al*, 2023; Canning, 2023) and European (Maassen *et al*, 2023) levels.

To a greater or lesser extent, these themes were reflected in the expert consultation. However, at a more nuanced level, differences in respondents' views could be identified according to the extent to which they emphasised direct as opposed to indirect factors.

The external environment was to the fore in most responses. Variations in emphasis, however, could be discerned ranging from the direct (for example, censorship, legislation, and the like) through to, more commonly, the indirect impact through political, policy, and financial 'steering.' There is, of course, a large literature on the subject of neo-liberal policies and the associated impact of NPM on universities and other institutions of higher education (summarised by, for example: Gumport, 2019; Douglass, 2020; Jones *et al*, 2020; Scott, 2021; Marginson, 2022). The sensitive balancing act is well described by von Lüde (2018).

It would be naïve to assume that professional academic administration would be possible independent of economic fundamentals. But it would be equally naïve to say economic principles that have proven effective in production and services could fully replace academic self-government.

(von Lüde, 2018, 160)

These tensions are highlighted by respondents.

In today's Europe, I see two main threats to academic freedom: commodification and commercialization of higher education and research; and illiberal political ideologies.

(Slovenia1)

Government legislation. (UK2)

Any type of censorship by funders (ministries, public funding bodies, private funders.

(Germany1)

Steering towards policy priorities through research funding and focus on rankings and the like featured prominently in responses to threats to academic freedom.

Strong and homogeneous modes of steering.

(Germany2)

Funding applied research only. Or themes on the political agenda. Or valuing quantitative over qualitative approaches. Using H index or other standardised instruments to evaluate the value of research or researcher.

(Switzerland1)

The orientation of research towards ratings and rankings. The subordination of research to market and political agendas on the mistaken assumption that scientific breakthroughs could be predicted and therefore be planned.

(Germany3)

Deciding priorities of research topics by politicians… a major threat to academic freedom is new public management; a second is the Bologna process- which set out to streamline all fields of education and research using the natural and health sciences as models- and third country-specific reforms of university governance linked to neo-liberal ideology.

(Sweden1)

One of the main threats is money. In Japan, universities are running out of research funds, and if they want to get more research funding, they have to apply for research projects proposed by the government, which is increasingly controlled by the government.

(Japan1)

One associated consequence of the issues of competition for research – and other forms of funding – is the challenge posed to collaboration.

> The business culture and the competitiveness of what now goes on within the higher education arena means that collaboration has become more difficult.
>
> *(UK1)*

Another theme to emerge focused more on the internal operation of universities.

> There are increasing numbers of examples of expanding constraints on speech, research and teaching, and university events that tend to exclude alternative thinking in some balanced way – particularly in the humanities and social science, but not exclusively.
>
> *(USA1)*

> ...increasing external policy prescriptions by politicians and the privatisation of HE more generally, cultivates a climate of fear, inducing silence and compliance rather than be *persona non grata* when decisions about research grants and promotions are being made.
>
> *(Ireland1)*

A final matter concerned what might be described as the impact of disciplinary 'fads.' At its heart, the right to academic freedom is based on recognition by peers in a relevant discipline. Disciplines, are, of course, themselves social constructs, subject to power struggles, fashions, 'splits,' etc. – well reflected in the title of the various editions of *Academic Tribes and Territories* (Becher, 1989; Becher and Trowler, 2001; Trowler, 2014) and as analysed by Bourdieu (1988) cited at the start of this chapter.

This matter of the strength, and weakness, of different disciplines, as well as wider academic culture, featured in responses on threats to academic freedom in practice:

> ...strong, dominant expectations and fashions about what to do in academia (again varying substantially by discipline and area of specialization.
>
> *(Germany2)*

> The 'World Class University' and ranking frenzy, focused on citation indices and publications in internationally recognized journals, has also been a force that shapes the topics that young and more established academics pursue.
>
> *(USA1)*

More generally what we find in the academic community is a pro liberal bias, so this can impact on researchers from different perspectives.

(Italy1)

The tension between maintaining academic independence while also being under some pressures to address or 'find answers to' current socially (and politically) constructed priorities is explored in the case of Mexico by Wietse de Vries (Chapter 6). This is particularly an issue in applied areas such as educational research, as highlighted by the respondent below.

While it is important that we constantly use critical analysis to investigate current practices and policies in order to find weaknesses in them, the whole idea then, I believe, is to help improve and develop better ones. It's a fallacy that's easy to fall into – to be the negative researcher with no vision, nothing to offer to policy or practice.

(Denmark1)

Reflecting on the impact of wider steering and funding mechanisms as identified above, a number of respondents drew more detailed attention to the ways such pressures work out in practice within institutions as posing a threat to academic freedom. At one level, this is associated with the ways in which appointments are made to the university.

Precarious and part-time positions. Requiring professors to focus on research [strategies] and management instead of doing research.

(Switzerland1)

This [tendency to the exclusion of alternative thinking] is also exemplified in litmus tests in hiring, and changes in the definition of academic freedom related to teaching that once valued balanced discourse on social topics to a relatively new tolerance for advocacy focused curriculum – not necessarily in all courses and academic programs, but a trend nonetheless.

(USA1)

Separating teaching from research; that is university positions dedicated only to teaching.

(Sweden1)

At another level, there is the experience of increasing bureaucratisation within universities. As an example, systems of ethical approval for research which may have arisen from other areas – for example, biological and medical research – are increasingly applied to social sciences. This is identified by one expert as a development which can have – presumably unintended – consequences on free enquiry.

> One of the growing threats to academic freedom lies in the ethical review of research. In many universities it has become excessive – nonsensical. Bureaucratic bodies are extending oversight and it takes a lot of time from researchers to meet these criteria. Also, research becomes prescriptive as pre-registration requires hypotheses to be registered in advance which may delegitimize research that is more exploratory.
>
> *(Italy1)*

And, beyond all such pressures, there is the wider impact of significant cultural changes.

> External threats tend to focus around cultural issues and a general decline in the faith and trust in 'experts,' academic or otherwise, that is exemplified by distrust and denial of climate change as well as the sense of universities and academics as elites, intolerant of conservative views, removed from the struggles of many within a nation and culturally out of step.
>
> *(USA1)*

> There are many [threats] but basically the development of so-called Cancel Culture…first especially around forms of feminism and gender identity/ideology and trans issues… and secondly the dangerous debates on anti-semitism (hard for me as a very conscious but secular Jew).
>
> *(UK3)*

> I would say social media is the main threat because more and more researchers don't want to engage with that part of the research task which is to interact with surrounding society…I don't participate in public debates, for example, in newspapers or social media: regrettably, that is simply the fact that I don't wish to receive threats to me or my family. This is a considerable reduction of democratic rights, but unfortunately it is where we are.
>
> *(Denmark1)*

In contrast to the latter point, another respondent suggested that in their experience working with national and international policy agencies, it could sometimes be more a question of what might be termed cautious, even self-censoring, behaviour on the part of academics that was a problem.

> I've had experiences of discussions with funders and policy agencies where they were rather critical of academics for being too conformist, not coming up with new ideas, but rather conforming to what they thought was going

to please. So, rather paradoxically in this respect I was getting a stronger concept of academic freedom from policy and funding agencies, than I sometimes got from the academics themselves.

(UK1)

In considering both safeguards and threats to academic freedom, some respondents spontaneously drew attention to changing employment practices and the increasing proportion of academic (and research) staff who were not in permanent positions. The next section goes on to consider responses to the direct question posed on this matter.

Expert consultation: implications for the exercise of academic freedom for those on part-time and temporary appointment

Along with the previously discussed growth in part-time and/or temporary positions, in some countries there has been the emergence of 'teaching only' contracts. Under neo-liberalism, rankings and competition between both institutions and individuals are associated with the weakening of the professoriate more generally – as hard-earned rights are diluted. Furthermore, in a highly competitive international environment, it is suggested that competition rather than solidarity can be discerned in relation to support – rather, lack thereof – offered for contingent faculty (Stromquist, 2017).

Despite differences in terminology and legal situation, the responses from the experts consulted indicated broadly similar trends across different European countries and other OECD states. Responses can broadly be characterised as emphasising one of three themes. First, a perception that some form of pyramid structure is inevitable in universities: as junior staff are in effect 'weeded out,' whether by choice – as they pursue a different career – or necessity, due to their failure to be promoted and/or appointed to a permanent role. Second, the emergence of new forms of temporary/part-time academic (and research) positions, largely as a result of direct or indirect pressures. Third, the implications for the relationship between individuals and their employing institutions: academics have (perhaps inevitably) divided loyalties between their commitment to their employing institutions and their commitment to their respective disciplinary networks. Some respondents highlighted what they saw as a qualitative shift in this latter delicate balance in the case of contingent faculty.

These three themes are considered in turn.

Traditional paths to achievement of full academic status

Some respondents regarded the progress from temporary to permanent roles as part of the traditional academic path. This can be conceived of as advancement from 'apprentice' to 'master,' with the implication that it is at the latter level – mastery in an academic discipline – that the individual has earned the right to profess and exercise academic freedom to the full.

In Germany, academics who aspire to a professorship have always been employed on a temporary and part-time basis. Academics without a completed doctorate may carry out scientific activities for six years, but then the dissertation should be completed. Once they have completed their doctorate, academics can be employed in the scientific field for a further six years during the postdoc phase.

(Germany3)

This, of course, leads to an inevitable pyramid structure as, whether by choice (such as moving in a different career direction), or force of circumstances (being unsuccessful in competitive appointment processes), more positions are available at the 'lower,' 'training' levels than at the more senior, professorial levels.

In my country this is only a case with PhD positions which give temporary employment for the time of doing PhD research, that is four to five years. Those researchers who graduate cannot be guaranteed a position afterwards. Thus, many PhD graduates cannot stay and continue their research at academic institutions.

(Sweden1)

One respondent regarded the matter as, in effect, one which recurred at different times depending on financial and policy conditions.

When I was Head of Department at [a university in London] in the 1970s and 1980s I had a bunch of part-time staff to whom I had to issue yearly measly contracts…terrible job for me…they were called hourly paid part-time staff….

(UK3)

Emergence of new forms of temporary and part-time academic positions

Most respondents, however, did identify a qualitative shift in both the numbers and patterns of people on temporary contracts. This shift particularly raised issues of academic freedom not only associated with the vulnerability of such employment contracts, but more broadly for their rights to be considered full members of the 'community of scholars.'

Those on precarious contracts are likely to be more cautious and not to assert their academic freedom for example, less controversial, less critical of government policy and speaking truth to power.

(UK2)

...the academic 'precariat' has expanded exponentially with the massifica-tion of higher education. These circumstances add to the fear factor men-tioned above. In the absence of a permanent contract, exercising one's academic freedom, speaking up and speaking out, may be too costly a price to pay. Thus, arguably, tenure, and the security it provides, is essential for the exercise of AF, and the health of an institution's culture.

(Ireland1)

If staff's employment situation is precarious, the time and effort to act, to resist, to innovate may not be possible, thus limiting the act of academic freedom.

(South Africa1)

Huge impact. How can one think and research freely when employed part-time or temporarily? This supports 'commanded' research.

(Switzerland1)

In the case of Germany, this matter has been taken up legally and is directly associated with institutional autonomy.

This is a development that has indeed led to claims that the right of 'scien-tific freedom' is curtailed. The courts have not sided with this argument but emphasized that the Länder, responsible for all matters regarding education, are free to organize (higher) education and the Constitution does prescribe or require a basic model of organization of universities (or other HE insti-tutions). There is one requirement however that the Constitutional Court has emphasized: When decisions are made within the HE Institution about matters relating to research, researchers (professors) must be in the majority.

(Germany1)

Implications for the relationship between academics and universities

A third theme raised by a number of respondents, focused on the relationship between temporary members of academic staff and their employing universi-ties. With 'loose ties' on both sides, employees can be particularly vulnerable. Despite the possible institutional benefits of flexibility, universities also can lose the benefits of loyalty which permanence provides.

This certainly has a negative impact on the exercise of academic freedom. By the very nature of their status, part-time employees have less ties to the institution, as well as a weaker identification with it, and this can result in the neglect of key elements of the institution's mission, which includes aca-demic freedom and institutional autonomy as its guardian.

(Slovenia1)

My sense is that the threat to academic freedom is greater for part-time faculty. This is because the employer values fidelity to the organization more than academic freedom....

(Japan1)

These are people who can be easily sanctioned...The problem for those who don't have tenure is that they don't have time so there are material obstacles in the conduct of their academic studies...They have to be careful about the effect on their teaching – today students are 'customers' so some systems have gone too far in their protection.

(Italy1)

Part-time and short-term employed academics might be more tempted to yield to the pressures of steering and to the pressures of mainstreams.

(Germany2)

In this context, to what extent does a term such as 'community of scholars' retain any meaning – if, in effect, many academics are excluded from engagement in governance, academic decision-making, and institutional policy development or the opportunity to pursue their individual interests in teaching and research?

I turn to a consideration of these matters in the final part of this chapter.

Concluding reflections: academic freedom and epistemic silences

In his analysis of academic creativity under the constraints of NPM, Marginson (2008), drawing on the work of Sen (1985), proposes what he calls a set of constituents of *self-determining academic freedom*. Three elements are identified: (a) agency freedom; (b) effective freedom, which is freedom as power or 'positive freedom'; and (c) freedom as control – that is freedom from constraint or 'negative freedom' (Marginson, 2008, 272). In pursuing this discussion, Marginson suggests that many part-time faculties might actively 'choose poorly paid temporary jobs rather than more secure and better paid employment elsewhere in order to pursue their vocation' (277). He suggests that this may be an example where agency freedom takes priority over well-being. The observation draws attention to the important point that part-time, temporary, contingent staff should not, automatically, be seen through a deficit lens.

However, while for some it may be a positive choice, allowing them freedom to pursue other opportunities in the form of a portfolio career, for many – probably most – it is not a question of agency and freedom of choice, but rather lack of opportunity to enjoy the wider benefits which permanency confers – not least in times of crisis such as the pandemic (Meliou and Lopes 2022). Large-scale surveys from Australia have shown that not only are many 'frustrated academics,' but also the gendered nature of casual status in university academic roles (Broadbent *et al*, 2013; May *et al*, 2013; Broadbent *et al*, 2017).

If stuck in such roles, many become, in a classic term from a 2007 article in *Nature*, 'taxi-cab professors,' as they rush from one part-time teaching job to another; they form

> an expanding club of non-tenure-track, or 'contingent,' teachers at universities and colleges around the world. Its members go by many names, depending on the institution and the country where they work. Officially, they may be called casual staff, adjunct professor, fixed-term worker or lecturer (which, confusingly, is a standard term for normal faculty posts in Britain). Unofficially, they're "gypsy scholars", "freeway flyers" or "taxi-cab professors".
>
> *(Ledford, 2007, 678)*

If universities are, at heart, about the creation and dissemination of knowledge, what are the implications if large sections of the academic community are in effect constrained to epistemic silence in important ways?

Four broad conclusions can be drawn from the foregoing discussion and analysis. Firstly, the right to academic freedom is universally held to be a cornerstone of the university in Western liberal democracies. Secondly, its definition is complex, varied and to some extent contested. Thirdly, academic freedom is under serious threat from a variety of directions. Fourthly, and the particular focus of concern in this chapter, a significant element in this catalogue of threats is the growing practice across most university systems of employing a variety of categories of staff who are on non-standard contracts: the so-called 'precariat.'

In this concluding section, the focus is upon the causative factors underlying the phenomenon of the 'precariat,' the implications this has for academic freedom, and the policy issues that arise.

Arguably, the development of mass systems of higher education in developed societies has made the creation of the 'precariat' almost inevitable. The rapid rise in student numbers has necessitated heavier teaching loads in most subject areas. This, combined with ever more intensive pressures to research and publish in high-quality academic journals, has led to full-time tenured staff having to give priority to their research productivity. Nor is this all: both the increasing load of administrative and managerial work, and the growing importance of securing major research grants (which involve considerable time in preparing often unsuccessful grant applications) have added to these problems. A second dimension to these issues, in the research context, is the increasingly explicit hierarchy of research publication outlets (discussed in detail in Chapter 10 by Ellen Hazelkorn) and the importance this has for academics' research profile, status, and hence promotion prospects.

The employment of part-time, often 'teaching only,' staff has acted as a 'safety valve,' enabling full-time tenured staff to cope with the pressurised context in which they find themselves. However, amongst other negative consequences, this often has an impact upon student expectations and experiences. When considering which university to apply to, a significant factor is frequently the presence of well-known professors on the academic staff. In the past, the most senior professors frequently taught first year students as this was seen as an essential part of their introduction to the discipline and university-level study.

Additionally, an unintended consequence of the increasing number of part-time staff is that it discriminates, in practice, against women academics. While the challenges and forms of discrimination facing women academics are complex (David, 2014), a disproportionate number of part-time and time-limited appointees are women who all too often find themselves in situations with limited choices – reinforcing the argument made by Burton and Bowman (2022) that, rather than understanding precarity simply as the preserve of those on insecure employment contracts, it is important to conceive of 'precarity as stemming from wider social inequalities' (500).

The overall effect of these changes in the profile of academic staff has been to exacerbate the already pronounced hierarchical structures of universities and to undermine the concept of 'collegiality.' The implications for the exercise of academic freedom are profound. Not only do the various categories of part-time, 'teaching only,' and research contract staff normally have little or no involvement in university governance (even at the departmental level), but also their teaching and research activities are largely preordained. Furthermore, it should also be noted that the 'precariat' phenomenon is by no means restricted to those universities which may be seen as of 'lower' status. On the contrary, some of the most prestigious institutions are those with the highest proportion of research contract staff, precisely because, as a key ingredient of their high-status position, they are successful in securing research grants.

There remain, therefore, important – and rarely asked – questions for universities to address. What rights, in terms of academic freedom, should such 'precariat' staff have? How can the problems posed by the increasingly hierarchical structures of universities best be addressed? And, assuming that it is undesirable to allow such flexible employment structures to remain – let alone for them to expand – how best, given the persisting pressures, can universities respond, in policy terms, to ensure that such colleagues are included in relevant academic governance structures and with associated protections to their academic freedom?

Acknowledgements

I am grateful to the 16 international experts from 11 different countries who gave so willingly of their time to explore the concept of academic freedom and associated implications for temporary, part-time, contingent academic staff/faculty. I regret that, due to limitations of space, only a fraction of the insights they provided could be incorporated, but I hope the analysis broadly does justice to their views. Responsibility for interpretation is entirely mine. Also, I would like to acknowledge the invaluable, enthusiastic, assistance provided by my colleague, Dr Lucia Vazquez Mendoza, Postdoctoral Researcher, Higher Education Research Centre, Dublin City University.

Note

1 Two notes on terminology. First, the discussion in this chapter is not country-specific, but much of the literature draws on work from the United Kingdom (which commonly refers to 'academic,' 'permanent,' 'part-time,' and/or 'temporary' academic staff) and the United States (where terms such as 'faculty,' 'tenure,' and 'contingent staff' are used). The discussion also refers to researchers on temporary contracts. While there are legal and technical distinctions, the implications for the exercise of academic freedom are broadly similar. Second, while recognising that a large part of the higher education system comprises many types of institutions of higher education, the main focus of the discussion is on universities.

References

AAUP (American Association of University Professors). (2022). *The 2022 AAUP Survey of Tenure Practices.* https://www.aaup.org/report/2022-aaup-survey-tenure-practices

Adekoya, R., Kaufmann, E., and Simpson, T. (2023). *Academic Freedom in the UK: Protecting Viewpoint Diversity.* London: Policy Exchange.

Altbach, P. G. (ed). (1996). *The International Academic Profession: Portraits of Fourteen Countries.* San Francisco: Jossey Bass.

Altbach, P. G. (2001). Academic freedom: International realities and challenges. *Higher Education, 41,* 205–19.

Becher, T. (1989). *Academic Tribes and Territories: Intellectual Enquiry and the Culture of Disciplines.* Buckingham: SRHE/Open University Press.

Becher, T., and Trowler, P. (2001). *Academic Tribes and Territories: Intellectual Enquiry and the Culture of Disciplines* (2nd ed.). Buckingham: SRHE/Open University Press.

Bourdieu, P. (1988). *Homo Academicus* (P. Collier, Trans.). Stanford: Stanford University Press.

Broadbent, K., Strachan, G., and May, R. (2017). Academic staff on insecure contracts and the interplay of gender in Australian universities. In K. Broadbent, G. Strachan, and G. Healy (eds), *Gender and the Professions: International and Contemporary Perspectives* (39–54). London: Routledge.

Broadbent, K., Troup, C., and Strachan, G. (2013). Research staff in Australian universities: is there a career path? *Labour and Industry, 23*(3), 276–95. https://doi.org/10.1080/10301763.2013.839082

Bruneau, W. (2019). Five defences of academic freedom in North American higher education. In P. Zgaga, U. Teichler, H. G. Schuetze, and A. Wolter (eds), *Higher Education Reform: Looking Back – Looking Forward* (2nd rev. ed., 184–9). Berlin: Peter Lang Verlag.

Burton, S., and Bowman, B. (2022). The academic precariat: understanding life and labour in the neoliberal academy. *British Journal of Sociology of Education*, 43(4), 497–512. https://doi.org/10.1080/01425692.2022.2076387

Canning, M. (2023, March 1). *Royal Irish Academy Presidential Discourse: 'The Critical University.'* https://www.ria.ie/news/discourse-series/watchback-presidential-discourse

Clancy, P. (2021). The governance of European higher education in transition. In H. Eggins, A. Smolentseva, and H. de Wit (eds), *Higher Education in the Next Decade: Global Challenges, Future Prospects* (167–85). Leiden Boston: Brill Sense.

Clark, B. R. (1983). *The Higher Education System*. Berkeley: University of California Press.

David, M. E. (2014). *Feminism, Gender & Universities, Politics, Passion & Pedagogies.* London: Ashgate.

Douglass, J. (2020). *Neo-nationalism and Universities: Populists, Autocrats and the Future of Higher Education.* Baltimore: Johns Hopkins University Press.

Farrington, D., and Palfreyman, D. (2021). *The Law of Higher Education* (3rd rev. ed.). Oxford. Oxford University Press.

Finkelstein, M. J., and Jones, G. A. (eds). (2019). *Professorial Pathways: Academic Careers in a Global Perspective.* Baltimore: Johns Hopkins University Press.

Frank, D. F., and Meyer, J. W. (2020). *The University and the Global Knowledge Society.* Princeton: Princeton University Press.

Gumport, P. J. (2019). *Academic Fault Lines: The Rise of Industry Logic in Public Higher Education.* Baltimore: Johns Hopkins University Press.

Hearn, J. C., and Burns, R. (2021). Contingent faculty employment and financial stress in public universities. *The Journal of Higher Education*, 92(3), 331–62. https://doi.org/10.1080/00221546.2020.1851570

Herbert, A., and Tienari, J. (2013). Transplanting tenure and the (re)construction of academic freedoms. *Studies in Higher Education*, 38(2), 157–73. https://doi.org/10.1080/03075079.2011.569707

Jones, D. R., Visser, M., Stokes, P., Örtenblad, A., Deem, R., Rodgers, P., and Tarba, S. Y. (2020). The performative university: 'targets', 'terror' and 'taking back freedom' in academia. *Management Learning*, 52(4), 1–15. https://doi.org/10.1177/1350507620927554

Ledford, H. (2007). Taxi-cab teaching. *Nature*, 445, 678–9. https://doi.org/10.1038/nj7128-678a

Maassen, P., Martinsen, D., Elken, M., Jungblut, J., and Lackner, E. (2023). *State of Play of Academic Freedom in the EU Member States. Overview of De Facto Trends and Developments.* European Parliamentary Research Service.

Marginson, S. (2008). Academic creativity under new public management: Foundations for an investigation. *Educational Theory*, 58(3), 269–87.

Marginson, S. (2022). Space and scale in higher education: The glonacal agency heuristic revisited. *Higher Education*, 84, 1365–95. https://doi.org/10.1007/s10734-022-00955-0

May, R., Peetz, D., and Strachan, G. (2013). The casual academic workforce and labour market segmentation in Australia. *Labour and Industry*, 23(3), 258–75. https://doi.org/10.1080/10301763.2013.839085

Meliou, E., and Lopes, A. (2022). Academic profession, contingent employment and career pathways during a crisis. Research Report. SRHE, Aston University and Newcastle University.

Scholars at Risk (SAR) (2022). *Free to Think. Report of the Scholars at Risk Academic Freedom Monitoring Project.* https://www.scholarsatrisk.org/resources/free-to-think-2022/

Scott, P. (2021). *Retreat or Resolution? Tackling the Crisis of Mass Higher Education.* Bristol: Policy Press.

Scott, W. J. (2022). What kind of freedom is academic freedom? *Critical Times, 5*(1), 1–19. https://doi.org/10.1215/26410478-9536460

Sen, A. (1985). Well-being, agency and freedom: the Dewey lectures 1984. *Journal of Philosophy, 82*(4), 169–221.

Sörensen, J. S., and Olsson, E. J. (2017). Academic freedom and its enemies: lessons from Sweden. In T. Halvorsen, H. Ibsen, H.-C. Evans, and S. Penderis (eds), *Knowledge for Justice: Critical Perspectives from Southern African-Nordic Research Partnerships* (57–70). Cape Town: African Minds.

Stromquist, N. P. (2017). The professoriate: the challenged subject in US higher education. *Comparative Education, 53*(1), 132–46.

Swedberg, R. (2018). How to use Max Weber's ideal type in sociological analysis. *Journal of Classical Sociology, 18*(3), 181–96. https://doi.org/10.1177/1468795X17743643

Swidler, E. (2017, October 30). The pernicious silencing of the adjunct faculty. *The Chronicle of Higher Education.* https://www.chronicle.com/article/the-pernicious-silencing-of-the-adjunct-faculty/

Teichler, U. (2022). *Higher Education Research - What Else? The Story of a Lifetime: In Conversations with Anna Kosmutky and Christine Rittgerott.* Berlin: Budrich Academic Press.

Teichler, U., Arimoto, A., and Cummings, W. K. (2013). *The Changing Academic Profession: Major Findings of a Comparative Survey.* Dordrecht: Springer.

Trowler, P. (2014). Academic tribes and territories: the theoretical trajectory. *Osterreichische Zeitschrift fur Geschichtswissenschaften, 25*(3), 17–26.

von Lüde, R. (2018). Academic freedom under pressure: from collegial governance to new managerialism. In P. Zgaga, U. Teichler, H. G. Schuetze, and A. Wolter (eds), *Higher Education Reform: Looking Back – Looking Forward* (2nd rev. ed., 156–67). Berlin: Peter Lang Verlag.

Weber, M. (1978). *Economy and Society: An Outline of Interpretive Sociology.* Berkeley: University of California Press.

Zapp, M., and Ramirez, F. O. (2019). Beyond internationalisation and isomorphism – the construction of a global higher education regime. *Comparative Education, 55*(4), 473–93. https://doi.org/10.1080/03050068.2019.1638103

10

INTERROGATING THE IMPLICATIONS OF RANKINGS, OPEN SCIENCE, AND PUBLISHING FOR ACADEMIC PRACTICE AND ACADEMIC FREEDOM

Ellen Hazelkorn

Introduction

The circumstances in which higher education institutions (HEIs) operate have changed significantly in recent decades, driven by the significance of knowledge and technological advances for social and economic advancement and the internationalisation of education and scientific research. This has elevated the reputational and prestige value of research and resource-intensive universities and global science as key differentiators in the national and global market. Critical to 'success' is the way in which academic activity and especially scholarship and scientific research are assessed. While global rankings are often used to measure and track changes, it is rarely considered in combination with or in relation to research assessment, open science and open access, and/or changes in the academic publishing industry, data analytics, and ultimately the impact on academic freedom. This is the subject of this chapter.

While global university rankings (GUR) only emerged in the early years of this century, rankings have featured for over 100 years. Early versions were influenced by aspects of eugenics and based on the idea of family attributes. James McKeen Cattell published *American Men of Science* which linked the 'scientific strength' of leading universities to the research reputation of their faculty members (Webster, 1986, 14; Usher, 2017). A turning point came during the post–World War II era, when the first big wave of massification helped transform the United States into the 'first high participation system (HPS) of higher education' (Cantwell, 2018, 227). Rankings began to rely on bibliometric and citation data drawn from the *Science Citation Index*, beginning in 1961, and the *Social Sciences Citation Index*, beginning in 1966. *US News and World Report*, then a weekly newsmagazine, produced its first *Best*

DOI: 10.4324/9781003363262-14

College Ranking in 1983. It was initially generated by a reputational survey of the opinions of university Presidents. After 1988, it utilised a wide range of different indicators. Its reliance on independent data was a defining moment.

GURs marked another historic turning point. Their arrival at the millennium reflected the acceleration of globalisation and increasing porosity of borders, leading to increased trade in goods and services and mobility of people – increasingly referred to as 'talent' – alongside the importance of knowledge creation and innovation as the engine of growth. As a result, nations are increasingly assessed according to the knowledge-producing and talent-attracting capacity and capability of their research-intensive universities. This in turn has placed a premium on academic and research 'stars.' Whereas previously knowledge creation was confined largely within national borders, in the global era it was only a matter of time before international comparability became important. Pursuance of 'world-class' status, determined according to standing within the top-100, is a shared ambition of individual scholars, universities, and nations. Today, there are over 20 different global rankings, although three dominate: 'Academic Rankings of World Universities' (ARWU), 'Times Higher Education World University Rankings' (THE), and 'QA World University Rankings' (QS) (IREG Observatory, 2021).

These developments have overlapped with, and reflected, calls for greater public accountability. It is not only what universities do that matter, but also how well they do what they do (Calhoun, 2006; Eaton, 2016). Traditionally, academic performance has been subject to expert judgment and peer review but academic self-regulation, like other forms of professional self-regulation, is less tolerated nowadays. There is ever-increasing interest in the use of public assets as well as ensuring a return on public investment and public benefits from those assets. This explains the preponderance of national and transnational frameworks, instruments, and 'governance indices' being developed as a growing aspect of public policy to monitor, measure, assess, and compare the outputs, outcomes, impacts, and benefits of higher education and research (Erkkilä and Piironen, 2009; Sauder and Espeland, 2009, 64). Moves towards open science, open access, open data, and open educational resources respond to an enhanced public accountability agenda as well as measures to democratise knowledge. At the same time, by challenging national, university, and individual claims of excellence, rankings and other forms of international comparability successfully highlighted the importance of independent data for institutional, national, and global governance. However, there are few, if any, reliable international comparability tools and there is no international database or agreed set of indicators or data definitions. Into this gap, rankings in partnership with publishing and data analytics companies have developed massive repositories of higher education and research information usually held behind pay-walls. In the process, major rankings have evolved from being a consumer tool to enhance student choice to a 'powerful, global data business' (PCG/Academia, 2022; Hazelkorn, 2024).

Using broad strokes, this chapter uses a multi-layered approach to help understand the way in which these developments have impacted on and transformed higher education and research practice – with implications for academic freedom. There are three distinct but intersecting strands and sections to this paper:

Part 1 looks at GURs. GURs purport to measure 'world-class' excellence but they predominantly measure research or scholarly productivity as a measure of faculty or institutional quality on the basis that academics and others believe it is a good or essential measure for comparing institutions. Given the absence of reliable international data, rankings rely predominantly on research and research-related activity using bibliometric indicators, and indexed journals listed by Scopus and Web of Science (WoS) and 'impact factors' as norms of quality. As a result, GURs have had an overarching influence on the academic enterprise, influencing where and what scholars research and publish with implications for academic prestige and for careers.

Part 2 looks at moves towards open science (OS), open data, and open access (OA). These developments reflect a desire to make the processes and the outcomes of publicly funded research widely accessible. The European Union (EU) Plan S open-access scheme was launched in 2018 (cOAlition, 2018). It was followed by 'Big Deal' read and publish agreements between publishers and university systems which were envisioned as transitionary arrangements to widen opportunities. The process has had many unintended consequences. This includes amplifying the role and authority of publishers, and narrowing publishing choices of scholars to those journals included within publishing agreements (Crotty, 2021; Kunz, 2022).

Part 3 looks at corporate consolidation between rankings, publishing, and data analytics which together form a lucrative knowledge intelligence business with huge repositories of data. Together they have developed sophisticated end-to-end software to accumulate and manage data, monetise and create new assets, and leverage analytics products to work across the entire academic knowledge production cycle from conception to publication, distribution, and subsequent evaluation together with reputation management (Chen and Chan, 2021). Research management systems encourage users (institutions, governments, and individuals) to participate in the process and then use the systems and outcomes for their own strategic purposes (Chen and Chan, 2021, 427). These developments raise fundamental questions about the use and ownership of data, regulation, and governance.

The conclusion seeks to draw these three strands together and consider their influence on how universities and governments go about their business, and the choices they make. More critically, the discussion reflects on the implications for academic and research practices and specifically academic freedom.

Ranking research

Despite sustained criticisms of rankings and the choice of methodology and data sources, GURs have succeeded in filling a huge information deficit about higher education by presenting the 'appearance of scientific objectivity' (Ehrenberg, 2002, 147). Prior to this, students and others made choices based on local intelligence, perceptions of quality, and/or the status-seeking attributes of specific choices. A measure of rankings' success can be illustrated by the wide range of user groups: students and their parents, policy- and decision-makers, HEIs, faculty and collaborators, business and employers, and investors and rating companies. According to the *New York Times*, 'as long as the rankings are taken seriously by applicants, they're going to be taken seriously by educators' (Diver, cited in Hartocollis, 2022).

Yet the significance of rankings goes further. Essentially, rankings measure the outcomes of historical advantage. Elite universities and nations benefit from accumulated public and/or private wealth and investment over decades if not centuries. These attributes are amplified by their simple ordinal format. By successfully linking the knowledge-producing and talent-attracting capability of universities to the ambitions of competitive nation states, they have played a formidable role in shaping academic behaviour and practice around the world as well as the strategic choices of universities and governments.

Global rankings principally measure research and reputation. Assuming a strong correlation between faculty reputation and research/research-related indicators (for example, academic reputation, Ph.D. awards, research income, citation, academic papers, faculty and alumni medals and awards, and internationalisation [Hazelkorn, 2015, 55]), then both ARWU and THE are 100% research-oriented and QS is 70%. Notably, ARWU specifically highlights *Nature* and *Science*, and Nobel Prizes or Fields Medals. THE and QS include reputational surveys but the methodology is criticised as being overly subjective, self-perpetuating, and easily conflated with historical advantage.

Some observations

1   Rankings highlighted the importance of data and use of quantitative indicators for measurement, comparison, and strategic governance, albeit the origins of this practice stretch back to the foundations of the modern nation state and the process of statecraft in the late nineteenth century. Over the decades, and especially in response to calls for enhanced accountability and public sector reform in the late twentieth century, there has been a proliferation of different types of rankings, ratings, and benchmarking instruments to drive, monitor, and evaluate actions and outcomes across all aspects of public life. Cooley and Synder (2015), Rottenburg *et al* (2015), Muller (2018), and Erkkilä and Piironen (2018) refer, in different ways, to

'ranking the world.' According to Cooley, 95 such indices were produced since 1990 'explicitly in the international realm targeting a diverse global audience of national policymakers, international bureaucrats, transnational activists, and media outlets' as part of the expansion of 'global governance networks' (Cooley, 2015, 9–11).

Rankings are part of this escalating set of policy and evaluation instruments introduced across education and research with the intention of measuring, assessing, improving, and comparing performance and productivity. They coincided with a growing desire to move beyond simply counting outputs to assessing quality and linking it to resources. Traditionally, this activity fell within the purview of the academy. Rankings were seen as an independent interlocutor. As such, they signalled a significant change in the relationship between higher education and the State (Dill and Beerkens, 2010, 51; Harman, 2011, 313–5; Hazelkorn, 2018).

2　Rankings purport to measure research excellence and impact by way of bibliometrics and journal impact factor (JIF). *WoS* or *Scopus* bibliometric databases include journal articles, conference proceedings, books, and other resources – albeit this is just a proportion of what is published. Because of differences in disciplinary practice, the main beneficiaries of this methodology are the physical, life, and medical sciences.

The JIF was developed by Garfield (1955, 1972) to distinguish between the importance of a journal and total publication or citation counts. It is used by funders and researchers to assess and fund research, to rank journals, etc. However, JIF has been subject to increasing criticism with strong warnings against using citation data without careful attention to the many phenomena that influence such rates. There are many reasons some research is more frequently cited, such as people referencing people they know or from their own country and/or countries where English is the native language and/or countries which publish the largest number of English-language journals (Wilsdon *et al*, 2015). New research fields, inter-disciplinary research, or ideas which challenge orthodoxy often find it difficult to be published or are less likely to be published in high-impact journals. Gender also influences citations practices, with implications for careers (O'Connor and O'Hagan, 2016).

This has led to growing concern that exceptional attention to high-impact journals and JIF is distorting research practice, with accusations of over/mis-interpretation, misconduct, and manipulation (Biagioli and Lippman, 2020). Recent years have seen moves towards open science and grey literature which are not captured in either Scopus or WoS.[1] Concerns have been highlighted by the *San Francisco Declaration on Research Assessment* (DORA, 2012) and the *Leiden Manifesto* (Hicks *et al*, 2015). Dutch universities and funding agencies and the Chinese government have renounced usage of citation counts for academic assessment, appointment, and promotion (VSNU *et al*, 2019; Creus, 2020). An indication of the competitive nature of this field is the recent announcement by Clarivate to radically expand the number of journals to be granted an impact factor to both respond to criticism and keep pace with Scopus (Cochran, 2022).

3 The net effect is that GURs help to (re)structure knowledge and knowledge products by their methodological choices (Marginson, 2010) with implication on academic practice. In addition to the points raised above, reliance on quantitative data that are easily measured rather than research outputs that are important, distorts research activity and assessment towards particular disciplines and what is more predictable. Fixation on traditional inputs and outputs reinforces a simplistic science-push view of innovation whereby research achieves accountability within the 'academy' rather than via social accountability. Because fundamental research is dominated by the biosciences, rankings reinforce a hierarchy of knowledge in which arts, humanities, and social sciences are less valued. Accordingly, universities with large STEM programmes and medical schools and those which emphasise international collaborations rather than regionally or culturally engagement are more likely to be highly ranked.

In so doing, rankings have helped create a global higher education landscape which favours resource- and research-intensive universities in global-north nations and perpetuates imbalances in the global knowledge system. Geopolitical tensions are not just highlighted but amplified. The recent decision by three Chinese universities to cease participation in global rankings is both a bold statement against Anglo-American defined hegemony in global science and a geo-political proclamation (Sharma, 2022).

Open science and open access

From the time of the earliest universities in Europe, scholarly and scientific inquiry were seen by political, ecclesiastical, and municipal authorities as being beneficial for policy, the economy, and helping to solve problems as well as being a status symbol (Rüegg, 1992). David (2008, 21) suggests the roots of open science lie in the era of the Scientific Revolution of the sixteenth century. Travelling scholars were common, journeying great distances and establishing connections between European, Asian, and North African centres of learning. By the nineteenth century, networks were becoming a normal part of scientific endeavour. Newman's idea that knowledge should be pursued 'for its own sake' was slowly overtaken by the Humboldtian principle of joining teaching and research (Anderson, 2009). Since the World War II era, the relationship between knowledge and society has become more tightly aligned. Publication of *Science, The Endless Frontier* in 1945 in the US was followed by the European Coal and Steel Community in 1951 (Reillon, 2015, 2). Both documents, in different ways, acknowledged that social and economic progress was dependent upon 'continuous additions to knowledge of the laws of nature, and the application of that knowledge to practical purposes' (Bush, 2020, 1; see also Guston, 2000), thereby transforming research into a public endeavour.

By the millennium, several issues had combined to catapult open science onto the political agenda reflecting emergent societal concerns: principles of accountability and transparency, sharing and using knowledge for problem-solving and evidence-based policymaking, and the desire to democratise knowledge by increasing public access and influence (Willinsky, 2006; Wouters *et al*, 2019). Open science is an umbrella concept.[2] Whereas knowledge creation was historically confined (if not restricted) within national borders, open science seeks to make 'everything in the discovery process fully and openly available, creating transparency and driving further discovery by allowing others to build on existing work' (LIBER, 2018, 6; see also Salmi, 2015). It advocates making research practice open so that others can collaborate and contribute, which includes sharing data, whereas open access refers to making the results of research widely disseminated.

The UN Millennium Development Goals (2000), followed by the EU Grand Challenges (2009)[3] and the UN Sustainable Development Goals (SDG) (2016), took the debate further acknowledging societal problems were territorially blind and no country had either the knowledge or research capacity or capability to solve such challenges on their own. In September 2018, the EU launched Plan S. Leading an international consortium of research funding and performing organisations, the objective was that all scientific publications resulting from publicly funded research must be published in Open Access journals or platforms by 2020 (cOAlition, 2018).

Timelines may have slipped, but by 2020, a third of all articles were published in open access format (STM, 2021). The global search for a vaccine for coronavirus – initially facilitated by early publication of a machine-readable genome of the COVID-19 virus by Chinese scientists – is a good demonstration of the potential of this ambition.[4]

Some observations

1 Facilitated by technological advances, platforms, and software, the transformation of academic publishing has quickened, spawning an expanding range of publishing models and tools. This has helped lower barriers to entry experienced by young researchers, emergent/developing countries, and smaller institutions as well as providing opportunities for public engagement with science. The launch of the Public Library of Science's PLoS in 2003 represented a 'breakthrough' (Willinsky, 2006, 1). Today, according to the Directory of Open Access Journals (DOAJ), there are 17,423 open access journals representing 130 countries, of which 12,273 operate with article processing charges (APCs).[5] The number of open access policies continues to expand, with Europe leading the way.[6]

2 Traditional print-based academic journals used to be sold to libraries and/ or to individuals on a subscription basis, otherwise known as pay-to-read. Open Science, however, requires the outcomes of all publicly funded research to be openly available, free of cost or any access barriers.

To get around these requirements, publishers began charging to publish: this has become known as an APC or the pay-to-publish model. This is hugely expensive for individuals, and thus negotiations, known as 'Big Deals,' have taken place between publishers and university systems and/or countries. The system works well for publishers as it locks-in subscribers. It also benefits people associated with universities/research organisations covered by the deal as long as they wish to publish in the journals covered by those publishers.

3 Open science is having a positive influence because it entails a shift from the standard practice of publishing research results in scientific journals, towards sharing all available data and knowledge at the earliest stages of the research process. It requires a move from 'publishing as fast as possible' to 'sharing knowledge as early as possible' (Wilsdon *et al*, 2017, 7). Preprints allow articles to be published at an early stage, albeit this can cause confusion about the scientific method when findings are changed. In addition, there is growing usage and readership of non-traditional or alternative forms of publishing, many of which are based on or facilitated by social media (Holmberg *et al*, 2020). Altmetrics seek to capture this activity (Wilsdon *et al*, 2017, 9–10).

However, these developments provoke questions about who has or can afford to have access or should have access. This has implications for cost, ownership, resourcing, and dissemination of knowledge with implications, *inter alia*, for copyright and intellectual property rights, as well as for governance and regulation. While OS and OA have expanded access, OA may be free to read but it is not free to publish. It still requires an APC to be paid. Open access journals may charge less, but they still charge.

More importantly, OA has increased the power of a cartel of major publishers which has eaten up a large share of the funding available for subscriptions or other deals, and has restricted publishing choices and opportunities for researchers operating outside these arrangements (Science Europe, 2018; Crotty, 2021). Smaller publishers, and academic societies with fewer resources, struggle to compete in this scenario, increasingly dominated by the big five academic publishers (Fyfe *et al*, 2017). Equally worrying is that large publishers have acquired some of the most innovative small open access publishes, such as F1000 (2020) and Hindawi (2021), thereby reducing competition and publishing opportunities (Burgelman, 2021). These developments are a long way from the original vision of open access.

Publishing, rankings, and data analytics

Globalisation and production of talent/graduate outcomes and knowledge creation for social and economic development and sustainability have transformed higher education and research from a nation-bound to an international activity with geopolitical implications. As a result, interest in the outcomes of higher education has created a 'global field of measurement that concerns knowledge governance more broadly' (Erkkilä and Piironen, 2021, 54). The shift to open science and use of digital platforms and artificial intelligence–driven analytics has further transformed the process of conceptualising, collecting, managing, warehousing, publishing, and analysing higher education and research information. There has been an exponential growth in the number and type of policy and commercial platforms, systems, and instruments and a whole array of people and organisations interested in this type of information for their own strategic and other purposes.

Since the millennium, five academic publishers have consolidated ownership of a disproportionate share of academic journals and papers in the natural and social sciences (Elsevier, Wiley-Blackwell, Springer, Taylor and Francis, and Sage). Via 'mergers and acquisitions of academic content,' Elsevier and Wiley have strengthened their position by focusing on 'academic services and data analytics' to create 'end-to-end systems.' They are designed to capture data across the 'entire academic knowledge production cycle from conception to publication and distribution and subsequent evaluation and reputation management' (Posada and Chen, 2018, 2, 4). As a result 'a small number of global publishers and online systems have grown to play major roles in the production, publication and distribution of research' (Coates *et al*, 2021, 417).

In the process, 'vast data lakes' containing 'triple-digit billions of data elements' have been created (Guhr, as cited in Siwinski, 2019). This has transformed the entire activity of handling and understanding data into a complex and sophisticated enterprise, far beyond the capacity and capabilities of most institutional research offices, and hence requiring the assistance of intermediaries. Understanding and using data is essential to being/staying competitive in the global landscape. Organisations which embrace an evidence-based decision-making approach are said to be more likely to 'outperform institutions that make decisions based on belief' (Guhr, as cited in Siwinski, 2019).

Some observations

1 GURs rely on public-available data supplemented with reputational data based on surveys by students, academic peers, or business, web-based data, and/or self-reported data by individual academics/researchers or by institutions. But the absence of internationally comparable data on higher education encouraged ranking organisations to begin to establish their own repositories.

The Global Institutional Profiles project was originally developed[7] in partnership between THE and Thompson Reuters in 2009. In 2014, THE announced its intention to establish the 'world's largest, richest database of the world's very best universities' (Baty, 2018). The *THE Data Points Portfolio* boasts holding 9 million data points from 3,500 institutions from over 100 countries (THE, n.d.). ARWU, now operating as a consultancy, created the Global Research University Profiles (GRUP) containing information on approximately 12,000 universities.[8] In contrast, U-Multirank is the only global ranking which is non-commercial; it operates as a project of the EU with additional financial support from non-profit foundations. Drawing on self-reported data, it provides open access to its data-warehouse of more than 1,700 universities from 96 countries.[9]

LinkedIn (Bergen and Hesseldahl, 2016) entered the rankings business using crowd-sourced data on graduate employment. The *THE Impact Rankings* requires universities to submit huge portfolios as evidence of their claim for SDG rating, which is then 'evaluated' behind closed doors (Hazelkorn, 2022), while universities seeking information for benchmarking are required to 'take a paid-up three-year subscription to the THE's dashboard' (Calderon, 2020).

2 Rankings are a commercial business; they are very successful at collecting data but this is an incredibly resource-intensive activity. The data is worthless without the capacity to monetise it through associated services. Publishers are also busy collecting data. Like rankings, their business model involves

> shifting from content provision to data analytics. This involves the tracking – that is, recording and storage – of the usage data generated by researchers...
>
> *(DFG-Committee on Scientific Library Services and Information Systems, 2021, 3–4)*

Research management systems operated by, for example, Elsevier encourage users (institutions, governments, and individuals) to participate in the process and then use the systems and outcomes for their own strategic purposes (Chen and Chan, 2021, 427). As Posada and Chen (2018, 12) argue, a deepening dependency relationship is being created 'through the integration of services [which] can have direct consequences on the decision making of individual researchers/lecturers and academic institutions' and governments.

The recent acquisition of US-based *Inside Higher Education* by *Times Higher Education* highlights another aspect of consolidation and concentration of the market (THE Reporters, 2022). It blurs the lines between independent commentary and rankings, which THE had arguably already overstepped by using its newspaper to promote its rankings. In this instance, the takeover facilitates THE getting access to the biggest higher education market. The prize is getting 'American universities hooked on the rankings THE produces' so they can 'sell their data division's analytical services – which are geared to helping institutions understand how to improve themselves in those rankings – in the world's richest higher education market' (Usher, 2022).

3 Academic publishing faces considerable criticism about predatory practices, high costs and large profit margins, aggressive use of impact factors, and the gaming that takes place to publish with a high impact factor. The move to embrace open access and alternative contractual and payment systems and structures could be interpreted as a move to democratise knowledge. However, the 'redirection of big publishers' business strategy towards the acquisition and integration of scholarly infrastructure, the tools and services that underpin the scholarly research life cycle, many of which are geared towards data analytics' is a shrewd and lucrative business move (Posada and Chen, 2018; Kunz, 2022). This explains publisher resistance to full-blown open access, and their continued efforts to restrict the way in which it operates even for those journals included within the Big Deal arrangements (Esposito, 2022). It also explains the ever-closer bond between rankings, publishers, and data analytics.

Conclusion

How are these different issues, individually and collectively, shaping and re-shaping academic practices and challenging academic freedom? This section reflects on some issues.

The higher education landscape is simultaneously collaborative and competitive. This has elevated the reputational and prestige value of rankings. Critical to their magnetic appeal has been holding out the tantalising hope that, by taking certain actions, the inherently unequal and asymmetrical relationship between diverse systems and institutions, and correspondingly their nations, could be altered (Cantwell, 2021). National excellence initiatives have sought to alter that narrative by seeking to position a few universities at the top of the global hierarchy (Salmi, 2017, 2021). In turn, this has helped elevate the importance of data collection and analysis, bringing it from the back-office and placing it at the centre of strategic decision making and performance measurement.

Despite considerable criticism, governments and universities, explicitly or implicitly, continue to 'obsess' about rankings (Diep and Gluckman, 2021; Jaschik, 2021). Table 10.1 below provides a summary of different ways rankings have been used to set strategic objectives and priorities and underpin resource allocation. This includes the introduction of tenure-track systems, prioritising research over teaching, rewarding high achievers and identifying weak performers, supporting or rewarding researchers who publish in high-impact journals, introducing distinctive teaching and research career paths,

TABLE 10.1 Examples of actions taken by universities to improve ranking position

	Examples of Actions
Governance and Organisation	Merge with another institution, for example, merge research institute with university, merge niche institutions with comprehensive university, etc.
	Develop/expand English-language facilities.
	Establish Institutional Research Unit.
	Embed rankings indicators as a Key Performance Indicator (KPI).
	Form task group to review and report on rankings.
Research	Recruit and reward academics who successfully publish in highly cited journals.
	Emphasis and funding placed on increasing output, quality, and citations.
	Publish in English-language journals.
	Set individual targets for academics and departments/colleges.
	Increase number/proportion of doctoral students.
Faculty	Recruit/head-hunt international high-achieving/HiCi scholars
	Include publications in highly cited journals as criteria for promotion or contractual arrangements.
	Create new tenure arrangements.
	Set market-based or performance/merit-based salaries.
	Reward high achievers and identify weak performers with higher salary, sources, labs, etc.
	Enable best researchers to concentrate on research
Students	Target recruitment of high-achieving students and international students, esp. Ph.D students.
	Offer scholarships and other benefits to high-achieving students.
	Include publications in highly cited journals as criteria for Ph.D.
	Expand international activities and exchange programmes.
	Open International Office and professionalise recruitment.
Public Image/ Marketing	Ensure common brand/institutional affiliation used on all publications.
	Professionalise admissions, marketing, and public relations.
	Expand internationalisation alliances and membership of global networks.
	Enhance reputational factors, incl. referencing to rankings, targeting potential peers.

focusing on STEM disciplines and discontinuing arts and humanities courses, recruiting post-graduate/Ph.D. students, and recruiting more elite, high-performing students who are likely to finish on time and go on to have influential employment, etc. (Hazelkorn, 2015; Yudevich *et al*, 2016).

How these changes are introduced and implemented have implications for academic freedom (Kinzelbach *et al*, 2021). Research assessment practices have had a profound (negative) impact on the way in which research organisations operate and the way in which research and researchers are funded, rewarded, and promoted (EUA, Science Europe, and European Commission, 2022). This puts faculty under pressure to publish more and publish in international high-impact journals to which their institutions subscribe rather than writing monographs or publishing in grey literature. In turn, publication records affect the way resources are distributed within or between departments, for example, using special funds to reward individual faculty, making 'iconic' appointments, recruiting 'star' scholars to particular units or building dedicated labs and other facilities, or rewarding individuals and departments which are especially productive or secure exemplary funding. Permission and funding to attend conferences or travel overseas may be targeted at individuals and departments which publish the most or publish in prestigious journals. Similarly, faculty may receive a financial reward or special benefits according to the citation impact of the journal in which the research is published. Publishing in English is especially favoured, especially in countries where English is not the native language. At the same time, research funding agencies or national research allocation models use the same criteria. In this way, there is again an implicit influence on academic research choices and publication choices – and hence academic freedom.

In addition to wider cultural effects, there are potential knock-on implications for the humanities and social sciences, as well as for disciplines such as agricultural and environmental sciences. These disciplines tend to have particular significance for local/national societies and for policymaking which can be lost or undermined when the research or publication focus is primarily on global reputation and status. Because research is reified by rankings, there is a perceived tendency to undermine teaching and/or to see teaching as a 'punishment' for weak researchers.

But faculty are not innocent victims. Years ago, Becher (1989) and Becher and Trowler (2001) detailed the way in which academics not only perceive themselves but also shape practice in their interest. There is plenty of evidence to suggest they are quick to use citation factors, journal prestige, and rankings to boost their own professional standing and are 'unlikely to consider research partnerships with a lower ranked university unless the person or team was exceptional.' Rankings are regularly used to expand the 'network of the academic superpowers and increases their competitive advantage' (Oprisko, 2012; Grove, 2022). As academic leaders, scholars, peer reviewers, recruiters, and journal editors, academics flex incredible muscle in shaping careers and determining the contours of scholarship (Irfanullah, 2021). In turn, rank, prestige, and reputation are used to determine government scholarships and visas (Jashik, 2022).

International collaboration and co-authorship is increasingly seen as a measure of excellence (Cahill, 2015; Kwiek, 2020), with co-authored papers more likely to be highly cited (Holmberg *et al*, 2020). This is strengthening existing global hierarchies with researchers around the world seeking to publish with scholars from a few Anglophone countries (Tijssen *et al*, 2017; Fu *et al*, 2022). The net effect is that regional and local collaboration, advocated by policy and institutional missions, is discouraged in favour of international partnerships. The same consolidation is evidenced in university networks and associations. These transnational partnerships have expanded significantly in recent years but not all networks are equal. Networks comprising 'research intensive and well-resourced universities from the most affluent nations tend to have greater public visibility'; these are also the networks with the most highest ranked universities (Calderon, 2021, 395–6).

Rankings and publishing reflect and reinforce widely perceived views about the academic status hierarchy. The debate around what constitutes 'excellence' may have broadened in recent years to focus more on teaching and to include actions that contribute to public value but this whole arena remains complex and complicated – and the indices used by academics, institutions, and funding agencies too often contradict these public good aspirations. It is much easier to capture the commercialisation of research through patents and licensing than societal impacts and civic engagements, contributions to public discourse or public behaviour, helping to build sustainable communities, etc. The losers are scholars in new and emerging countries and less elite universities/ HEIs, those studying in the arts, humanities and social sciences, those focused on local or regional problems, and women more so than men (Paasi, 2015). Despite attempts to broaden criteria around academic decisions, research continues to influence career trajectories and choices.

Open access and open data are making a significantly positive impact on science and public life. One need look no further than efforts to find a vaccine and public health responses to COVID-19 (Lee and Haupt, 2021). But, as Brand – the director and publisher of MIT Press– asks, how did open access become a system underpinned by 'myriad pay-to-publish models, which protect publisher profits but systematically disadvantages researchers from less well-funded institutions, academic societies and disciplines?' The growth of platform services creating a major content, systems, and services business has effectively 'colonised' higher education. 'Their contractual relationships with some universities even give them the right to exploit university-generated content and data for other business purposes' (Brand, 2022).

These developments, individually and collectively, carry significant implications for academic freedom. Some effects are more obvious – such as closing down departments or re-allocating resources to improve in the rankings which itself carries benefits – while others are more obscure – research management software tools or 'Big Deal' arrangements which create a wrap-around data capture system. So should we consider ranking universities according to commitment to academic freedom? There have been several initiatives which have sought to do just this. U21 system rankings measures the overall governance and policy environment, and includes questions about the degree of freedom with respect to choosing the CEO of a public research university or appointing foreign academics (Williams and Leahy, 2020, 30). The Academic Freedom Index housed at the University of Gothenburg has a global data set which tracks how well commitments to academic freedom are delivered (Kinzelbach *et al*, 2021; Quinn *et al*, 2021). These are fundamental issues but the problem with any ranking remains – they are simplistic approaches to complex issues which can quickly lead to distortion. As the era of self-regulation comes to an end, is it time to grasp the nettle and consider regulation, governance, and data ownership issues of the rankings, publishing, and data analytics business?

Notes

1 Scopus does not include HAL Archives, which is likely to include more social science/humanities and locally/regionally impactful research.
2 https://www.fosteropenscience.eu/foster-taxonomy/open-science-definition
3 Lund Declaration – Global Challenges. https://cordis.europa.eu/article/id/31013-swedish-presidency-research-must-focus-on-grand-challenges
4 https://ec.europa.eu/info/research-and-innovation/strategy/strategy-2020-2024/our-digital-future/open-science_en
5 https://doaj.org
6 https://roarmap.eprints.org/dataviz2.html
7 https://clarivate.com/webofsciencegroup/globalprofilesproject/
8 https://www.shanghairanking.com/rankings/arwu/2023
9 https://www.umultirank.org/press-media/umultirank-news/u-multirank-provides-open-access-to-data/

References

Anderson, R. (2009). The "Idea of a University" today. In K. Withers (ed), *First Class? Challenges and Opportunities for the UK's University Sector*. https://www.history-andpolicy.org/policy-papers/papers/the-idea-of-a-university-today

Baty, P. (2018, January 16). This is why we publish the World University Rankings. *Times Higher Education*. https://www.timeshighereducation.com/blog/why-we-publish-world-university-rankings

Becher, T. (1989). Academic Tribes and Territories Intellectual Enquiry and the Cultures of Disciplines. Society for Research into Higher Education.

Becher, T. and Trowler, P. (2001) *Academic Tribes and Territories*, 2nd ed. Buckingham: SRHE/ Open University Press.

Bergen, M., & Hesseldahl, A. (2016, June 14). Microsoft's big LinkedIn purchase puts the pressure on Google to respond. *CNBC*. https://www.cnbc.com/2016/06/14/microsofts-big-linkedin-purchase-puts-the-pressure-on-google-to-respond.html

Biagioli, M., and Lippman, A. (eds). (2020). *Gaming the Metrics. Misconduct and Manipulation in Academic Research*. https://doi.org/10.1017/CBO9781107415324.004

Brand, A. (2022, April 8). Open access loses when publishers are vilified. *Times Higher Education*. https://www.timeshighereducation.com/opinion/dont-be-pound-foolish-over-pensions

Burgelman, J.-C. (2021, January 28). Scholarly publishing needs regulation. *Research Professional News.*

Bush, V. (2020). *Science, The Endless Frontier. 75th Anniversary Edition.* https://www. nsf.gov/about/history/EndlessFrontier_w.pdf

Cahill, T. (2015). *Measuring the Value of International Research Collaboration. Report Prepared for the Department of Industry and Science.* https://www.humanities.org. au/wp-content/uploads/2017/04/AAH_Measuring-Value-2015.pdf

Calderon, A. (2020, May). Sustainability rankings show a different side to higher education. *University World News.* https://www.universityworldnews.com/post. php?story=2020050409591134

Calderon, A. (2021). The geopolitics of university rankings: not all regions and university networks stand equal. In E. Hazelkorn and G. Mihut (eds), *Research Handbook on University Rankings: History, Methodology, Influence and Impact* (382–98). Cheltenham: Edward Elgar. https://www.e-elgar.com/shop/gbp/research-handbook-on-university-rankings-9781788974974.html

Calhoun, C. (2006). The university and the public good. *Thesis Eleven, 84*(7), 7–43. http://www.nyu.edu/ipk/calhoun/files/calhounTheUniversityAndThePublic-Good.pdf

Cantwell, B. (2018). Broad access and steep stratification in the first mass system: high participation higher education in the United States of America. In B. Cantwell, S. Marginson, and A. Smolentseva (eds), *High Participation Systems of Higher Education* (227–65). Oxford: Oxford University Press.

Cantwell, B. (2021). Ideas for theorizing the geopolitics of higher education in the global rankings era. In E. Hazelkorn and G. Mihut (eds), *Research Handbook on University Rankings. Theory, Methodology, Influence and Impact* (354–65). Cheltenham: Edward Elgar.

Chen, G., and Chan, L. (2021). University rankings and governance by metrics and algorithms. In E. Hazelkorn and G. Mihut (eds), *Research Handbook on University Rankings. Theory, Methodology, Influence and Impact* (425–43). Cheltenham: Edward Elgar.

cOAlition, S. (2018). *Making Open Access a reality by 2020.* https://oa2020.org/wp-content/uploads/pdfs/B14-11-Robert-Jan-Smits.pdf

Coates, H., Liu, L., and Hong, X. (2021). Reputation risk rating and the commercialisation of higher education. In E. Hazelkorn and G. Mihut (eds), *Research Handbook on University Rankings. Theory, Methodology, Influence and Impact* (413–24). Cheltenham: Edward Elgar.

Cochran, A. (2022, July 26). The end of journal impact factor purgatory (and numbers to the thousandths). *The Scholarly Kitchen.* https://scholarlykitchen. sspnet.org/2022/07/26/the-end-of-journal-impact-factor-purgatory-and-numbers-to-the-thousandths/?informz=1andnbd=c0f6fa5c-0a3d-48cb-81f4-de2a8861ca76andnbd_source=informz

Cooley, A. (2015). The emerging politics of international rankings and ratings. A framework for analysis. In A. Cooley and J. Synder (eds), *Ranking the World. Grading States as a Tool of Global Governance* (1–38). Cambridge: Cambridge University Press.

Cooley, A., and Synder, J. (eds). (2015). *Ranking the World. Grading States as a Tool of Global Governance.* Cambridge: Cambridge University Press.

Creus, G. J. (2020, March 21). Will others follow China's switch on academic publishing? *University World News*. https://www.universityworldnews.com/post.php?story=2020031810362222

Crotty, D. (2021, December 14). Market consolidation and the demise of the independently publishing research society. *The Scholarly Kitchen*. https://scholarlykitchen.sspnet.org/2021/12/14/market-consolidation-and-the-demise-of-the-independently-publishing-research-society/

David, P. A. (2008). The historical origins of "Open Science": an essay on patronage, reputation and common agency contracting in the scientific revolution. *Capitalism and Society*, 3(2). https://doi.org/10.2202/1932-0213.1040

DFG-Committee on Scientific Library Services and Information Systems. (2021). *Data Tracking in Research: Aggregation and Use or Sale of Usage Data by Academic Publishers*. https://doi.org/10.5281/zenodo.5937995

Diep, F., and Gluckman, N. (2021, September 13). Colleges still obsess over national rankings. For proof, look at their strategic plans. *The Chronicle of Higher Education*. https://www.chronicle.com/article/colleges-still-obsess-over-national-rankings-for-proof-look-at-their-strategic-plans?cid=gen_sign_in

Dill, D. D., and Beerkens, M. (2010). Reflections and conclusions. In D. D. Dill and M. Beerkens (eds), *Public Policy for Academic Quality. Analyses of Innovative Policy Instruments* (313–35). Dordrecht: Springer.

DORA. (2012). *The San Francisco Declaration on Research Assessment*. https://doi.org/10.1242/bio.20135330

Eaton, J. S. (2016). The quest for quality and the role, impact and influence of supranational organisations. In E. Hazelkorn (ed), *Global Rankings and the Geopolitics of Higher Education* (324–38). London and New York: Routledge.

Ehrenberg, R. G. (2002). Reaching for the brass ring: the U.S. News and world report rankings and competition. *The Review of Higher Education*, 26(2), 145–62. https://eric.ed.gov/?id=ED470061

Erkkilä, T., and Piironen, O. (2009). The iron cage of governance indicators. In R. W. Cox (ed), *Ethics and Integrity in Public Administration. Concepts and Cases* (125–45). Armonk: M. E. Sharpe.

Erkkilä, T., and Piironen, O. (2018). *Rankings and Global Knowledge Governance. Higher Education, Innovation and Competitiveness*. Basingstoke: Palgrave Macmillan.

Erkkilä, T., and Piironen, O. (2021). Rankings and global knowledge governance. In E. Hazelkorn and G. Mihut (eds), *Research Handbook on University Rankings. Theory, Methodology, Influence and Impact* (54–66). Cheltenham: Edward Elgar.

Esposito, J. (2022). Return of the big brands: how legacy publishers will coopt open access. *The Scholarly Kitchen*. https://scholarlykitchen.sspnet.org/2015/10/14/return-of-the-big-brands/

EUA, Science Europe, and European Commission. (2022). *Agreement on Reforming Research Assessment*. https://eua.eu/downloads/news/2022_07_19_rra_agreement_final.pdf?utm_source=flexmailandutm_medium=e-mailandutm_campaign=mailing20julyagreementonreformingresearchassesment1211publicationoftheagreem2andutm_content=document

Fu, Y. C., Marques, M., Tseng, Y. H., Powell, J. J. W., and Baker, D. P. (2022). An evolving international research collaboration network: spatial and thematic developments in co-authored higher education research, 1998–2018. *Scientometrics, 127*, 1403–29. https://doi.org/10.1007/s11192-021-04200-w

Fyfe, A., Coate, K., Curry, S., Lawson, S., Moxham, N., and Røstvik, C. M. (2017). *Untangling Academic Publishing. A history of the relationship between Commercial Interests, Academic Prestige and the Circulation of Research.* https://doi.org/10.5281/zenodo.546100

Garfield, E. (1955). Citation indexes to science: A new dimension in documentation through association of ideas. *Science, 122*(3159), 108–11.

Garfield, E. (1972). Citation analysis as a tool in journal evaluation - journals can be ranked by frequency and impact of citations for science policy studies. *Science, 178*, 471–9.

Grove, J. (2022, August 3). Academic reputation 'still driven by journal prestige' – survey. *Times Higher Education.* https://www.timeshighereducation.com/news/academic-reputation-still-driven-journal-prestige-survey?utm_source=newsletterandutm_medium=emailandutm_campaign=editorial-dailyandmc_cid=7b41f8875candmc_eid=6adc09098d

Guston, D. H. (2000). *Between Politics and Science. Assuring the Integrity and Productivity of Research.* https://assets.cambridge.org/97805216/53183/sample/9780521653183wsn01.pdf

Harman, G. (2011). Competitors of rankings: new directions in quality assurance and accountability. In J. C. Shin, R. K. Toutkoushian, and U. Teichler (eds), *University Rankings. Theoretical Basis, Methodology and Impacts on Global Higher Education* (35–54). Dordrecht: Springer.

Hartocollis, A. (2022, March 17). U.S. News ranked Columbia no. 2, but a math professor has his doubts. *New York Times.*

Hazelkorn, E. (2015). *Rankings and the Reshaping of Higher Education: The Battle for World-class Excellence* (2nd ed.). https://doi.org/10.1057/9781137446671

Hazelkorn, E. (2018). The accountability and transparency agenda: emerging issues in the global era. In R. Pricopie, L. Deca, and A. Curaj (eds), *European Higher Education Area: The Impact of Past and Future Policies* (423–39). Dordrecht: Springer.

Hazelkorn, E. (2022, April 30). Are the SDGs being used to rank impact or monetise data? *University World News.* https://www.universityworldnews.com/post.php?story=20220429114637871

Hazelkorn, E. (2024). Putting global university rankings in context: the internationalisation of accountability and measurability and the geo-politicisation of higher education and research. In L. Engwall (ed), *The Internationalization of Higher Education Institutions* (pp. 55–73). Cham: Springer.

Hicks, D., Wouters, P., Waltman, L., De Rijcke, S., and Rafols, I. (2015). Bibliometrics: the Leiden manifesto for research metrics. *Nature, 520*(7548), 429–31. https://doi.org/10.1038/520429a

Holmberg, K., Hedman, J., Bowman, T. D., Didegah, F., and Laakso, M. (2020). Do articles in open access journals have more frequent altmetric activity than articles in subscription-based journals? An investigation of the research output of Finnish universities. *Scientometrics, 122*(1), 645–59. https://doi.org/10.1007/s11192-019-03301-x

IREG Observatory. (2021). *IREG Inventory of International University Rankings.* https://ireg-observatory.org/en/

Irfanullah, H. (2021, September 2). The north is drawing the south closer, but, this is not the whole picture of geographical inclusion. *The Scholarly Kitchen*. https://scholarlykitchen.sspnet.org/2021/09/02/the-north-is-drawing-the-south-closer-but-this-is-not-the-whole-picture-of-geographical-inclusion/?informz=1

Jaschik, S. (2021, April 21). Ex-dean at temple indicted on charges of manipulating rankings. *Inside Higher Ed*.

Jaschik, S. (2022, May 31). Britain to give visas to graduates of top universities world-wide. *Inside Higher Ed*.

Kinzelbach, K., Saliba, I., and Spannagel, J. (2021). Global data on the freedom indispensable for scientific research: towards a reconciliation of academic reputation and academic freedom. *The International Journal of Human Rights*, 26(10), 1723–40. https://doi.org/10.1080/13642987.2021.1998000

Kunz, R. (2022, March 18). Threats to academic freedom under the guise of open access: The power of publishers, data tracking in science, and the responsibilities of public actors. *VerfBlog*. https://verfassungsblog.de/threats-to-academic-freedom-under-the-guise-of-open-access/

Kwiek, M. (2020). What large-scale publication and citation data tell us about international research collaboration in Europe: changing national patterns in global contexts. *Studies in Higher Education*, 46(12), 2629–49. https://doi.org/10.1080/03075079.2020.1749254

Lee, J. J., and Haupt, J. P. (2021). Scientific globalism during a global crisis: research collaboration and open access publications on COVID-19. *Higher Education*, 81, 949–66. https://doi.org/10.1007/s10734-020-00589-0

LIBER. (2018). *LIBER Open Science Roadmap*. https://zenodo.org/record/1303002#.W0iLj8J9i71

Lim, M. A. (2021). The business of university rankings: the case of times higher education. In E. Hazelkorn and G. Mihut (eds), *Research Handbook on University Rankings. Theory, Methodology, Influence and Impact* (444–54). Cheltenham: Edward Elgar.

Marginson, S. (2010). University rankings, government and social order: managing the field of higher education according to the logic of the performance present-as future. In M. Simons, M. Olssen, and M. Peters (eds), *Re-reading Education Policies: Studying the Policy Agenda of the 21 Century* (584–604). Rotterdam: Sense.

Muller, J. Z. (2018). *The Tyranny of Metrics*. Princeton: Princeton University Press.

O'Connor, P., and O'Hagan, C. (2016). Excellence in university academic staff evaluation: a problematic reality? *Studies in Higher Education*, 41(11), 1943–57. https://doi.org/10.1080/03075079.2014.1000292

Oprisko, R. (2012). Superpowers: The American Academic Elite. *Georgetown Public Policy Review, December 3*. http://gppreview.com/2012/12/03/superpowers-the-american-academic-elite/

Paasi, A. (2015). Academic capitalism and the geopolitics of knowledge. In J. Agnew, V. Mamadouh, A. Secor, and J. Sharp (eds), *The Wiley-Blackwell Companion to Political Geography*. Wiley-Blackwell, pp. 509–23.

PCG/Academia. (2022, January 24). Times Higher Education acquires Inside Higher Ed. *PCG/Academia*. https://pcgacademia.pl/en/news/times-higher-education-acquires-inside-higher-ed/

Posada, A., and Chen, G. (2018). *Inequality in Knowledge Production: The Integration of Academic Infrastructure by Big Publishers.* https://doi.org/10.4000/proceedings. elpub.2018.30

Quinn, R., Spannagel, J., and Saliba, I. (2021, March 11). Why university rankings must include academic freedom. *University World News.* https://www.universityworldnews. com/post.php?story=20210311071016522#:~:text=In%20the%20absence% 20of%20academic,but%20sometimes%20commercial%20or%20communal

Reillon, V. (2015). Overview of EU funds for research and innovation. *Briefing.* https://www.europarl.europa.eu/RegData/etudes/BRIE/2015/568327/EPRS_ BRI(2015)568327_EN.pdf

Rottenburg, R., Merry, S. E., Park, S.-J., and Mugler, J. (eds). (2015). *The World of Indictors. The Making of Governmental Knowledge Through Quantification.* Cambridge: Cambridge University Press.

Rüegg, W. (1992). Themes. In H. de Ridder-Symoens (ed), *A History of the University in Europe: Volume 1, Universities in the Middle Ages* (3–34). Cambridge: Cambridge University Press. https://books.google.ie/books?id=5Z1VBEbF0HAC&pg=PR5 &source=gbs_selected_pages&cad=1#v=onepage&q&f=false

Salmi, J. (2015). *Study on Open Science: Impact, Implications and Policy Options.* https://doi.org/10.2777/237283

Salmi, J. (2017). Excellence strategies and world-class universities. In E. Hazelkorn (ed), *Ranking and the Geopolitics of Higher Education. Understanding the Influence and Impact of Rankings on Higher Education, Policy and Society* (216–43). Cheltenham: Routledge.

Salmi, J. (2021). Do rankings promote academic excellence? World-class universities in perspective. In E. Hazelkorn and G. Mihut (eds), *Research Handbook on University Rankings. Theory, Methodology, Influence and Impact* (455–72). Cheltenham: Edward Elgar.

Sauder, M., and Espeland, W. N. (2009). The discipline of rankings: tight coupling and organizational change. *American Sociological Review, 74*(1), 63–82. http://asr. sagepub.com/cgi/content/abstract/74/1/63

Science Europe. (2018). *Challenging the Current Business Models in Academic Publishing: Accelerators and Obstacles to the Open Access Transition.* http:// www.scienceeurope.org/wp-content/uploads/2018/06/SE_WS_Report_OA_ Big_Deals.pdf

Sharma, Y. (2022, May 11). Three major universities quit international rankings. *University World News.*

Siwinski, W. (2019, June 10). University rankings organisations need to do more. *Chronicle of Higher Education.* https://www.universityworldnews.com/post. php?story=20190527120509757

STM. (2021). *STM Global Brief 2021 – Economics and Market Size.* https://www.stm-assoc.org/2022_08_24_STM_White_Report_a4_v15.pdf

Roller, E. (2020, March 27). Dutch funders move away from journal impact factor. Retrieved July 23, 2020, from Research Professional News website: https:// www.researchprofessionalnews.com/rr-news-europe-netherlands-2020-3-dutch-funders-move-away-from-journal-impact-factor/

THE. (n.d.). *THE Data Points Product Portfolio.* https://www.timeshigheredu-cation.com/sites/default/files/standard-page-paragraphs/attachments/the_ datapoints_0.pdf

THE Reporter. (2022, January 10). Times Higher Education acquires Inside Higher Ed. *Times Higher Education.*

Tijssen, R., Lamers, W., and Yegros, A. (2017). *UK Universities Interacting with Industry: Patterns of Research Collaboration and Inter-sectoral Mobility of Academic Researchers* (No. 14). www.researchcghe.org

Usher, A. (2017). A short global history of rankings. In E. Hazelkorn (ed), *Global Rankings and the Geopolitics of Higher Education. Understanding the Influence and Impact of Rankings on Higher Education, Policy and Society* (23–53). London and New York: Routledge.

Usher, A. (2022, February 2). Two rankings stories you may have missed. *One Thought to Start Your Day.* https://myemail.constantcontact.com/One-Thought-to-Start-Your-Day--Two-Rankings-Stories-You-May-Have-Missed.html?soid=11030805200 43andaid=rRSz_U8ZNmE

VSNU, NFU, KNAW, NWO. and ZonMw. (2019). *Room for everyone's talent.* https://www.nwo.nl/sites/nwo/files/media-files/2019-Recognition-Rewards-Position-Paper_EN.pdf

Webster, D.S.A. (1986) *Academic Quality Rankings of American Colleges and Universities.* Springfield: Charles C. Thomas.

Williams, R., and Leahy, A. (2020). *U21 Ranking of National Higher Education Systems 2020.* https://universitas21.com/rankings

Willinsky, J. (2006). *The Access Principle: The Case for Open Access to Research and Scholarship.* https://doi.org/10.3201/eid1209.060643

Wilsdon, J., Allen, L., Belfiore, E., Campbell, P., Curry, S., Hill, S., and Johnson, B. (2015). *The Metric Tide: Report of the Independent Review of the Role of Metrics in Research Assessment and Management.* https://doi.org/10.13140/RG.2.1.4929.1363

Wilsdon, J., Bar-Ilan, J., Frodeman, R., Lex, E., Peters, I., and Wouters, P. (2017). *Next-generation Metrics. Report of the European Commission Expert Group on Altmetrics.* https://doi.org/10.2777/337729

Wouters, P., Ràfols, I., Oancea, A., Caroline, S., Kamerlin, L., Britt, J., and Jacob, M. (2019). *Indicator Frameworks for Fostering Open Knowledge Practices in Science and Scholarship.* https://doi.org/10.2777/445286

Yudevich, M., Altbach, P. G., and Rumbley, L. E. (eds). (2016). *The Global Academic Rankings Game. Changing Institutional Policy, Practice and Academic Life.* New York: Routledge.

11

CONCLUDING REFLECTIONS ON ACADEMIC FREEDOM

Maria Slowey and Richard Taylor

At the level of generality, two broad conclusions can be drawn from the fore-going analyses and discussions: firstly, that the principles and practice of academic freedom are a central, indeed defining, characteristic of the university in liberal democracies; and, secondly, that for a variety of reasons in the twenty-first century, it is under severe threat. This threat is, of course, most apparent in autocratic and war-torn parts of the world, where academics are in danger of expulsion, imprisonment, or worse. However, even in liberal democracies, recent years have seen the rise of neo-nationalism and populist, illiberal movements, and, in many cases, elected governments representing these interests. In the university context, this has been accompanied by tendencies to increased interventions from external forces – government, commercial interests, the conceptualisation of the student as 'customer,' and other related aspects of the marketisation of higher education. As we discussed in some detail in Chapter 1, all this has meant that there is a greater need than ever for 'eternal vigilance' to ensure that the hard-won rights to academic freedom are protected and developed.

The pressures on higher education are thus considerable. Peter Scott (Chapter 2), in tracing the historical development of the concept of academic freedom, discusses how, in contemporary times, even in liberal democracies, many governments are introducing ever more intrusive systems of accountability. Four broad justifications are given: first, that governments, as the supposed guardians of the interests of the taxpayers, must ensure 'value for money'; second, governments, representing the interests of the students as 'customers' of higher education, need to regulate the universities, as the providers of 'knowledge products' and services; third, that governments have a responsibility to ensure the academic quality of the higher education and research that

DOI: 10.4324/9781003363262-15

they fund, whether directly or indirectly; and fourth, that, competing in the international market place, characterised by the 'global knowledge economy,' governments in democratic societies are entitled to set the broad priorities that universities and, consequently, individual scholars should follow.

This is the context in which our book raises the rhetorical question as to whether academic freedom should be seen as a 'core value' or an 'elite privilege.' The answer, of course, is that in certain respects it is both. All our authors – varied as they are in disciplinary backgrounds, professional contexts, national, geographic locations, and ideological outlook – are firmly committed to the principles and practice of academic freedom: all of them – and both of us as editors – agree that it is indeed a core value. We hope that the preceding chapters in this book clearly indicate the reasons why, and how, this is the case.

What is perhaps less obvious is why academic freedom may also in certain respect be considered by some to be an elite privilege. The notion of 'elite privilege' can be interpreted in at least three different ways: professional status, institutional status, and hierarchical structures within the university. These are considered below.

In the first place, the notion of 'privilege' can be associated with the benefits accruing to individual academics of the status they hold as members of valued institutions in society. Despite an arguably declining status, declining relative remuneration, increased pressures for accountability, and the associated frustrations of the new 'public management' and the like, running through the chapters in this book is a recognition that being a university academic is indeed a privileged occupation, in the sense that it brings high personal rewards in terms of the freedom to pursue passions in research and teaching. There is also value attached to the professional kudos of holding an academic position in institutions which are generally highly regarded by local communities and the wider society – as is evidenced, for example, by the numerous campaigns in towns and regions to establish a local institution of higher education. David Watson, in reviewing six and a half centuries of university development, observes that universities have always changed in response to perceived social and economic needs, and they have always remained the same – the worldly 'instrumental' side to our business has always been matched by an independent, value-laden side.

The latter is most eloquently, as well as practically, expressed through civic and community engagement. What brings these two together is the time-honoured concept of a 'liberal' higher education (Watson, 2007; Watson, 2014).

But how far does this liberal concept of the university apply to all types of institutions? A second way in which the extent of academic freedom can, in practice, operate relates to an individual institution's place in the (international) 'league tables.' Differentiation in status affects profoundly the degree to which academic freedom can, in practice, be exercised in elite, as opposed to less prestigious, institutions.

The contributors to this book occupy, or have recently occupied, different positions in different types of universities – and, of course, in different countries. In general, the more elite the university, the greater the level of autonomy in both research and teaching. These issues are analysed in some detail by Ellen Hazelkorn (Chapter 10), who points out that, as the contemporary higher education landscape is simultaneously collaborative and competitive, the reputational and prestige value of 'rankings' has grown in importance in recent decades. As a result, 'excellence initiatives' seek to alter national positions by investing disproportionately in a few selected universities at the 'top' of the global hierarchy. This has led inexorably to resources becoming ever more concentrated in those institutions which are already well-endowed. The inevitable consequence has been that policy and practice in the less prestigious universities tend to be shaped to a much greater extent by short-term government, business, commercial, and/or societal pressures. In this respect, opportunities for the full exercise of academic freedom is, in practice, not available equally to all, with the better resourced institutions being in a more advantageous position to withstand instrumental, short-term external pressures.

A third way in which academic freedom is circumscribed in the context of this elite/privileged spectrum lies in the inequality between individual academics. In any profession, there are, of course, status hierarchies: generally, lengthy 'apprenticeships' with a narrowing of the occupational pyramid from junior to senior positions. As we elaborated in Chapter 1, the right to exercise academic freedom has to be earned through peer assessment, based upon an extensive period of obtaining academic qualifications, publishing in recognised journals or publishing houses, engaging with the relevant disciplinary research community, and the like. The troubling trend now evident, however, is for an increasing proportion of academics to hold short-term, contingent positions – the 'taxi-cab' teachers or researchers, employed on specific grants outside mainstream academic/tenure tracks. Maria Slowey discussed in Chapter 9 the constraints under which the latter operate. This means that, in effect, those who hold tenured or permanent positions are, for all practical purposes, privileged in relation to the exercise of academic freedom *vis-a-vis* the growing proportion of their colleagues who are on temporary and/or part-time contracts. As one of the respondents in the expert consultation she conducted commented: 'academic freedom is not an elite privilege but to be an academic is a privilege'. This raises the question as to what it means to be 'an academic,' when in many systems over a half of those so employed are likely to be in situations where they teach courses over whose syllabuses and overall orientation they have little or no control and/or are engaged in research projects largely designed and supervised by other, more senior, colleagues.

Some aspects of these developments are undoubtedly a result of the expansion of higher education and the shift, in Burton Clark's typology, from a 'mass' to a 'universal' system. This has negative implications in the teaching and learning context for what should be the close relationships between tutors and students and the associated possibilities for 'Socratic' dialogue and learning through exposure to often uncomfortable ideas and theories. Other aspects are more associated with the permeation of neo-liberal policies and public management approaches. In some countries, the marketisation of universities has reached a stage where, due to the imposition of fees, many students come to see themselves as 'customers' in the marketplace of higher education. In such an environment, a key criterion for 'success' can all too easily become equated with the acquisition of certification and instrumental forms of knowledge, orientated largely towards future employment prospects.

Related to this growth of an individualist culture has been the rise of 'identity politics' and the foregrounding of individuals' self-definitions in relation to, for example, sex, ethnic, social, or dis/ability status. This has led to major debates in the public arena based upon so-called 'cancel culture' (or 'No Platforming') as discussed in the British context by Evan Smith in Chapter 5.

In reviewing the literature on the constraints on academic freedom for this book, as editors we found that much of the critique tended to come from those on the Left of the political spectrum. Two of the case studies focus upon contrasting ideological examples. In Chapter 4, Richard Taylor explores the alleged discrimination against Marxists and members of the Communist Party of Great Britain in the early years of the Cold War in British university adult education. However, as Wietse de Vries describes in Chapter 6, arguably not dissimilar pressures can also be applied by populist, left-leaning governments: recent experience in Mexico shows the ways in which government can shape national research agendas through construction of research funding mechanisms.

Such politically contentious situations relate to another difficult issue relevant to the proper exercise of academic freedom by members of the academy. All are agreed that suitably qualified academics have the right, indeed the duty, to engage in the public domain in the subject areas in which they have expertise. The question arises, however, as to how far, if at all, academics should exercise a similar right to express opinions on issues, and in fields, in which they are not specialists or experts. Of course, as *citizens* they have the same rights as anyone else. But how far should they use their established academic position to try to assert authority in areas in which they are clearly non-expert? On occasion, this is not directly the result of the actions by the individuals concerned, but is, in reality, an assumption by the wider society that they have a legitimacy, as public intellectuals, to pronounce authoritatively upon a wide range of issues of social concern. In the North American context, it has generally been accepted that academics, as public intellectuals, do indeed have the right, if not duty, to speak and write in the public sphere on matters of social, political, religious, and moral concern. (Noam Chomsky is a case in point. Although a specialist in linguistics, he has been better known in wider society as a fierce, radical critic of US foreign policy. More recently, he has commented on the vexed question of the implications of AI [Chomsky *et al*, 2023]. In this latter context, he could be argued to have appropriate expertise, given the clear links between the field of linguistics and some aspects of the AI phenomenon.)

Many similar examples of such an approach can be cited in Western European societies. For example, in the UK, Bertrand Russell, a philosopher specialising in mathematical logic, was far better known in wider society for both his peace activism and for his views on sexual and educational topics. An analogous case is that of Richard Dawkins, the eminent life scientist, who has been outspoken in his atheistic views. Although acknowledged by his peers as an accomplished scientist in his field, his excursions into theological and philosophical areas may have been regarded with more scepticism by specialists in those latter areas.

This is clearly a matter of ongoing debate: but, in our view, academics should always err on the side of caution, if not diffidence, in claiming any special authority outside their specialist areas.

We have adopted throughout this wide-ranging book a *longue duree* approach to the topic of academic freedom, rather than discussing the fast moving, contemporary controversies. Having said that, two chapters in this book highlight crucial, pivotal points of change: the case of Hong Kong (Liz Jackson in Chapter 7) and Hungary (Rebecca Bakos and Andrea Pető in Chapter 8). So, while our focus is primarily on higher education in liberal democracies, we are all too aware that, just as the fostering and protecting of academic freedom requires continuous vigilance, so also do the values underlying liberal democracy require protection and fostering: today's democratic state can all too readily become tomorrow's autocracy.

Some on the left have argued, in our view mistakenly and dangerously, that academic freedom and other related liberties enjoyed in liberal democracies are to be derided as 'bourgeois.' Ralph Miliband, the political sociologist and Marxist theorist, was unequivocal in his rejection of such views. On the contrary, as his biographer, Michael Newman, explains, his overriding concern was that the left should see such liberties 'as an integral part of socialism' (Newman, 2002, 179).

The defence of the liberal approach, defined in broad terms of political philosophy rather than specific political parties, is a central task across the whole of society for those who advocate progressive views. In Chapter 3, Alan Haworth discusses the influential ideas of J.S. Mill in his classic 1859 text, *On Liberty*, and some of the still relevant issues and dilemmas over free speech and academic freedom that this raises.

There can be little doubt that, at the time of writing, liberal values are under the most severe threat since the end of the Cold War – arguably even since 1945. These threats manifest themselves in almost all developed societies in a variety of social and political contexts, ranging from the 'Trump phenomenon,' through religious fundamentalism, to some of the more exclusionary aspects of identity politics. It is on this broader canvass that the threats to academic freedom have to be seen. Our universities are now called upon to play a central role in society: their liberal culture has not only to be defended, but further developed as a high priority.

In this book we have attempted to identify the risks and threats to academic freedom in a variety of contexts. We conclude by citing one of the classic advocates for academic freedom, John Dewey, whose perspective is, in our view, as relevant today as it was in 1902:

> Any attack, or even restriction, upon academic freedom is directed against the university itself. To investigate truth; critically to verify fact; to reach conclusions by means of the best methods at command, untrammelled by fear or favour, to communicate this truth to the student; to interpret to him [sic] its bearing on the questions he [sic] will have to face in life – this is precisely the aim and object of the university. To aim a blow at any of these operations is to deal a vital wound to the university itself…Since freedom of mind and expression are the root of all freedom, to deny freedom in education is a crime against democracy.
>
> *(Dewey, 1902)*

References

Chomsky, N., Roberts, I., and Watumull, J. (2023) Noam Chomsky: The False Promise of ChatGPT. *New York Times*. 8 March.

Dewey, J. (1902). Academic freedom. *Educational Review*, 23(3), 1–14.

Newman, M. (2002). *Ralph Miliband and the Politics of the New Left*. London: Merlin Press.

Watson, D. (2007). *Managing Civic and Community Engagement*. Maidenhead. SRHE/Open University Press.

Watson, D. (2014). *The Question of Conscience: Higher Education and Personal Responsibility*. London: Institute of Education.

INDEX